Wilhelm

Deutscher Kaiser u. König von Preußen.

FACSIMILE REPRODUCTION OF THE KAISER'S VISITING CARD

Wilhelm

Kronprinz des Deutschen Reiches und

Kronprinz von Preußen.

THE VISITING CARD OF THE CROWN PRINCE,
REPRODUCED IN FACSIMILE

FACE TO FACE WITH KAISERISM

JAMES W. GERARD

THE KAISER AND VON TREUTLER
TAKEN IN THE NORWEGIAN TOWN OF ODDE IN 1910

FACE TO FACE WITH KAISERISM

BY

JAMES W. GERARD

LATE AMBASSADOR TO THE GERMAN IMPERIAL COURT
AUTHOR OF "MY FOUR YEARS IN GERMANY"

NEW YORK
GEORGE H. DORAN COMPANY

TO

COLONEL EDWARD M. HOUSE

STATESMAN AND FRIEND

THE AUTHOR

DEDICATES THIS BOOK

INTRODUCTORY NOTE

In some measure this book is a continuation of MY FOUR YEARS IN GERMANY, the narrative here being carried up to the time of my return home, with some observations on the situation I have found in the United States.

What I want especially to impress upon the people of the United States is that we are at war because Germany invaded the United States—an invasion insidiously conceived and vigorously prosecuted for years before hostilities began;—that this war is our war;—that the sanctity of American freedom and of the American home depend upon what we do *NOW*.

JAMES W. GERARD.

NEW YORK,
APRIL FIRST, 1918.

CONTENTS

ix

CONTENTS

ILLUSTRATIONS

ILLUSTRATIONS

FACE TO FACE WITH KAISERISM

FACE TO FACE WITH KAISERISM

CHAPTER I

PERSONALITY OF THE KAISER AND SOMETHING OF THE KING BUSINESS

TO the American mind the Kaiser is the personification of Germany. He is the arch enemy upon whom the world places the responsibility for this most terrible of all wars. I have sat face to face with him in the palace at Berlin where, as the personal representative and envoy of the President of the United States, I had the honor of expressing the viewpoint of a great nation. I have seen him in the field as the commanding general of mighty forces, but I also have seen him in the neutral countries through which I passed on my return home and in my own beloved land—in the evidence of intrigue and plotting which this militaristic monarch has begotten and which is to-day "the Thing," as President Wilson calls it, which has brought the American people face to face with kaiserism in the greatest conflict of all history.

What manner of man is he? What is his character? How much was he responsible for what has

13

happened—how much his General Staff? What of the Crown Prince and what of the neutral peoples and their rulers whom Germany has intimidated and would fain subjugate if it suited her purpose? These are the questions I shall attempt to answer out of my experiences in Germany and my contacts with the rulers of other countries in my journeys to and from Berlin and Washington.

To illustrate the craft of the Kaiser, I believe I can perform no better service to Americans than to reveal an incident which has not hitherto been published. It occurred at the New Year's reception of 1914 when the Ambassadors of all the foreign countries represented at the German court, were ranged in a large room at the Palace. They stood about six feet apart in the order of their residence in Berlin. The Kaiser and his aides entered the room, and the Emperor spoke a few minutes to each envoy. He tarried longest with the Turkish Ambassador and myself, thereby arousing the curiosity of the other diplomats who suspected that the Kaiser did more than merely exchange the greetings of the season. He did.

What the German Emperor said to me interests every American because it shows his subtlety of purpose. *The Kaiser talked at length to me about what he called Japan's designs on the United States. He warned me that Mexico was full of Japanese spies and an army of Japanese colonels.* He also spoke about France, saying that he had made every effort to make up with France, that he had extended his hand to that country but that the French

14

had refused to meet his overtures, that he was through and would not try again to heal the breach between France and Germany!

All this was in 1914, six months before the outbreak of the European War. Little did I know then what the purpose was back of that conversation, but it is clear now that the Emperor wished to have the government of the United States persuaded through me that he was really trying to keep Europe at peace and that the responsibility for what was going to happen would be on France. The German is so skilful at intrigue that he seeks even in advance of an expected offensive to lay the foundation for self-justification.

But the reference to Japan and alleged hostility against us on the part of fanciful hordes of Japanese in Mexico made me wonder at the time. There were many evidences subsequent to that New Year's Day reception of an attempt to alienate us from Japan. As a climax to it all, as a clarification of what the Emperor had in mind, came the famous Zimmermann note, the instructions to the German Minister in Mexico to align both Japan and Mexico against us when we entered the war against Germany!

Plotting and intriguing for power and mastery! Such is the business of absolute rulers.

I believe that had the old Austrian Kaiser lived a little while longer, the prolongation of his life would have been most disastrous both for Austria and Hungary. I believe after the death of Franz Ferdinand at Sarajevo and after a year of war the

15

German Emperor and autocracy were brooding over a plan according to which, on the death of Francis Joseph, the successor should be allowed to rule only as King or Grand-Duke of Austria, the title of Emperor of Austria to disappear and German Princes to be placed upon the thrones of Hungary and of a new kingdom of Bohemia. These and the king or grand-duke of Austria were to be subject-monarchs under the German Kaiser, who was thus to revive an empire, if not greater, at least more powerful, than the empires of Charlemagne and of Charles the Fifth. Many public utterances of the German Kaiser show that trend of mind.

Emperor William deliberately wrote and published, for instance, such a statement as this: "From childhood I have been influenced by five men, Alexander the Great, Julius Cæsar, Theodoric II, Frederick the Great and Napoleon. Each of these men dreamed a dream of world empire. They failed. I have dreamed a dream of German world empire and my mailed fist shall succeed."

Could any declaration of a life's ambition be more explicit? It seems impossible for human ambition to stand still. Either a man loses all stimulus of self and becomes as spiritless as a fagged animal or ambition drives him always on—he is never content with any success achieved. The millionaire to whom the first million, when he was a boy, seemed the extreme limit of human wealth and desire, presses on insatiably with the first million in his pocket, more restless, more dissatisfied, than the hungry farmer's boy who first carries his ambitions to the great city.

When these zealous, scheming men gain the power of kingship, they usually bring disaster to their country. Their subjects find no compensation in the personal ambitions which hurry a nation into the miseries of war. Better Charles II, dallying with his ringletted mistresses, than an Alexander the Great; better Henry the Fourth of France, the "ever-green gallant," than Frederick the Great, bathing his people in blood. "Happy nations have no history."

William the Second, the present German Emperor, might well be called the Restless Emperor. He is never satisfied to remain more than a few days in any place or in any occupation. He commands his armies in person. He has won distinction as a writer and a public speaker. He is an excellent shot. He has composed music, written verses, superintended the production of a ballet, painted a picture; the beautiful Byzantine chapel in the Castle of Posen shows his genius for architecture; and, clothed in a clergyman's surplice, he has preached a sermon in Jerusalem. What ruler in all history has exhibited such extraordinary versatility?

In my conversations with the Emperor I have been struck by his knowledge of other countries, lands which he had never visited. He was familiar not only with their manners, customs, industries and public men, but with their commercial problems. Through his conversation one can see the keen eye of the Hanseatic trader looking with eager envy on the trade of a rival merchant. The Emperor, incidentally, while instinctively commercial, has an inborn contempt, if not for the law, at least for lawyers. In October, 1915, for instance, he remarked to me, "This is a lawyers' war, Asquith and Lloyd George in England, Poincaré and Briand in France."

In appearance and conversation Emperor William is very manly. His voice is strong, with a ring in it. He is a good rider. Following the German custom, he puts on his nightshirt every afternoon after lunch and sleeps for two hours—for the German is more devoted to the siesta than the Spaniard or Mexican. The hours of the Berlin Foreign Office, for example, were from eleven to one and from four to eight. After a heavy lunch at one o'clock all the officials took a nap for an hour or two. Also, the hours of the bank where I did business were from ten to one and from four till six. This meant that after six o'clock the clerks had to sit until perhaps eight making up the books for the day.

In 1916, the Olympic games were to have taken place at Berlin, and in September, 1913, before sailing for Germany, I attended a luncheon at the New York Athletic Club, given by President Page, with the members of the German Commission who had come to America to study athletics and to see what could be done in Germany so that the Germans could make a good showing at the games in their own city.

After my arrival in Germany one of the members of this commission told me that it was impossible, he believed, to organise the Germans as athletes until German meal and business hours had been changed. He said that with us in America young men leaving business at four-thirty, five or five-thirty, had time in which to exercise before their evening meal, but that in Germany the young men ate so much at the midday meal that they required their siesta after it, and that they did not leave their offices until so late in the evening that exercise and practice were impossible.

On the Emperor's table his wine glasses or rather cups are of silver. Possibly this is because he has been forbidden by his physician to drink wine. The Germans maintain the old-fashioned custom of drinking healths at meals. Some one far down the table will lift his glass, look at you and smile. You are then expected to lift your glass and drink with him and then both bow and smile over the glasses. As the Emperor must reciprocate with every one present, his champagne and wine are put in silver cups in order that those drinking wine with him do not see that he consumes no appreciable quantity of alcoholic liquor on the occasion of each health drinking. Some people in America may have often wished for a similar device.

The Emperor is out of uniform only on rare occasions. Occasionally, when in a foreign country, he has appeared in civilian dress, as shown in the accompanying photograph, taken in 1910 at the small town of Odde in Norway, where he had landed from his yacht. He appears to much better advantage in uniform than in civilian attire. Although uniformed while at sea as an Admiral, his favourite uniform is really that of the Hussars. In this picture he is accompanied by Baron von Treutler, Prussian Minister to Bavaria and Foreign Office representative with the Kaiser. Von Treutler is a German of the world. I met him at the Great General Headquarters, at the end of April, 1916, when the submarine question was being discussed. He came to dinner several times at the Chancellor's house, undoubtedly reporting back what was said to the Emperor, and I believe that his voice was against the resumption of ruthless submarine warfare and in favour of peace with America. Shortly after this period he fell into disfavour and went back to occupy his post of Minister in Munich.

In conversation, the Emperor reminds one very much of Roosevelt, talking with the same energy, the same violence of gesture and of voice so characteristic of our great ex-President. When the Emperor talks all his attention is given to you and all his mental energy is concentrated on the conversation. In this violence of manner and voice he seems not at all German. The average German is neither exuberant nor soft-spoken.

His favourite among his ancestors is William of Orange. Once he attended a fancy-dress ball in costume and make-up copied from the well-known picture of that Prince. The Emperor is strongly built and is about five feet nine inches tall. He sits well on his horse and walks, too, with head erect and shoulders thrown back—a picture of military precision.

A friend of mine who was present at Kiel with his yacht, in 1910, tells me that when all the yachts and warships had been assembled along the long narrow waterway which constitutes that harbour, with the crews lined up on deck or manning the yards, with bands crashing and banners floating, the *Hohenzollern* slowly steamed into the harbour and passed lazily and majestically through the waiting ships. Alone on the upper bridge stood the Monarch, attired in full military uniform, with white coat and tight breeches, high top boots, shining silver breastplate and silver helmet, surmounted by an eagle, the dress of the Prussian Guard Regiment so dear to those who portray romantic and kingly rôles upon the stage, a figure on whom all eyes were fixed, as splendid as that of Lohengrin, drawn by his fairy swan, coming to rescue the unjustly accused Princess. And, alas, the Germans like all this pomp and splendour. It appeals to something in the German heart and seems to create a feeling of affection and humility in the German breast.

When I talked at length one day with President Wilson on my visit to America in October, 1916, he remarked, half to himself, in surprise at my tale of war, "Why does all this horror come on the world? What causes it?" "Mr. President," I answered, "it is the king business."

I did not mean nominal kings as harmless as those of Spain and England. I was thinking of the pow-

erful monarchs. A German republic would never
have embarked on this war; a German Congress
would have thought twice before sending their own
sons to death in a deliberate effort to enslave other
peoples. In a free Germany teachers, ministers and
professors would not have taught the necessity of
war. What German merchant in a free Germany
would have thought that all the trade of the East,
all the riches of Bagdad and Cairo and Mosul could
compensate him for the death of his first-born or
restore the blind eyes to the youngest son who now
crouches, cowering, over the fire, awaiting death?
For there was no trade necessity for this war. I
know of no place in the world where German merchants were not free to trade. The disclosures of
war have shown how German commerce had pene-
trated every land, to an extent unknown to the best
informed. If the German merchants wanted this
war in order to gain a German monopoly of the
world's trade, then they are rightly suffering from
the results of overweening covetousness.

Experts in insanity say that the Roman Emperors
as soon as they attained the rule of the world were
made mad by the possession of that stupendous
power. The sceptre of Emperor William is mighty.
No more autocratic influence proceeds from any
other monarch or ruler. But you will say how about
our President in time of war? Great power can
safely be given to a president. Our presidents have
all risen from the ranks. Usually they have gone
through the school of hard knocks. And there are
ways of keeping them abreast of the people.

It is told that hidden from public view, crouched down in the chariot in which the successful Roman pro-consul or general drove triumphantly through the crowded streets of Rome, was a slave celebrated for his impertinence, whose duty it was to make the one honoured feel that, after all, he was nothing more than an ordinary mortal blessed with a certain amount of good luck. Probably as the chariot passed by the forum the slave would say, after a thunderous burst of applause from the populace: "Do not take that applause too seriously. That is the T. Quintus Cassius Association whose chief received a hundred sesterces from your brother-in-law yesterday, on account, with a promise of a hundred more in case the Association's cheers seemed loud and sincere."

So in America the press, serious and comic, takes the place of the humble slave and throws enough cold water on the head of any temporarily successful American to reduce it to normal proportions. Besides, the President knows that some day he must return to the ranks, live again with his neighbours, seek out the threads of a lost law practice or eke out a livelihood on the Chautauqua circuit in the discomfort of tiny hotels, travelling in upper berths instead of private cars and eating on lunch stools in small stations instead of in the sumptuous surroundings of presidential luxury. These are sobering prospects.

Kings, on the other hand, come to look on their subjects as toys. A post-card popular in Austria and Germany showed the old Emperor, Francis Jo-

23

seph, seated at a table with a little great-grand-nephew on his knee, teaching the child to move toy soldiers about on the boards; and it is unfortunately true that the same youngster—should the system of the Central Empires be perpetuated—will be able to move his subjects across the map of Europe just as he did the toy soldiers on his great-grand-uncle's table. He will be able to tear men from their work and their homes, to seize great scientists, great chemists, great inventors—men who may be on the eve of discoveries or remedies destined to rid the human race of the scourge of cancer or the white plague—and send them to death in the marshes of Macedonia or the fastnesses of the Carpathians because some fellow-king or emperor has deceived or outwitted him.

In a monarchy all subjects seem the personal property of the monarch and all expressions of power become personal. This extends throughout all countries ruled by royalty.

When, for example, a member of the royal family dies, even in another country, it must be lamented by the court circle of other lands. Here is the official notice sent to all diplomats and members of the Imperial German Court on the occasion of the death of the Queen of Sweden.

"The Court goes into mourning today for Her Majesty the Queen-Mother of Sweden for three weeks up to and including the 19th of January, 1914.

"Ladies wear black silk dresses, for the first fourteen days, including January 12th, with black hair ornaments, black gloves, black fans and black jewelry; the last eight days with white hair ornaments, grey gloves, white fans and pearls.

"Gentlemen wear the whole time a black band on the left sleeve. Civilians wear with the embroidered coat, during the first fourteen days, including January 12th, on occasions of Grand Gala, black buckles and swords with black sheathes. During the last eight days bright buckles; on occasions of 'Half Gala' gold or silver embroidered trousers of the color of the uniform and in the one as in the other case gold or silver embroidered hat with white plume; with the 'small' uniform, however, black trousers (or knee-breeches, black silk stockings, shoes with black bows and the 'three-cornered' hat with black plume). During the first fourteen days gentlemen wear black woolen vests and black gloves, in the last eight days black silk vests and grey gloves.

"Berlin, December 30, 1913.
                         "The Ober-Ceremonienmeister.
                              "Graf A. Eulenburg.

"By command of His Majesty the Emperor, mourning will be suspended for New Year's Day and the 17th and 18th of January."

So, it is apparent what a close corporation all the royal families make and the peoples are simply viewed as the personal property of the ruling princes. In his telegram which the German Kaiser wrote to President Wilson on August tenth, observe that all is personal. The Kaiser says, "I telegraphed to His Majesty the King, *personally,* but that if, etc., I would employ *my* troops elsewhere. . . . His Majesty answered that he thought *my* offer. . . ."

25

He speaks of the King of the Belgians "having refused *my* petition for a free passage." He refers to "*my* Ambassador in London."

This telegram shows, on the other hand, another thing,—the great ability of the Kaiser. Undoubtedly he knew why I was coming to see him—to present the offer of mediation of President Wilson—but from our conversation I do not think that he had even in his mind prepared the answer, which sets forth his position in entering the war.

He said, "Wait a moment, I shall write something for the President." Then taking the telegraph blanks lying on the table, he wrote rapidly and fluently. It was a message in a foreign language, and, whatever we may think of its content, at any rate it is clear, concise, consecutive and forceful.

The personal touch runs through that extraordinary series of telegrams in the famous "Willy-Nicky" correspondence between Kaiser Wilhelm and the last of the Romanoffs, discovered in Petrograd by Herman Bernstein. These reveal, moreover, the surpassing craft of the German Kaiser. He was the master schemer. Touting for German trade, always for his advantage, he twists the poor half-wit of the Winter Palace like a piece of straw.

Emperor William was not satisfied with a quiet life as patron of trade. As he studied the portraits of his ancestors, he felt that they gazed at him with reproachful eyes, demanded that he add, as did they, to the domains of the Hohenzollerns, that he return from war in triumph at the head of a victori-

26

ous army with the keys of fallen cities borne before him in conquering march.

One-tenth of Frederick the Great's people fell, but to the poverty-stricken peasant woman of Prussia, lamenting her husband and dead sons, did it matter that the rich province of Silesia had been added to the Prussian Crown? What was it to that broken mother whether the Silesian peasants acknowledged the Prussian King or the Austrian Empress? Despots both. And what countless serfs fell in the wars between the King and the Empress! I once asked von Jagow when this war would end. He answered, "An old history of the Seven Years' War concludes, 'The King and the Empress were tired of war, so they made peace.' That is how this war will end." Will it? Will it end in a draw, to be resumed when some king feels the war fever on him? No, this war must end despots, and with them all wars!

It is all such a matter of personal whim. For instance before Bulgaria entered the war on the side of Germany, even the best informed Germans predicted that King Ferdinand would never join Germany because of an incident which occurred in the Royal Palace of Berlin. This is how it happened:

It is the custom for one monarch to make his pals in the King business officers of his army or navy. Thus the German Emperor was General Field Marshal and Proprietor of the 34th "William the first, German Emperor and King of Prussia" Infantry, and of the 7th "William the Second, German Emperor and King of Prussia" Hussars, in the Austro-

Hungarian Army; Chief of the "King Frederick William III St. Petersburg Life Guards," the 85th "Viburg" Infantry and the 13th "Narva" Hussars, and the "Grodno" Hussars of the Guard, in the Russian Army; Field Marshal in British Army; Hon. Admiral of the British Fleet and Colonel-in-Chief 1st Dragoons; General in the Swedish Army and Flag Admiral of the Fleet; Hon. Admiral of the Norwegian and Danish Fleets; Admiral of the Russian Fleet; Hon. Captain-General in the Spanish Army and Hon. Colonel of the 11th "Naumancia" Spanish Dragoons; and Hon. Admiral of the Greek Fleet.

The King of Bulgaria was Chief of the 4th Thuringia Infantry Regiment No. 72, in the Prussian Army. As per custom, on a visit to Berlin he donned his uniform of the Thuringian Infantry. He had put on a little weight, and military unmentionables, be it known, are notoriously tight. So as he leaned far out of the Palace window to admire the passing troops, he presented a mark so tempting that the Emperor, in jovial mood, was impelled to administer a resounding spank on the sacred seat of the Czar of all the Balkans. Instead of taking the slap in the same jovial spirit in which it was given the Czar Ferdinand, a little jealous of the self-assumed title of Czar, became furiously angry—so angry that even the old diplomats of the Metternich school believed for a time that he never would forgive the whack and even might refuse to join Germany. But Czar Ferdinand, believing in the military power of Germany, cast his already war-worn people in the

war against the Allies, much to the regret of many
Bulgarian statesmen who, having been educated at
Robert College, near Constantinople, a college
founded and maintained by Americans, and having
imbibed somewhat of the American spirit there,
were not over-pleased to think of themselves arrayed against the United States of America.

But there is no monarch in all Europe who is more
wily than Czar Ferdinand. At a great feast in Bulgaria at which Emperor William was present, Czar
Ferdinand toasted the Emperor in Latin and alluded
to him as *"Miles Gloriosus"*—which all present took
to mean "glorious soldier"; but the exact Latin
meaning of "gloriosus" is "glorious" in its first
meaning and "boastful" in its second, a meaning
well known in Berlin where, at the "Little Theatre,"
in a series of plays of all ages, the *"Miles Gloriosus"*
of Plautus had just been presented—a boastful,
conceited soldier, the *"Miles Gloriosus,"* the chief
character of the comedy.

Nothing illustrates more vividly the belief of the
royal families of the Central Empires in their God-
given right to rule the plain people than those few
words of Maximilian written before his ill-fated
expedition to Mexico. Speaking of the Palace at
Caserta, near Naples, he wrote, "The monumental
stairway is worthy of Majesty. What can be finer
than to imagine the sovereign placed at its head,
resplendent in the midst of these marble pillars,—
to fancy this monarch, like a God, graciously per-
mitting the approach of human beings. The crowd
surges upward. The King vouchsafes a gracious

glance, but from a very lofty elevation. All powerful, imperial, he makes one step towards them with a
smile of infinite condescension. Could Charles V,
could Maria Theresa appear thus at the head of this
ascending stair, who would not bow their heads before that majestic, God-given power?"

What was the condition of the people under
Maria Theresa, whom Maximilian spoke of as
possessing a power that, according to him, was so
God-given no one could fail to bow the head
before her majestic presence? The peasants,
under her rule, were practically slaves, as they could
not leave the lord's lands nor even marry without
his permission, nor could they bring their children
up to any profession other than that of labourer. In
other words, the children of the slave must remain
slaves.

Poor Maximilian! He was a brother of the late
Emperor Francis Joseph and a member of that
Kaiserbund and royal system which, while America
was busy with domestic difficulties between the
North and South, sought to wrest from Mexico
her liberty. I wonder if the Mexicans have forgotten the incident and its implications.

But one-man power always fails in the end. No
man, king or president, whatever he may himself
think, has a brain all powerful and all knowing.
There is wisdom in counsel. Too much of some
favourite dish may lead to indigestion and that to
bad judgment at a critical time and disaster. Napoleon III, just before 1870, was suffering from a
wasting disease and so allowed himself to be ruled

by the beautiful, narrow, fascinating, foolish Spanish Empress whom he gave to the French in a moment of passion because, as she said to him, "The way to her room lay through the church door." Colonel Stoffel, the French Military Attaché to the Berlin Embassy, wrote confidentially report after report to the Emperor telling him of the immense military strength of Prussia and of her readiness for immediate war. But most of these reports were afterwards found unopened in the desk of the doting, sick and fallen Emperor.

For, after all, however divine the King, Emperor or Kaiser may consider himself, he is but a vulnerable human being—and no accident of birth should give even a small number of people on this earth into the hands of a single mortal.

CHAPTER II

WHO DOES THE KAISER'S THINKING AND WHO DECIDED ON THE BREAK WITH AMERICA?

BECAUSE the German Emperor possesses talents of no mean order, because of his fiery energy, because of the charm of his conversation and personality, his ambitions for world conquest are most dangerous to the peace of the world.

Certainly of all the ruling houses of the world, the Hohenzollerns have shown themselves the most able, and of the six sons of the Kaiser there is not one who is unable or unworthy from the autocratic standpoint to carry on the traditions of the house. They are all young men who in any field of human endeavour are more than a match for men of their age, and by reason of these qualities, so rare in kings and princes, it has been easy to arouse a great feeling of devotion for the royal house of Prussia among all classes in Germany, with the possible exception of the Social Democrats. The other kings and princes of Germany have been overshadowed, mere puppets in the king business, by the surpassing talents of the Hohenzollerns, and so the task of those who, in Germany and out, hope for that evolution towards liberalism or even democracy which alone can make the nations of the world feel

32

safe in making peace with Germany, is beset with numerous difficulties.

Before the war the Emperor turned much of his enterprising talent into peaceful channels, into the development of commercial and industrial Germany. No one has a greater respect for wealth and commercial success than the Emperor. He would have made a wonderful success as a man of business. He ought to be the richest person in the Empire, but the militaristic system which he fostered gave that distinction to another. For the richest person in Germany before the war was Frau Krupp-Bohlen, daughter of the late manufacturer of cannon. She inherited control of the factories and the greater part of the fortune of her father and was rated at about $75,000,000. It was a contest between Prince Henckel-Donnersmarck and the Emperor for second place, each being reputed to possess about sixty to sixty-five million dollars. Most of the Emperor's wealth is in landed estates, and of these he has, I believe, about sixty scattered through the Empire. The Emperor is credited with being a large stockholder in both the Krupp works and the Hamburg-American Line. What a sensation it would make in this country were the President to become a large stockholder in Bethlehem Steel or the Winchester Arms Company!

The earnings of the Krupp's factory since the war have been immense and doubtless the fortune of the Krupp heiress since then has more than doubled. The subscriptions to war loans and war charities, thrown by Frau Krupp-Bohlen and the

33

Krupp directors as sops to public opinion, are mere nothings to the fat earnings made by that renowned factory in this war.

And what a sensation, too, would be caused in America if the Bethlehem Steel Company or the United States Steel Corporation were to purchase newspapers or take over The Associated Press in order to control public opinion! Yet the German nation stands by, apathetic, propagandised to a standstill, stuffed and fed by news handed them by the Krupps and the alliance of six great industrial iron and steel companies of western Germany.

A question which interests every inhabitant of the world to-day is, where does the ultimate power reside in Germany?

Where is the force which controls the country? The Reichstag, of course, has no real power; the twenty-five ruling princes of Germany, voting in the Bundesrat through their representatives, control the Reichstag, and the Chancellor is not responsible to either but only to the Emperor.

Consider, for a moment, the personality of von Bethmann-Hollweg, Chancellor of the Empire for eight or nine years. He lacked both determination and decision. Lovable, good, kind, respected, the Chancellor, to a surprising degree, was minus that quality which we call "punch." He never led, but followed. He sought always to find out first which side of the question seemed likely to win,—where the majority would stand. Usually he poised him-

34

self on middle ground. He could not have been the ultimate power in the State.

I have a feeling that the Kaiser himself always felt in some vague way that his luck lay with America, and I imagine that he himself was against anything that might lead to a break with this country. What, then, was the mysterious power which changed, for instance, the policy of the German Empire towards America and ordered unrestricted submarine war at the risk of bringing against the Empire a rich and powerful nation of over a hundred million population?

The Foreign Office did not have this decision. Its members, made up of men who had travelled in other countries, who knew the latent power of America, did not advise this step—with the exception, however, of Zimmermann, who, carried away by his sudden elevation, and by the glamour of personal contact with the Emperor, the Princes and the military chiefs, yielded to the arguments of military expediency.

The one force in Germany which ultimately decides every great question, except the fate of its own head, is the Great General Staff.

On one side of the Königs-Platz, in Berlin, stands the great building of the Reichstag, floridly decorated, glittering with gold, surrounded by statues and filled, during the sessions of the Reichstag, with a crowd of representatives who do not represent and who, like monkeys in a cage, jibber and debate questions which they have no power to decide. Across the square and covering the entire block in a building that resembles in external appearance a jail, built of dark red brick without ornament or display, is the home of the Great General Staff. This institution has its own spies, its own secret service, its own newspaper censors. Here the picked officers of the German army, the inheritors of the power of von Moltke, work industriously. Apart from the people of Germany, they wield the supreme power of the State and when the Staff decides a matter of foreign policy or even an internal measure, that decision is final.

The peculiar relations of the Emperor to the Great General Staff make it possible for him to dismiss in disgrace a head of the Staff who has failed. But at all times the Kaiser is more or less controlled in his action by the Staff as a whole and at a time when the chief of the Great General Staff is successful, the latter, even on questions of foreign policy, claims the right then to make a decision which the Emperor may find it difficult to disregard. This is because in an autocratic government, as in any other, personality counts for much. Von Tirpitz controlled all departments of the navy, although only at the head of one. The Ludendorff-Hindenburg combination, especially if backed by Mackensen, can bend the will of the Emperor.

Yet while the head of the Great General Staff may fall, the system always remains. An unknown, mysterious power it is, unchanging, and relentless, a power that watches over the German army with unseen eyes. It seeks always additions to its own ranks from those young officers who have dis-

THE IRON CROSS. IN THE EXPECTATION OF A SHORT WAR
THOUSANDS OF THESE CROSSES WERE DISTRIBUTED IN
THE FIRST MONTHS OF THE WAR AND THE PRECEDENT
THUS ESTABLISHED HAS LED TO THE GIVING OF PERHAPS
HUNDREDS OF THOUSANDS OF THESE DECORATIONS

tinguished themselves by their talents in the profession of arms. What does it mean to them?

It is January twenty-seventh, the birthday of the Kaiser in a German garrison town. The officers of the regiment are assembled in the mess-hall, the regimental band plays the national air of Prussia, "Heil Dir im Sieger Kranz" (Hail, thou, in the conqueror's wreath). (The music is familiar to us because we sing it to the words of "America." The British sing the air to the words of "God Save the King." This music was originally written for Louis XIV.) The health of the Emperor is proposed and drunk with "Hurrahs" and again "Hurrahs," and then comes a telegram from Berlin announcing the promotions and decorations granted to some of the officers of the regiment: the most envied of all is that younger officer, perhaps the student among them, who receives the laconic despatch telling him that he is detailed to the Great General Staff!

Then commences for the young officer a life of almost monastic devotion. No amusements, no social obligations or entertainments must interfere in the slightest with his earnest work in that plain building of mystery which so calmly, and with such mock modesty, faces the garish home of the Reichstag on the Königs-Platz, in Berlin.

Who decided on the break with America? It was not the Chancellor, notoriously opposed; it was not the Foreign Office, nor the Reichstag, nor the Princes of Germany who decided to brave the consequences of a rupture with the United States on the submarine question. It was not the Emperor;

but a personality of great power of persuasion. It was Ludendorff, Quartermaster General, chief aid and brains to Hindenburg, Chief of the Great General Staff, who decided upon this step.

Unquestionably a party in the navy, undoubtedly von Tirpitz himself, backed by the navy and by many naval officers and the Naval League, advocated the policy and promised all Germany peace within three months after it was adopted; unquestionably public opinion made by the Krupps and the League of Six (the great iron and steel companies), desiring annexation of the coal and iron lands of France, demanded this as a quick road to peace. But it was the deciding vote of the Great General Staff that finally embarked the German nation on this dangerous course.

I do not think the Emperor himself, unless backed by the whole public opinion of Germany, would dare to withstand the Great General Staff which he himself creates. They are so much his devotees that they would overrule him in what they consider his interest.

Whatever thinking the Emperor does nowadays is more or less on his own account. There is to-day no shining favourite who has his ear to the exclusion of others. The last known favourite was Prince Max Egon von Fürstenberg, a man now about fifty-four years old, tall, handsome, possessed at one time of great wealth and a commanding position in Austria as well as Germany, with the privilege of citizenship in both countries. The Prince in his capacity as Grand Marshal accompanied the Em-

38

peror, walking in his train as the latter entered the
White Hall at a great ball early in the winter of
1914. The Emperor was stopping at the Prince's
palace in southern Germany at Donnaueschingen
when the affair at Zabern and the cutting down
of the lame shoemaker there shook the political
and military foundations of the German Empire.
Prince Max together with Prince Hohenlohe,
Duke of Ugest, embarked, however, on a career
of vast speculation in an association known as
the Princes' Trust. They built, for instance, the
great Hotel Esplanade in Berlin, and a hotel of the
same name in Hamburg, and an enormous com-
bined beer restaurant, theatre and moving picture
hall on the Nollendorff Platz in Berlin. They organised banks, and the name of the princely house
of Fürstenberg appeared as an advertisement for
light beer. They even, through their interest in a
department store on the east end of the Leipziger
Strasse, sold pins and stockings and ribbons to the
working classes of Berlin. As this top-heavy structure of foolish business enterprise tumbled, the favour of Prince Max at the Imperial Court fell with
it. For the Emperor never brooks failure.

During the present war Von Gontard, related by
marriage, I believe, to brewer Busch in St. Louis;
von Treutler, who represented the Foreign Office;
von Falkenhayn, for a while head of the Great General Staff and Minister of War, and the Prince of
Pless, and von Plessen with several minor adjutants, have constituted the principal figures in the
surroundings of the Emperor. Falkenhayn fell be-

cause of his failure in the attack of Verdun, ordered by him or for which he was the responsible commander. Von Treutler probably told the truth; he was against the breaking of the submarine pledges to America; and Prince Pless, who remains still in favour, never took a decided stand on any of these questions. Prince Pless, as Prince Max was, is rich. His fortune before the war, represented mostly by great landed estates in Silesia, mines, etc., amounted approximately to thirty million dollars. His wife is an Englishwoman, once celebrated as one of the great beauties of London, daughter of Colonel and Mrs. Cornwallis-West, and sister of the Duchess of Westminster and Cornwallis-West, formerly married to Lady Randolph Churchill, and now the husband of Mrs. Patrick Campbell, the well-known actress. And therefore the position of Princess Pless has not been enviable during this war.

Emperor William does not, like many kings and dictators, confine himself in his search for general information regarding men and conditions to the reports of a few persons. He always has been accessible, seeking even to meet strangers, not merely his own people but foreigners, thus escaping the penalty of those rulers who shut themselves up and who have all their information and thoughts coloured for them by the preferences and desires of prejudiced counsellors.

The chiefs of the army are always in close touch with the Kaiser, but he is consulted on army com-

mands and promotions much less than on civil and
even naval promotions.

Always with him is the head of the Civil Cabinet,
who advises with the Emperor on all appointments
and promotions on the civil side of the Government,
helping even to make and unmake Ambassadors and
Chancellors. Admiral von Mueller, head of the
Marine Cabinet, is constantly in the Emperor's company. He is a shrewd, capable, reasonable man; for
a long time Admiral von Mueller was against taking
the chance of war with America and perhaps, even
to the end, persisted in this course. After the fall
of von Tirpitz, von Mueller acquired more real
power. But in a sense it is incorrect to speak of the
forced retirement of von Tirpitz as a "fall," because from his retirement he was able to carry on
such a campaign in favour of "ruthless" submarine
war that the mass of the people, Reichstag deputies,
the General Staff, and all came over to his point of
view and von Bethmann-Hollweg, who had brought
about his dismissal, was forced officially to adopt
the policy first sponsored by this skilful old sea-dog
and politician.

CHAPTER III

WHO SANK THE "LUSITANIA"?

WHO is responsible for the sinking of the *Lusitania,* for the deliberate murder which has always remained deep in the consciousness of every American, and which at the outset turned this great nation against Germany?

In the first place there was no mistake—no question of orders exceeded or disobeyed. Count von Bernstorff frankly, boldly, defiantly, and impudently advertised to the world, with the authority of the German Government, that the attempt to sink the *Lusitania* would be made. The Foreign Office, no doubt, acquainted him with the new policy. Von Tirpitz, then actual head of the Navy Department and virtual head of the whole navy, openly showed his approval of the act, and threw all his influence in favor of a continuation of ruthless tactics. But a question which involved a breach of international law, a possible break with a friendly power, could not be decided by even the Foreign Office and Navy together.

The Great General Staff claims a hand in the decision of all questions of foreign policy which even remotely affect the conduct of the war. Similarly it was the duty of the Foreign Office to point out

42

the possible consequences under the rules of international law; but when the question of submarine warfare was to be determined, the consultation was usually at the Great General Headquarters. At these meetings von Tirpitz or the navy presented their views and the Great General Staff sat with the Emperor in council, although it was reported in Charleville at the time of the settlement of May, 1916, that Falkenhayn, speaking in favour of submarine war, had been rebuked by the Emperor, and told to stick to military affairs.

All the evidence points to the Emperor himself as the responsible head who at this time ordered or permitted this form of murder. The orders were given at a time when the Emperor dominated the General Staff, not in one of those periods, as outlined in a previous chapter when the General Staff, as at present, dominated the Emperor. When I saw the Kaiser in October, 1915, he said that he would not have sunk the *Lusitania,* that no gentleman would have killed so many women and children. Yet he never disapproved the order. Other boats were sunk thereafter in the same manner and only by chance was the loss of life smaller when the *Arabic* was torpedoed. It is argued that, had the Emperor considered beforehand how many noncombatants would be killed, he would not have given the order to sink that particular boat. But what a lame excuse! A man is responsible for the natural and logical results of his own acts. It may be too that Charles IX, when he ordered, perhaps reluctantly, the massacre of St. Bartholomew, did not know that so many would be killed, but there can be no Pilate-washing-of-the-hands,—Emperor William was responsible. He must bear the blame before the world.

Blood-shed in honorable war is soon forgotten; but the cowardly stroke by which the Kaiser sought to terrorise America, by which he sent to a struggling death of agony in the sea, the peaceful men and women and children passengers of the *Lusitania,* may ever remain a cold boundary line between Germany and America unless the German people utter a condemnation of the tragedy that rings true and repentant.

We want to live at peace with the world when this war is over, to be able to grasp once more the hands of those now our enemies, but how can any American clasp in friendship the hand of Germans who approve this and the many other outrages that have turned the conscience of the world against Germany?

To Americans in Berlin, the sinking of the *Lusitania* came like a lightning stroke. No Bernstorff warnings had prepared us. I believed I would be recalled immediately. In making preparations to leave, I sent a secretary to see the head of one of the largest banks in Germany, a personal friend, to ask him, in case we should leave, to take for safekeeping into his bank our silver, pictures, etc. He said to my secretary, "Tell Judge Gerard that I will take care of his valuables for him, but tell him also, that if the *Mauretania* comes out to-morrow we shall sink her, too."

That was the attitude of a majority of the business men of Germany. German casualties at that time had been great so that the mere loss of human life did not appal as would have been the case in a country unused to the daily posting of long lists of dead and wounded. Consequently the one feeling of Germany was of rejoicing, believing indeed that victory was near, that the "damned Yankees" would be so scared that they would not dare travel on British ships, that the submarine war would be a great success, that France and England deprived of food, steel and supplies from America soon would be compelled to sue for peace, especially since the strategically clever, if unlawful, invasion of France by way of Belgium had driven the French from the best coal and iron districts of their country.

I do recall that one Imperial Minister, a reasonable individual whose name I think it best not to mention, expressed in private his sorrow, not only for the deed itself, but for the mistaken policy which he saw, even then, would completely turn in the end the sympathies of America to the Entente Allies. And there were others,—among the intellectuals, and, especially, among the merchants of Hamburg and Frankfort who had travelled in the outer world both on pleasure and business, who realised what a profound effect the drowning of innocent men, women and children would have on our peace-loving people.

Many of these men said to me, "The sinking of the *Lusitania* is the greatest German defeat of all the war. Its consequences will be far-reaching; its impression, deep and lasting."

The Teutonic Knights, from whom the ruling class of Prussia is descended, kept the Slavic population in subjection by a reign of physical terror. This class believes that to rule one must terrorise. The Kaiser himself referring to the widespread indignation caused by German outrages of the present war, has said: "The German sword will command respect."

Terrorism — "Schrecklichkeit" — has always formed a part, not only of German military inclination, but of German military policy. I often said to Germans of the Government, "Are you yourselves subject to being terrorised? If another nation murdered or outraged your women, your children, would it cause you to cringe in submission or would you fight to the last? If you would fight yourselves, what is there in the history of America which makes you think that Americans will submit to mere frightfulness; in what particular do you think Americans are so different from Germans?" But they shrugged their shoulders.

I have heard that in parts of Germany school children were given a holiday to celebrate the sinking of the *Lusitania*. I was busy with preparations, too anxious about the future to devote much time to the study of the psychology of the Germans in other parts of Germany at this moment, but with the exception of the one Cabinet Minister aforementioned, and expressions of regret from certain merchants and intellectuals, it cannot be denied that a

46

great wave of exultation swept over Germany. It was felt that this was a master stroke, that victory was appreciably nearer and that no power on earth could withstand the brute force of the Empire.

Mingled with this was a deep hate of all things American inculcated by the Berlin Government. And we must understand, therefore, that no trick and no evasion, no brutality will be untried by Germany in this war. It was against the rules of war to use poison gas, but first the newspapers of Germany were carefully filled with official statements saying the British and French had used this unfair means. Coincidentally with these reports the German army was trying by this dastardly innovation to break the British lines. It was not a new procedure. Months before the *Lusitania* crime, the newspapers and people had been poisoned with official statements inflaming the people against America, particularly for our commerce with the Entente in war supplies.

It was the right, guaranteed by a treaty to which Germany was a signatory, of our private individuals to sell munitions and supplies, but as Prince von Buelow once remarked on December 13th, 1900, in the Reichstag, "I feel no embarrassment in saying here, publicly, that for Germany, right can never be a determining consideration."

Indeed the tame professors were let loose and many of them rushed into government-paid print to prove that, according to law, the murders of the *Lusitania* were justified. A German chemist friend of mine told me that the chemists of Ger-

47

many were called on, after poison gas had been met by British and French, to devise some new and deadly chemical. Flame throwers soon appeared together with more insidious gases. And it is only because of the vigilance of other nations that German spies have not succeeded in sowing the microbes of pestilence in countries arrayed against lawless Germany.

Remember there is nothing that Kaiserism is not capable of trying in the hope of victory.

CHAPTER IV

THE talents and ability and agreeable personality of the German Emperor must not blind us to the fact that he is the centre of the system which has brought the world to a despair and misery such as it never has known since the dawn of history. We must remember that all his utterances disclose the soul of the conqueror, of a man intensely anxious for earthly fame and a conspicuous place in the gallery of human events; envious, too, of the great names of the past, his ears so tuned for admiration and applause that they fail to hear the great, long drawn wail of agony that echoes around the world. His eyes are so blinded with the sheen of his own glory that they do not see the mutilated corpses, the crime, the pestilence, the hunger, the incalculable sorrow that sweeps the earth from the jungles of Africa to the frozen plains of the North, from Siberia to Saskatchewan, from Texas to Trieste, from Alaska to Afghanistan—everywhere he has brought the dark angel of mourning to millions upon millions of desolate homes.

Do you remember that picture of the Conquerors, Cæsar and Alexander, Attila and Napoleon, Charlemagne and Cambyses, astride their horses or in chariots in the centre of the picture, dark, gloomy, menacing? On each side of them, lining a vast plain that fades in the distance, lie the dead—stiff, cold, grey, reproachful;—yet all the victims of those conquerors, as well as all their battalions do not equal the countless number that have already drenched a forgiving earth with their dying blood in this war:—victims all of the vain-glorious ambition of a single mortal—the German Kaiser.

But the despot who sends his subjects to die, as Frederick the Great said, "in order to be talked about" is not indigenous to any one particular country. Like conditions produce like results. The career of Louis XIV, the "Sun King," for instance, whose wars and extravagances sowed the seeds of the French Revolution, is epitomised in two phrases uttered by him: "I am the State" and "I almost had to wait."

After the French Revolution, another despot, the first Napoleon, not only sought the conquest of the world, but made his ex-waiter and ex-groom marshals and his washerwomen duchesses ape the manners and customs of the old régime. Despotism has been characteristic of many generations but the world had thought itself rid of the worst offenders.

Royalty still lives to torture and retard civilisation. Its methods of perpetuation are unchanged from the middle ages. What is lèse-majesté but a survival of feudalism, a kind of slavery to inviolable tradition—the immunity of the monarch and his family from that criticism and freedom of discussion which is the essence of democracy?

THE UNITED STATES EMBASSY STAFF, BERLIN; MR. GERARD IN THE CENTER

To commit lèse-majesté, to speak slightingly of royalty in Germany, is a very serious offence.

I have taken the following examples of decisions in lèse-majesté cases not from the records of the lower courts, the decisions of which may be reversed, but from the records of the Imperial Supreme Court at Leipzig, the highest court in the land.

For instance: The defendant, a speaker at a meeting consisting chiefly of sympathisers with the socialist cause, made the following statement in reference to a speech of the Kaiser:

"Under the protection of the highest power of the State the gauntlet has been flung before the (socialist) Party, the gauntlet which means a combat for life and death. Well, then, so far as the insult concerns our Party, we are so far above it, that the mudslinging—no matter from what direction it may come—cannot touch us."

The defence pointed out that the defendant "had considered each word carefully before he had made the speech, and that in doing so, wanted to avoid any possibility of lèse-majesté."

The Supreme Court held that although the defendant carefully selected his words and tried to evade prosecution, he must be adjudged guilty, because his audience could not have misunderstood the insinuation. The sentence was affirmed.

Dangerous as it is to say anything that can be construed as derogatory of the authority of the Kaiser it is equally dangerous to attack the dead members of the Royal House.

51

119463

The editor of the *Volkswacht* had published in his paper an article entitled "The German Characteristics of the Hohenzollerns" which the Lower Court interpreted to be a reply to a statement of the Kaiser, which had referred to a group of people considered unworthy by him to be called "Germans." Without doubt the editor was alluding to the Kaiser's speech, made at Koenigsberg to the newly enlisted army recruits, in which he called the socialists "vaterlandslose Gesellen," i.e., scoundrels without any country. The writer, however, discussed "the conduct of the Elector Joachim of Brandenburg and of his brother Albrecht, Elector of Mainz, before and during the election of Emperor Charles V."

The defence claimed that the defendant could not be held guilty of lèse-majesté against the Kaiser since the defendant "criticised the Kaiser's ancestors and not the Kaiser himself." But the Court held that it was the intent of the defendant to discredit the "House of the Hohenzollerns, and that the Kaiser by implication, being the living head of the Hohenzollern family, was thereby insulted." The Court further states that the defendant's article could not be regarded as a scientific or historical contribution since the *Volkswacht's* subscribers, consisting chiefly of workingmen, had neither any understanding of nor interest in dynastic intrigues of the sixteenth century."

Even those Americans who have expressed themselves freely about the Kaiser will, after the war is over, be compelled to take their "cures" in some country other than Germany, for in one case it was held that an American citizen was rightfully convicted in Baden of lèse-majesté because of statements made by him in Switzerland.

The Court held that the judgment of the Lower Court must be sustained, since the German Imperial Laws have precedence over any treaties engaged in by the Grand Duchy of Baden and the United States and "that the fact that the defendant had become a citizen of the United States does not exempt him from prosecution in the German Imperial Courts."

In another case a newspaper editor criticised a speech delivered by the Kaiser before the Reichstag on December 6th, 1898. The defendant did not refer to the person of the Emperor himself, but simply attacked and ridiculed the propositions and proposals made by His Imperial Majesty. The defence pointed out that the Kaiser's speech was not an act of the Kaiser's own personal will, but only an act of government for which the Imperial Chancellor should be responsible, and that the defendant was not conscious of the fact that the criticism contained in his article could be an insult to the person of the Kaiser.

It was held, however, by the Court that a criticism of the Kaiser's speech at the opening of the Reichstag is *always* to be regarded as a criticism of the Kaiser's person, and that the plea that the Imperial Chancellor should be responsible for acts of government of this sort is not sustained.

In other words it is, in Germany, a crime to criticise or ridicule any proposition uttered by the sacred lips of the Kaiser.

If the Kaiser announces that two and two make five, jail awaits the subject who dares to ridicule that novel arithmetical proposition.

It is because of these convictions for lèse-majesté that the Berliners, when discussing the Emperor at their favourite table or "Stammtisch" in the beer halls and cafés, always refer to him as "Lehmann."

CHAPTER V

An Unpublished Diary

KAISERDOM is an institution with which the American people are really unacquainted—a complex institution the parallel of which does not exist elsewhere. How it sought to play double with the United States is in a general way familiar to Americans, but I think the record of what happened in the eighteen months preceding our break with Germany will illustrate exactly the currents and cross-currents of official opinion which led the United States to be scrupulously cautious in its course before entering the war. As I talked with the Emperor or the Chancellor or the Foreign Minister, I jotted down from time to time notes of their conversation as well as brief summaries of the information available to me from other sources. Naturally I cabled to the Department of State the most significant news, but much of this was not published because our Government was proceeding cautiously and did not wish to be embarrassed by publicity of its negotiations. There is every reason now, however, why the facts should be known. I am reproducing here the diary I kept from June,

55

1915, to the end of January, 1917, when unrestricted submarine warfare was resumed and our break with Germany came. I did not have the idea then of ever publishing my memoranda, so my comments were written without restraint. They show, I am sure, what the general trend of sentiment was in Germany for and against submarine warfare and disclose, too, that while the Emperor was often in the background and seemingly not the most powerful factor in the situation, it was his system that dominated Germany, his spirit that bred the lust for military gain at whatever cost—even the respect of the whole civilised world. Here are the notes as I penned them at the time:

June, 1915. Lincoln never passed through a crisis greater than that with which the President is contending. He is fighting, first, for humanity and some decency in war, and, second, determining whether a European Emperor shall or shall not dictate the political attitude of certain of our citizens.

It is regrettable to be compelled to think that the German nation knows no treaty or law except the limit of its own desires.

We are still awaiting the second *Lusitania* note and I fear that Germany will never consent to abandon its present hideous method of submarine war. It is extraordinary to hear Germans of all classes extoll mere brute force as the only rule of international life. It is a warning to us to create and increase our fleet and coast defences.

The Germans not only do not fear war with us,

but state frankly they do not believe we dare to declare it, call us cowardly bluffers and say our notes are worse than waste paper. Breaking diplomatic relations means nothing.

Von Wiegand, the newspaper correspondent, is just back from Przemysl and says the Russians were defeated by woful lack of artillery and ammunition. Their power for offence is broken for many months. From the West I hear the French are rather discouraged.

Germany has ample food and gets all copper, etc., necessary for war purposes through Sweden in exchange for potash and other commodities.

An officer of the war ministry, who comes to see me about prisoners, etc., told me last night that because the French have kept several hundred Germans as prisoners in Dahomey and other places in Africa, fifteen thousand French prisoners will be sent to work in the unhealthy swamps of Holstein. I have cabled the State Department often about this Dahomey business, transmitting the request of Germany that these prisoners be sent to Europe. Germans cannot be beaten on reprisals.

Two or three German-Americans have attacked the President, Secretary Bryan and our Government, some publicly. I have ordered their passports taken away and hope to be sustained. To permit them to continue poisoning the atmosphere would be taken as a sign of weakness here. No one who abuses his own country, its government or its Chief is entitled to protection from that country.

We have the visiting of British prisoners in good shape now, that prohibition put on our visiting and inspecting the camps was abolished in March by the "treaty" I arranged between England and Germany. It was not until March twenty-ninth that we finally got passes to visit camps under the "treaty." The prisoners say they are badly treated when they are first captured, but we know only of their treatment in the camps.

I do not believe all the atrocity stories; but one of our servants in this house came back from the East front recently and said the orders were to kill all Cossacks. Our washerwoman reports that her son was ordered to shoot a woman in Belgium and I myself have heard an officer calmly describe the shooting of a seven-year-old Belgian girl child, the excuse being that she had tried to fire at an officer.

If the *Lusitania* business settles down, I hope the suggestion made to me by the authorities here and cabled to the State Department, will be carried into effect. This was that each American and Spanish Ambassador, having charge of prisoners in belligerent countries, should meet in Switzerland and discuss the whole prison situation. Each Ambassador would be accompanied by representatives of whatever authorities deal with prisoners (here the War Ministry) in the country to which he is accredited. To prevent unseemly discussions the actual talking would be done by the Ambassadors (coached by those representatives). In addition to doing away with many misunderstandings and helping the prisoners, there are great possibilities in such a meeting. We could all give each other useful "tips" on the caring for prisoners, inspections, camps, package delivery, mail, etc.

There is plenty of food in Germany now and enough raw materials to carry on the war. Raw materials for peaceful industries are needed.

A suggestion—why not start a great government chemical school or give protection for a certain number of years to dyestuffs, medicine, chemical, and cyanide material? All these industries are run here by the trustiest trusts that ever trusted, and by their methods keep American manufacturers from starting the business. A Congressman represents one of the best firms, hence his statements that it is impossible to start such manufactures in America. Our annual tribute to these trusts is enormous. One dyestuff company here employs over five hundred chemists. Only big or protected business can compete. This war has shown that we should not be dependent on other countries for so many manufactures.

Gifts from America within the last week have been refused in Saxony.

I fear that Germany will not give up its present method of submarine war. Each month new and more powerful submarines are added.

Perhaps it is worth a war to have it decided that the United States of America is not to be run from Berlin.

Germans in authority feel that our "New Freedom" is against their ideas and ideals. They hate President Wilson because he embodies peace and learning rather than war.

In regard to prisoners, Mr. Harte reports prisoners in Russia and Siberia better treated than was reported.

I hear for the first time of growing dissatisfaction among the plain people, especially at the great rise in food prices. Germany is getting everything she wants, however, through Sweden, including copper, lard, etc. Von Tirpitz and his Press Bureau were too much for the Chancellor; the latter is not a good fighter. Zimmermann, if left to himself, would, of course, have stopped this submarine murder.

I hope the President never gives in on the embargo on arms; if he ever gives in on that, we might as well hoist the German Eagle on the Capitol.

July, 1915. I think that the firm tone of the President's note (of June 9, 1915) will make the Germans climb down. There seems a general disposition to be pleased with the note and an expectation that matters can be arranged. The great danger is that the Germans may again get the idea that we do not dare to declare war. In such case they will again become difficult to handle.

Zimmermann and von Jagow are both quite pleased with the tone of the note.

60

They both talk now of keeping Belgium, the excuse being that the Belgians hate the Germans so that if Belgium again became independent it would be only an English outpost. Meyer Gerhard, Bernstorff's special envoy, has arrived and has broken into print over the sentiment in America. I am afraid he makes it too peaceful, and, therefore, the Germans will be encouraged to despise America.

While the authorities here think the idea of freedom of the seas good, they think the idea of freedom of land too vague. They want to know exactly what it means and say the seas should be free because they belong to no one, but that land is the private property of various nations. They compare the situation to a city street, where every one is interested in keeping the streets free but would resent a proposal that private houses also should be made common meeting ground if not common property. Unfortunately for Germany and the world, the German armies are winning and this will be considered a complete vindication of the military and caste system and everything which now exists. As Cleveland said, we are confronted by a condition, not a theory. *Germany, unless beaten, will never directly or indirectly agree to any freedom of land or disarmament proposal.*

The Emperor probably will see me soon. He has been rabid on the export of arms from the United States to the Allies, but like all Germans, when they see we cannot be scared into a change of policy, he is making a nice recovery.

Was told by a friend at the Foreign Office that the German note would contain a proposition that regular passenger ships should not be torpedoed without notice, but must carry no cargo other than passengers' baggage. Have heard Marine Department rather opposes this, but may favor proposition as to ships inspected and certified to carry no arms or ammunition. No note until after July fourth, they say at Foreign Office, on tip from Washington. (Note—German note was delivered to me July 8, 1915.)

Chancellor and von Jagow have been in Vienna, probably over Balkan question. The situation there hinges on Bulgaria. Germany wants a direct strip of territory for itself or Austria to Constantinople. Thirteen million pounds in gold sent recently by Germany to Turkey to keep the boys in line. Principal Socialist paper, the *Vorwaerts,* has been suppressed because it spoke of peace; reason given is that this kind of talk would encourage enemies of Germany.

The Germans are becoming more strict, even women now entering Germany must strip to the skin and take down their back hair. The wife of Hearst's correspondent here had to submit to this the other day.

At first, newspaper correspondents had to promise they would not go to enemy territory, next that they would not go to neutral territory (after one correspondent went to Denmark and sent out dispatches about the movement against annexing Belgium). Now the correspondents must promise not to go home. This is to keep secret the internal conditions. The women stormed a butter shop here the other day and our Consul reports, in Chemnitz, quite a serious food riot. The military were called out and the fire department turned hose on the crowd.

In Austria, I hear men up to fifty-five are being called to the colours and even the infirm taken for the army. There are said to be seven German and five Austrian army corps invading Servia. The losses of the invaders are reported to be heavy. To date, the German dead in this war number about seven hundred thousand. People who offered private hospitals at the beginning of the war and who were told these were not needed, have been requested to open them. I was told the remaining civil population of Vouziers, France (in German hands), had been removed to make room for German wounded.

The note of July 21, 1915, in which the President said he would regard the sinking of ships without warning as "deliberately unfriendly," is received with hostility by press and Government. Of course, the party of frightfulness has conquered those of milder views, owing largely to the aggressive newspaper campaign conducted by von Tirpitz, Reventlow and Company. The Germans generally are, at present, in rather a waiting attitude, perhaps anxious to see what our attitude toward England will be——but this will not affect their submarine policy. The Foreign Office now claims, I hear, that I am hostile to Germany, but that claim was to be expected. Of course, I had no more to do with the American note than they did, but it is impossible to convince them of that, so I shall not try.

Germany has the Balkan situation well in hand. Roumania can do nothing in the face of recent Russian defeats and has just consented to allow grain to be exported to Austria and Germany, but has, I think, not yet consented to allow the passage of ammunition to Turkey. The pressure, however, is great. If not successful, perhaps German troops will invade Servia so as to get a passage through to Turkey.

A minister from one of the Balkan States told me the situation of Roumania, Greece and Bulgaria was about the same, each state can last in war only about three months, so all are trying to gauge three months before the end and then come in on the winning side.

The Bulgarian Minister of the Public Debt got in here by mistake the other day, insisting he had an appointment; he *had* an appointment with the Treasurer, Helfferich, whose office is nearby. This shows, perhaps, that Bulgaria is getting money here.

Also the Germans are sending back to Russia, Russians of revolutionary tendencies, who were

64

prisoners here, with money and passports in order that they may stir up trouble at home.

The Germans are making a great effort to take Warsaw, even old Landsturm men are in the fighting line; I think they will get it, and then they hope to turn two million men and strike a great blow in France—thus they expect to end the war by October.

I notice now a slight reaction from annexation toward giving up all or part of Belgium; but I must say I hear very little of popular dissatisfaction with the war. Everything seems to be going smoothly; but they are scraping the bottom of the box on getting men for the army.

It is not pleasant to be hated by so many millions. The Germans naturally make me the object of their concentrated hate. I received an anonymous letter in which the kindly writer rejoices that so many Americans were drowned in the Chicago disaster. This shows the state of mind.

The Emperor is at the front, "Somewhere in Galicia." They keep him very much in the background, I think, with the idea of disabusing the popular mind of the idea that this is "his war." After all, accidents may happen, and even after a victorious war there may be a day of reckoning. The Chancellor went to the front yesterday, probably to see the Emperor about the American question.

65

August, 1915. I had a conversation last week of one hour and a half with the Chancellor. He sent for me because I had written him to take no more trouble about my seeing the Emperor. He explained, of course, first that he did not know I wanted to see the Emperor, and second that it was impossible to see the Emperor. They keep the Emperor well surrounded. *Now* I do not want to see him. He is hot against Americans and the matters I wanted to talk of are all settled—one way. I cabled an interesting report on the Emperor's conversation re America.

The Chancellor is still wrong in his head; says it was necessary to invade Belgium, break all international laws, etc. I think, however, that he was personally against the fierce Dernburg propaganda in America. I judge that von Tirpitz, through his press bureau, has egged on the people so that this submarine war will continue. *An official confessed to me that they had tried to get England to interfere, together with them, in Mexico, and Germans "Gott strafe" the Monroe Doctrine in their daily prayers of hate.*

Warsaw, as I predicted officially, long ago, will soon fall.

No great news—we are simply waiting for the inevitable submarine "accident."

Unless there is a change of sentiment in the Government I think the submarine commanders will be careful.

66

The Chancellor talked rather freely but again said it was impossible to leave Belgium to become an outpost of the English, but possibly with Germans in possession of the forts, the railways and with commercial rights in Antwerp it might be arranged.

There is a faction here led by deputy Bassermann, Stresemann, Fahrmann, etc., who are attacking the Chancellor. They represent great. industrials who want to annex Belgium, Northern France, Poland and anything else that can be had, for their own ultimate advantage. A man named Hirsch is hired by the Krupp firm to "accelerate" this work. Krupps also pay the expenses of the "Oversea Service" which is feeding news to America.

A paper against annexation of Belgium has been signed, I am told, by Dernburg, Prince Hatzfeld and others, and will be presented to the Chancellor to-day. I believe many are to sign it; but of those who have signed are Hatzfeld, who is one of the three big Dukes of Prussia; Prince Henkel-Donnersmarck, who is the second richest subject in Germany—(85 years old, he was in 1870 first Governor of Lorraine)—von Harrach, who is a man of great ability, highly respected, as is also Professor Delbrück.

The Reichstag meets in a few days. The Socialists are holding daily caucuses, but have not yet decided on any party action. Undoubtedly they will vote for the new ten milliard loan, with Liebknecht and a few others dissenting. Probably a split will also develop in the National Liberal Party; Basserman and others have been attacking the Chancellor, but I think other members will dissent. It is quite probable that there will be a discussion about the *object* of the war, and permission will be asked for public discussion, the Socialists perhaps claiming that they have consented to a defensive war only, and that now that the war is on enemy territory peace should be at least discussed. There may also be talk about the annexation of Belgium and food prices. The Socialists are greatly incensed at those who are holding food for high prices.

Personally, I think that Germany now wants peace but does not want to say so openly.

A relative of a Field Marshal told me to-day that Germany's killed to date were 600,000 and 200,000 crippled for life.

I must say that the plain people still seem perfectly tame and ready to continue the war. However, there may also be a protest in the Reichstag about the treatment by non-commissioned officers of Landsturm men who have never served but who now, in the process of scraping the box, are called to the colors.

The Germans hope by a great movement to capture a great part of the Russian army; probably they will fail. They also entertain hopes that in such case Sweden will enter Finland and two Balkan States declare for them. Balkan Ministers here tell me the defeat of Russia makes it impossible for Roumania to enter, but they fear an invasion by the Germans. All diplomatic work is now centred in the Balkans.

Successes in Russia have made the people here very cocky. Hence, probably, the torpedoing of the *Arabic*. Also great hope of Bulgaria coming in with Germany; there is no more dissatisfaction heard over the war. I have as yet received nothing from Washington regarding the *Arabic*.

I have just spent four half days at Ruhleben, where civilian Britishers are interned, so as to give every prisoner a chance to speak to me personally.

There is much talk of creating an independent Poland. The Reichstag session has developed no opposition.

A fac-simile of that infernal advertisement * of the Cleveland Automatic Tool Company in the *American Machinist* was laid on the desk of every member of the Reichstag; and the papers are full of accounts of great deliveries of war munitions by America, possibly preparing people for a break. If Bulgaria comes in, Germany will undoubtedly take a strip in Servia and keep a road to Constantinople and the East. The new Turkish Ambassador has just arrived. The old one was not friendly to Enver Bey and so was bounced.

* This was an advertisement in an American newspaper about machines for the manufacture of particularly deadly shells and was much used in Germany to show how America was helping the Entente.

he remains here, however, as he fears if he went to Turkey he would get some "special" coffee. The hate for Americans grows daily.

All rumours are that in the recent council at Posen the Chancellor, advocating concessions in submarine war, won out over von Tirpitz. But von Tirpitz will die hard, and there will be trouble yet, as the Navy will be very angry if the present methods are abandoned. Members of the Reichstag have telegraphed backing up the Chancellor; but it is hard for any civilian idea to prevail against Army or Navy.

Probably the Admiralty will say that the submarine which torpedoed the *Arabic* was lost, in order to avoid disgracing an officer.

If the *Arabic* question is not complicated with the *Lusitania* a solution will be easier. The common people have been aroused by von Tirpitz's press bureau and it will be simpler for the Chancellor to "back track," taking as an example a case like the *Arabic* when the ship was going West and carried no ammunition.

The defeat of the Russians is undoubtedly crushing. Is England waking up too late? There will be a big offensive soon against the West lines.

I have heard nothing up to to-day from the State Department re the *Arabic,* except one cable asking me to request a report.

A correspondent has just been in and says that

the General Staff people threaten to expel him because he went to Copenhagen and sent out news about the petition to the Chancellor not to annex Belgium. The Foreign Office had no objection; this shows how the line is forming between the Chancellor and the Military. All correspondents to-day say the Germans are trying to dragoon them into sending only news which the General Staff wants sent, and the Military have added their censorship to that of the Foreign Office.

An official told me that Bernstorff, while not exactly exceeding his instructions in his *"Arabic Note"* (of Sept. 1, 1915), had put the matter in a manner they did not approve.

Orders have now, apparently, been given to all German officials to say that the war will last a long time—at least a year and a half.

It is expected that Persia will come in under German leadership and attack India.

Our Military Attaché, Colonel Kuhn, was finally presented to the Kaiser and had a pleasant chat with him. Colonel Kuhn says all fighting on the West is with artillery and hand grenades. Rifles are thrown aside.

Germans have spies "piking off" our Embassies in Paris, London and Petrograd.

Great airship attacks on London may be expected. In one of the recent attacks nine thousand eight hundred bombs (fire and explosive) were dropped. I get this from good authority.

71

Foreign Office quite elated over their Balkan triumph. Personally, I think it was one of the most effective bits of German "diplomacy" in the history of the Empire.

CHAPTER VI

THE INSIDE OF GERMAN DIPLOMACY

The Diary Continued

*O*CTOBER, *1915.* There is a tendency here to
say Bernstorff went too far. But this is all
for the public, von Jagow told a correspondent so to-
day; but, of course, he did not know about the note
of Austria to Servia either! The Marine people
are positively raging. The paper which Reventlow
writes for, the *Tages Zeitung,* was suppressed yesterday; I hear on account of an article on this
Arabic settlement, but I am not yet sure.

There is talk now of marching to Egypt.

More and more men are being called to colours.
But Germany seems to be able to take care of all
fronts. The Emperor is now in the West. The
Foreign Office leads the rejoicing over the Entente's
invasion of Greece and the violation of its neutrality and says that talk about Belgium is now shown
to be *cant.*

Weather is rotten and we shall have a melancholy winter. Feel the war more—deaths and
prices. Six hundred and eighty thousand killed to
October first, and many crippled. Food way up,
but they cannot starve Germany out.

Suppression of the *Tages Zeitung* means that the Chancellor has at last exhibited some backbone and will fight von Tirpitz. The answer of Germany depends on the outcome of this fight. It is possible that von Falkenhayn and the army party may sustain the Chancellor as against von Tirpitz. It is quite likely that a sort of safe conduct will be offered in the note for ships especially engaged in passenger trade. Much stress will be laid on English orders to merchant ships to ram submarines.

The Kaiser is at Pless, a castle of Prince of Pless, in Silesia, near Breslau, where he moved after the attempt of French fliers to bombard him at Charleville on the West Front. The Germans probably will have Lemberg in a few days. This may prevent Roumania coming in. There is talk here of an attempted revolution in Moscow. There is said to be jealousy of Hindenburg and on account of this, Mackensen was put forward to be the hero of the Galician Campaign. Captain Enochs, one of our observers in Austria, was forced out of Austria because of German pressure and our other military observers will follow soon.

Many commercial magnates have arrived in town to argue with the government against war with America; but some are in favor of the continuance of bitter submarine war, notably one who sees his Bagdad railway menaced by possible English success in the Dardanelles.

November, 1915. A man who saw Tisza tells me the Serbs inquired if they could get peace and

74

retain their territories. They were answered, "No."

It is said that Italy has also felt out for peace, but was answered that she must deal with Austria alone—and Austria says that she will not include Italy in any general peace but will wallop her alone after general peace is made.

I am working hard to get British prisoners properly clothed. Winter is already here. Efforts to starve Germany will not succeed. We shall be on meat and butter cards, but that is only a precaution. The people still are well in hand. Constant rumours of peace keep them hopeful. Men over forty-five not yet called. They seem to have plenty of troops. The military are careless of the public opinion of neutrals; they say they are winning and do not need good opinion. I am really afraid of war against us after this war—if Germany wins. We had snow, ice, and cold weather at the end of October.

There have been uneasy movements among the people in Leipzig, a great industrial centre, and the *Volkzeitung,* a Socialist paper there, has been put under permanent preventive censorship.

All these movements start with the question of the price of food.

The Prussian Junkers, however, are really benefited by the war. They get, even with a high "stop price," three times as much as formerly for their agricultural products and pay only a small sum, sixty pfennig daily, for the prisoners of war who now work their fields. They may, in addition, have to pay the keep of the prisoners, but that is very small. Camp commanders are allowed sixty-six pfennig per head per diem.

There is much talk of peace. The shares of the Hamburg-American Line and the shares of the Hamburg-South American Line have risen enormously in price from fifty-six to one hundred and forty in one case. This may be caused by an advantageous sale of some shares of the Holland-American Line or by promise of a subsidy, or by hopes of peace.

There is no question but that every man under forty-five that can drag a rifle has been drafted for the army, with the possible exception of men working in railways, munitions, etc.

Yesterday I noticed many women working on the roadbed of the railway.

The new Peruvian Minister is named von der Heyde; his father was a German.

The Greek Minister still thinks Greece will stay out of the war. His father is one of the cabinet.

The Germans are very glad to get rid of Brand Whitlock. For some time they have been looking for an excuse to expel him.

The dyestuff and other chemical manufacturers are getting quite scared about possible American competition. I hope the Democrats will give protection to these new industries and will also enact some "anti-dumping" legislation.

76

The German cities are adding to the general weight of debt by incurring large debts for war purposes, such as relief of soldiers' families, etc.

The former Turkish Ambassador, who is against the Young Turks, is living here. He is afraid to go back and also the Germans are keeping him in stock in case the Young Turks go out of power, and possibly to stir up trouble in Egypt, as his wife is a daughter of one of the Khedives.

There are lots of suspicious looking Spaniards about, possibly cooking up an attack on Gibraltar.

Any German peace talk includes payment of a large subsidy by England, Russia, and France; Italy to be left to Austria to finish.

The export of gold has now been formally forbidden.

There is no doubt whatever that the population in the conquered portion of Poland has been for a long time in need of food.

Our Military Attaché, Colonel Kuhn, just back from Servia, says the Germans have, literally, stacks of ammunition and had begun preparing last spring for the present attack, even little mountain wagons and new harness being all ready. Only about six German corps are there.

The hate against Americans here is deep-seated and bitter. Hans Winterfeldt, a prominent German banker, with American citizenship, just came in to tell me that at the annual meeting to-day of the great Allegemeine Electricitäts Gesellschaft a fight was started against him because of his American citizenship, and he was not, therefore, re-elected a director. He thinks of resigning from all banks, etc., and returning to America.

December, 1915. Red Cross Doctor Schmidt just in from Servia says Belgrade was completely plundered.

Having lots of difficulty getting the Germans to give the English prisoners clothes.

Hate of Americans worse than ever.

Germans are not resentful when I fight to get things for English prisoners; they only say they hope our Ambassadors are doing the same for Germans.

Much disappointment at Dr. Snoddy's mission not yet being permitted to work in Russia.

Last Tuesday night I ran into quite a peace demonstration, called by placards the night of the Peace Interpretation in the Reichstag. Soon disbanded by the police with many arrests. One man told me that they were tired of a silly war and days without meat. There has been nothing in the papers about these demonstrations; of course, each arrest makes an anarchist for life.

It is hard to get butter. The women storm the butter shops and market.

In a new building (where the Consulate is) they are taking off the *copper* roof.

Of a sudden—peace talk. The Chancellor is waiting to address the Reichstag, waiting to get the sentiment of the members who are all in Berlin,

ORDER.

The unheard-of and rough treatment, which, according to reliable information, has been accorded to civilian prisoners, and particularly German women and children who remain in England, has caused the withdrawal of all privileges formerly granted to English Prisoners of War. On this account, permission for all kinds of amusements and games has been cancelled

The time for bathing has been limited to 10 minutes.

The English Prisoners of War, Mc Lachlan, was shot dead early on the 7th. August, whilst attempting to escape.

The English Prisoner of War, Orton, has been summoned to a Military Trial owing to resistance against to Authority.

Alberti

Oberst und Kommandant
des Gefangenenlagers Döberitz.

FACSIMILE OF AN ORDER ISSUED BY COMMANDER OF GERMAN PRISON CAMP OF DOEBERITZ. MANY CAMP COMMANDERS, WITHOUT AUTHORITY, UNDERTOOK TO MAKE PRISONERS SUFFER FOR ALLEGED AND UNPROVED MISDEEDS OF THE BRITISH. I HAD GREAT TROUBLE IN WATCHING FOR ORDERS OF THIS CHARACTER AND SECURING THEIR ANNULMENT

and then swim with it. Many members, who are not Socialists, favour peace, and the Chancellor will be forced to make some sort of a declaration on why they are fighting and for what.

A Reichstag member told me the Reichstag will say and do things it did not dream of doing six months ago. There are many quiet meetings of members going on.

Hindenburg is out with an interview saying it is not yet time for peace. This is a Government measure to stamp out peace talk among the Reichstag members.

Am having a hard fight to get the British prisoners properly clothed for the winter. Of course, the Germans have rather a difficult time with so many prisoners, but that is no excuse if men die of cold. The weather is and has been bitterly cold.

Saw von Jagow lately, but only on business and commercial questions. Zimmermann lunched here to-day. Roeder, of the *World,* is here making a study of German industrial conditions. I introduced him to Gutmann, of the Dresdner Bank; Rathenau, head of the Allegemeine Electricitäts Gesellschaft; Dr. Solf, Colonial Minister, and others. I think his report will be very sound and worth reading.

There is no question but that there is a deep-seated hatred of America here, *which must be reckoned with sooner or later.*

I don't expect things to be easy, but I wish to goodness all Americans would stay at home.

Greek Minister still thinks Greece will remain neutral.

Probably greatest need of Germany is lubricating oil for machines, etc. Germans claim to have a copper mine in Servia. I never heard of one there.

Dr. Ohnesorg, U. S. N., and Osborne back from inspecting camps. They report bad conditions; they were not allowed (contrary to our "treaty") to talk out of hearing of camp officers to the prisoners in Lemburg Camp. These prisoners are 2,000 Irish, and the reason, of course, for the refusal of the usual permission is that the Germans, through the notorious Sir Roger Casement, have been trying to seduce the Irish, and do not want the soldier prisoners to tell us about it. I have learned, through other sources, that the Germans seduced about 30 Irish. I told von Jagow what I had learned and asked what the Germans had done with these victims—whether they were in the German army or not. He said, "No, most of them had been sent to Ireland to raise hell there." I suppose they were landed from submarines.

I think the German press has received orders to step softly on the von Papen-Boy-ed recall. The greatest danger now lies in Austria, and over the *Ancona* note. There is a large body of manufacturers, ship-owners, etc., here who at the last moment declare themselves against war with the U. S. A. and use their influence to that end, but in Austria no such interests exist to help toward peace. However, pressure from Germany may be brought to bear.

I think Germany will not send successors to von Papen and Boy-ed even with safe conduct; whether they will ask the recall of our attachés is another question not yet decided.

An official tells me confidentially that Rintelen was sent to America to buy up the product of the Dupont Powder Company, and that if he did anything else he exceeded his instructions.

Shop people in Berlin with whom I have talked are getting sick of the war.

I hear rumours that Germany is trying, through its Minister in China, to come to an understanding with Japan and Russia.

The banks are sending circulars to all safe-deposit box holders, trying to get them to give up their gold.

An American clergyman has just told me the German church body has refused to receive an American Church deputation and has written a very bitter letter.

An official has told me that no new Military Attaché will be sent to America. The naval people have not yet decided.

I am very glad to hear Colonel House is coming over. There are many things I want to tell the President but which I do not dare to commit to paper.

A newspaperman supposed to be of the *New York* ———— had an interview with Zimmermann the other day, and Zimmermann sent some messages by him to the President. I do not know what the messages are. We all suffer much from amateur diplomats.

Anthony Czarnecki, a very intelligent Chicagoan, an American of Polish descent, is here representing Victor Lawson and the *Chicago Daily News*. He informs me that the Spy Nest is contemplating an attack on the Administration because of the taking away of Archibald's and others' passports.

My impression is that the Austrians, owing to pressure from here, will eventually give in on the *Ancona* business. I think the present a good time to force the settlement of the *Lusitania* question.

NOTE. I do not suppose that any Ambassador ever suffered as much from amateur "super Ambassadors" as I did.

The German Foreign Office, trying to be modern and up-to-date at times, paid more attention to the tales of pro-German American correspondents than they did to the utterances of President Wilson.

Of course, the Germans succeeded in taking many of those correspondents in their camp. In the Hotel ——— in Berlin an agent of the German Government who possessed American citizenship was always ready to arrange trips to the front or to make an advance of money to an American correspondent who would promise to be "good."

Some received cash, some were paid in interviews with prominent officials, some received both, before all was continually dangled the blue ribbon—the hope of an interview with the Kaiser—and some, thank God, were real Americans and refused all the offered temptations—news or money.

An American gentleman who lived for a time at this hotel has given me a written statement which throws a light on the activities of certain of these gentry and which I may some day use. In this he states how one of these gentlemen claimed that the Imperial Chancellor always sent for him to consult him on his attitude towards America and that he had advised him to make a bold front and bluff. Hence, perhaps the note of January thirty-first which suddenly announced the ruthless submarine war.

I have proof that one of this traitorous gang went about Berlin personating me. What scheme he was cooking up I do not know.

Zimmermann was particularly weak in being advised by one of these shady individuals.

I think the German Government will allow Ford or any of his angels to come here, but the Peace Ark seems pretty well wrecked.

Provincial and small newspapers are much more bitter against America than the larger ones.

Von Jagow told me the other day that he thought the feeling here against America was so bitter that, eventually, war would be inevitable.

Received following anonymous letter:

"I am enabled to-day to give your Excellency news of the utmost importance, Germany is at the end of its forces and the Imperial Government is inclined to make peace cost what may! One of the most prominent and influential members of the Reichstag has assured me, that the general conviction of the parliament is dominated by the absolute necessity, to pull back and to strive for peace as soon as possible. The financial aspect given by Dr. Helfferich is disastrous, the military situation, taken in the whole, unsatisfactory and the confidential information, given by Herr von Jagow in the committee with regard to the Egyptian expedition, discouraging if not hopeless. The Government and particularly Herr von Bethmann wish for peace, but believe themselves restrained by public opinion and by the fear of the Pan-Germanists. It's now the psychological moment for intervention by the United States and there can be no doubt, that it should and will be exercised in favour of humanity, culture and freedom, in favour of the prevalence of the Anglo-Saxon race and the future development of the new world against Prussian barbarity, Imperial despotism and Teutonic slavery!

22. XII. 1915.   OLD GENTLEMAN."

83

CHAPTER VII

The Diary Continued

JANUARY, 1916. Many of the intelligent rich are expressing the fear that after this war the Socialist high price system, governmental seizure of food, control of raw materials, etc., will be continued and also that the owners of large landed estates will be compelled to subdivide them.   .

We are getting vague and conflicting reports in the newspapers here about the sinking of the *Persia.* There seems to be no end to this business. Perhaps it is best to have the inevitable *come now.* The hate of America has grown to such an extent under careful Government stimulus that I am quite sure we will be the first attacked after the war. Therefore, if it is to come, it had better come now when we would start with a certain fleet in command of the seas, making it impossible for agitators, dynamiters, and spies to be sent to Mexico and South America and into the U. S. A. through Canada and Mexico. From the highest to the lowest I get intimations that at the first chance America will be attacked.

84

There is still a spirit of confidence in ultimate success, amply justified, it would seem, by the military situation.

A lot of dyestuffs mysteriously left Germany recently in spite of the embargo, and got to Holland, billed to America, where it remains, awaiting a permit from the British. Perhaps the Germans are getting worried about the possible building-up of the industry at home. The profits of the German dyestuff "trust" are certainly great enough to tempt the trust to do anything to keep the monopoly. Hardly a company pays less than 24 per cent. dividends.

The Kaiser is still laid up with a boil on his neck.

I am waiting the arrival of Colonel House, who, I suppose, will be here in ten days or so.

S. S. McClure of the good ship *Nutty* (Proprietor Ford), Hermann Bernstein and Inez Milholland Boissevain, likewise of the crew, have been here. Their stories are most amusing. Apparently, now, the nuttiest have voted to remain a permanent committee at The Hague; salary (five thousand suggested) to each to be paid by Ford— with washing and expenses.

The Reichstag, sitting in "Budget Commission," is getting quite worked up over the censorship and the Socialists are demanding the freedom of the press.

Yesterday one member said he thought it would

do the U. S. A. good if they knew what the Germans really thought of Americans.

The spy system here is very complete and even the President and Cabinet at home in America are surrounded. Heydebrand, leader of the Conservative Party, called the uncrowned King of Prussia, said yesterday in the Prussian Chamber that "America was among the worst enemies of Germany." I am convinced that Germany, as now advised, either will attack America or land in South America, if successful in this war. Falkenhayn, Chief of the General Staff, said, referring to America, "It is hard to stop a victorious army."

I have just returned from three days in Munich. I visited two prison camps and the American Red Cross Hospital in Munich and conferred with Archdeacon Nies (of the American Episcopal Church), who is permitted to visit Bavarian prison camps, talk to prisoners, and hold services in English. These Bavarian camps are under Bavarian, not Prussian, rule.

Munich seems lively and contented. I saw great quantities of soldiers there and at Ingolstadt.

I expect Colonel House about the 26th, and shall be very glad to see him.

Morgenthau was here for a day. I took him to see von Jagow, where we talked for an hour. Later, through some Germans, he met Zimmermann, who asked him if he did not think the German-Ameri-

86

cans in America would rise in rebellion if trouble came between Germany and America.

Von Jagow was very explicit in saying that Germany had made no agreement with us about submarine commanders. He said distinctly that Germany reserved the right to change these orders at any time. On the general question, he again said that the submarine was a new weapon and that the rules of international law must be changed, apparently claiming the right for Germany to change these rules at will and without the consent of any other power involved.

Morgenthau sailed Sunday, the sixth, from Copenhagen. The newspapers to-day and last night print articles to the effect that the negotiations are taking a more favourable course.

February, 1916. I dined last night at von Jagow's. He said I would get a note to-day which would accept all Bernstorff's propositions except, as he put it, one word, viz.: Germany will acknowledge liability for the loss of American lives by the sinking of the *Lusitania,* but will not acknowledge that the act of sinking was illegal. He said that international law had to be changed, that the submarine was a new weapon, and that, anyway, if a break came with America, that they had a lot of new submarines here and would make an effective submarine blockade of England. To-day a cipher from the German Foreign Office came in to be forwarded to the State Department for Bernstorff, so I suppose this is what he referred to. Probably the Germans are in earnest on this proposition. It

87

is now squarely up to the American people to decide.

Of course, I am very much disturbed at the turn of affairs, but I am doing nothing except repeating to Lansing what is said to me, and trying to convince the Germans that we are in earnest.

I was very glad to see Colonel House in Berlin, for many reasons, and, especially, that the President may get his view of the situation here. He had long talks with the Chancellor, von Jagow, and Zimmermann, and also met Dr. Solf, the Colonial Minister; von Gwinner, head of the Deutsche Bank; Gutmann, of the Dresdner Bank; and Dr. Rathenau, head of the Allegemeine Electricitäts Gesellschaft and many corporations, who is now engaged with the General Staff in providing raw materials for Germany.

I think the Germans are getting short of copper and nickel, especially the latter. Copper lightning rods of churches have been taken and an effort was made to take the brass reading desk in the American Church and the fittings in the Japanese Embassy.

I think from underground rumours that the Germans and the propagandists will endeavour to embroil us with Japan.

Baroness von Schroeder, a von Tirpitz spy, stated the other day that Japan would send a note to the United States of America making demands on the U. S. in regard to the Japanese immigration question.

There was a well-defined report that Germany

would issue a manifesto stating that enemy merchant ships would be fired on without notice and this because of orders alleged to have been found on British ships ordering merchant ships to fire on submarines at sight.

The Chancellor told me he was ready for peace but that all his emissaries had met with a cold reception in the Allied countries of France, England and Russia.

A fight against the Chancellor has been started in the home of the Junkers—the Prussian Chamber. The powerful liberal papers are jumping hard on the disturbers and the Chancellor hit back quite hard. These Junkers are demanding unlimited submarine war and are stirred up by von Tirpitz. It is one of their last kicks as soon a real suffrage will have to be introduced in Prussia. The Chancellor foreshadowed this in opening this Prussian Chamber; hence the tears!

The visit of Colonel House here was undoubtedly, from this end, a success; and I am glad that he can give the President a fresh and impartial view.

March first we go on a milk and butter card regime. I have put the Polish question (food) up to Zimmermann, and asked informally whether proper guarantees against the direct or indirect taking of food and money from Poland will be stopped, if relief is sent; no answer yet.

In spite of what I was told by certain exalted personages last autumn, I think that if the war

89

continues much longer the President will be welcomed as a mediator. In fact, there are a number of cartoons and articles appearing in the newspapers which, in tone, are against the President because he does not insist on peace.

I think that we may soon look for a very strong German attack on the West Front, an endeavour to break through before the time when the French and English are contemplating their offensive, which is probably some time in March.

At or about the same time there will probably be great Zeppelin attacks on London and on other English centres. It is reported that in their next offensive the Germans will use a more deadly form of poison gas.

I had the grippe, went to Partenkirchen for a few days, but the first night in country air since July, 1914, was too much for me and filled me with such energy that I tried skiing, fell down and broke my collar-bone, came to Berlin and can sit at my desk, but am very uncomfortable.

I think Germany was about to offer to sink no merchant ships without notice and putting crews, etc., in safety, if England would disarm merchant ships, but now, since the President's letter to Stone, both the Chancellor and von Jagow say they are convinced that America has a secret understanding with England and that nothing can be arranged.

Captain Persius points out in to-day's *Tageblatt* that it is not submarines alone that are now, without notice, going to sink armed merchant ships, but cruisers, etc., will take a hand.

It is reported that the Kaiser went to Wilhelmshafen to warn submarine commanders to be careful and that submarines will hunt in pairs, one standing ready to torpedo while the other warns. The German losses at Verdun are small as artillery fire annihilated enemy first. I think an attack will be made now in another part of the front.

Germany has forbidden the *import* of many articles of luxury; this is to keep exchange more normal and keep gold in the country. This probably will continue after the war.

Some newspaper men just in from Verdun report the Germans saving men—losses small—going at it with artillery, probably over 1,000 guns, and making a slow and almost irresistible push. Some military attachés think there may be a strong attack somewhere else on the front.

This Verdun attack was undoubtedly made to keep Roumania out.

I think the food question here is getting very serious, but before they are starved out they will starve six million Belgians, eleven million Russians and Poles and two million prisoners; so that, after all, this starvation business is not practical.

There was a Grand Council of War last week at Charleville to determine whether von Tirpitz's proposition, to start an unlimited submarine blockade of England, should be started or not—i. e., sink all ships, enemy and neutral, at sight. Falkenhayn was for this, the Chancellor against, and von Tirpitz lost. The decision, of course, was made by the Emperor.

Great advertising efforts are being made on the question of the Fourth War Loan. It will, of course, be announced as successful.

There are undoubtedly two submarine parties in Germany and there may be an unlimited blockade of England.

I think Germany, as at present advised, is willing, if merchant ships are disarmed, to agree to sink no boats whatever without warning and without putting passengers and crew in safety. The Admiralty approves of this.

One of the American correspondents publishes an article in the *Lokal Anzeiger* on America, in which he makes some statements no loyal American should make just now.

The "illness" of von Tirpitz is announced. I think it means his resignation, and have just cabled, although it is possible that his resignation may never be publicly announced. For one thing, the Kaiser and army people began to think it was a bad innovation to have any officer or official appealing to cheap newspapers and the "man in the street" in a conflict with superior authority.

I heard that at Charleville conference both the Chancellor and von Jagow said they would resign if von Tirpitz's policy of unlimited submarine war on England was adopted.

The food question is becoming really acute—the village people are about starving in some sections and are not as well off as the people in the big towns; it is the policy to keep the people in the cities as content as possible in order to prevent riots, demonstrations, etc.

Some Germans have asked me if the sending of a German "Colonel House" to America would be agreeable to the President. Probably the Envoy would be Solf, and he could talk informally to the President and prominent people. If sent he would require a safe conduct from England and France.

I hear the submarines now are mostly engaged in mine laying, at the mouth of the Thames.

Events are beginning to march. At first von Tirpitz's "illness" was announced, then came his resignation. Yesterday was his birthday and a demonstration was expected; there were many police out, but I could see no demonstrators. The row may come in the Reichstag.

There are two sources of danger; first, a failure at Verdun and the new food regulations may make people ready to accept Tirpitz's guarantee that if he is allowed his way the war can be won and ended. He has a large following already who favour this plan; second, there are some Reichstag members and others who think the Tirpitz people can never be reconciled unless there is a new Chancellor.

The Chancellor sent for me Friday. I think the Chancellor wants to keep peace with America and also wishes to make a general peace. He talked, or rather I talked, a little about terms. He still wants to hang on to Belgium, but I think will give most of it up; but is fixed for an indemnity from France. The loss of life here is affecting every one, the Chancellor is a very good man, and I think honestly desires an honourable peace.

Potatoes are restricted from to-day, 10 pounds per head in 12 days, not much, bacon and lard practically not to be had, butter only in small quantities and meat out of reach of the poor.

I told the Chancellor I thought a great source of danger to the good relations of Germany and U. S. A. was in Mexico, that if we had trouble there, had to raise a large army and rouse the military spirit at home, the President might find it hard to hold the people. This struck him as a new view, as most Germans think that Mexican troubles are to their advantage, and I am sure Villa's attacks are "made in Germany."

I shall not come home; both the Chancellor and von Jagow have begged me not to go.

I sent a cable about the possible stirring up of our coloured people by propagandists. I notice that there are great fires in many cities of the South.

It is reported that Prussian State Railways were given the banks as additional security for the last loan, but I do not see how this could be, as the railways are Prussian and the Loan Imperial.

Several South American diplomats here think that in case of war between U. S. and Germany public opinion in their countries will demand the seizure of the German ships and possible war.

April, 1916. I am just off to the Reichstag where the Chancellor is to speak. I have no news here and none from America, but it seems to me five boats sunk almost at once will rather strain things at home. Here they do not want war with America. Perhaps von Tirpitz before leaving gave these submarine commanders these orders to sink at sight.

I think the Germans will eventually encircle and take Verdun, mostly now for moral effect.

Von Jagow will shortly give Conger (*Associated Press*) an interview disclaiming any intention on Germany's part of attacking America after the war. "A guilty conscience, etc.," and "Qui s'excuse, s'accuse."

Every night fifty million Germans cry themselves to sleep because all Mexico has not risen against us.

Part of Germany goes soon on meat ration. The food question is becoming acute, but they will last through here.

I think that the Germans would now, in spite of previous statements by a high authority, welcome the intervention of the President looking toward peace. Colonel House is so relied on here that he

95

would be doubly welcome as the bird with the olive branch.

It looks more and more as if the issue of the campaign would be peace or war! On this issue the Germans at the last moment will have to side with the President.

The recent sessions of the Reichstag have been lively. Liebknecht caused a row on several occasions. Once by interrupting the Chancellor to imply that the Germans were not free, next to deny that the Germans had *not* wished the war, and another time by calling attention to the attempts of the Germans to induce Mohammedan and Irish prisoners of war to desert to the German arms, the Irish being attacked through Sir Roger Casement. Liebknecht finally enraged the Government by calling out that the loan subscription was a swindle.

The German-American spies and traitors are hard at work at 48 Potsdammer Strasse and also at the Oversea News Service, a concern paid for by Krupps. Mr. ———, in addition, gains money by getting permits for goods to go out of Germany, capitalising his "pull" as it were. Some of the money for their dirty work is given them by Roselius of Bremen, proprietor of the "Caffee Hag." ———, a traitor, who also writes against the President, also works with the gang.

This cry in America that German babies have not sufficient milk is all rot. One of our doctors has reported on the subject. The cry is only raised to get a hole in the British blockade.

The Germans are going at Verdun carefully, and an imitation of each French position or trench they wish to take—planned from airmen's and spies' reports—is constructed behind the German lines and the German soldiers practise taking it until they are judged letter perfect and are put to work to capture the original.

It is said the Germans have developed a submarine periscope so small as to be almost invisible, which works up and down so that only at intervals, for a second or so, does it appear above the water. Also, it is said the wireless vibrations by means of copper plates at each end are transmitted through the boat, and every member of the crew learns the wireless code, and no matter where working can catch the vibrations.

Note about the *Sussex* and other four ships just in. I think Germany is now determined to keep peace with America as the plain people are convinced that otherwise the war will be lengthened—a contingency abhorrent to all.

May, 1916. I delivered the last American note to von Jagow to-day. He said they probably would not answer, and then engaged me in gossipy conversation.

These people want peace and will gladly accept the President as mediator.

The Pope, they think, will want brokerage—a "Makler Lohn"—as they call it—concessions for the church, such as the return of the Jesuits, etc.

If they get good and sick of war here, perhaps

they may not feel like revenge after all—but there is an ever-present danger we must prepare for.

The fact that I was given detailed instructions as to leaving, etc.—which they undoubtedly learned, with their wonderful spy system—helped the *Sussex* settlement.

The Chancellor and I became great friends as a result of my stay at the Hauptquartier. The League of Truth gang attacked me lately. The Government published a certificate in the *Official Gazette* to the effect that I was their fair-haired boy, etc.—very nice of them. I really think they recognise that the propaganda was an awful failure and want to inaugurate the era of good feeling.

I did not go to the front at the Hauptquartier as reported. I had enough to do in Charleville, but did witness the splendid relief work being done by the Americans who are feeding 2,200,000 of the population of Northern France. Twenty thousand of the inhabitants of Lille, Roubaix-Tourcoing, are being sent under circumstances of great barbarity to work in the fields in small villages. I spoke to the Chancellor and he promised to remedy this.

Germans say they will take Verdun. A military treaty with Sweden is reported; a large Swedish Military Commission is now here, receiving much attention.

While at Charleville, in connection with American work, I asked, at one village, to see the German Army stores so as to convince myself that the German Army was not using the stores from America.

I saw that one-half the stores came from *Holland*.

I think the psychological moment is approaching when Colonel House should appear as the President's White Emissary of Peace.

While the food question here is pressing, the harvest will be good, if present indications continue. Rye is the principal crop and this is harvested about July 12th. I think, however, Germany can last, and in very desperation may try a great offensive which may break the French lines and change the whole position. The people here, although tired of war, are well disciplined and will see this thing through without revolution.

We are rather in calm after the last crisis. The Chancellor sent for me and said he hoped we would do something to England or propose a general peace, otherwise his position here will become, he thinks, rather hard. Delbrück, vice-chancellor, very hostile to America, is out—failure as Minister of Interior to organise food supply is the real reason.

Yesterday I had a talk with the Chancellor. The occasion was the Polish Relief question which I shall now take up direct with Helfferich, who, as I predicted, is the new Minister of the Interior and Vice-Chancellor. He is a very business-like man and did much for the favourable settlement of our last crisis.

The Chancellor seemed rather downcast yesterday, without apparent cause. He says that Germany from now on will have two months of hardship on the food question, but that after that things will be all right. The crops, as I have seen on my shooting place, are magnificent and the rye harvest will probably begin even before July 15th.

Mrs. Gerard has just returned from a week in Budapest with her sister. The Hungarians are once more gay and confident. The Italians, their hereditary foes, are being driven back, and on the Russian front there seems to be a sort of tacit truce —no fighting and visiting in trenches, etc.—terms of great friendliness.

(This was the beginning of the fraternisation which led, a year later, to the collapse of Russia.)

At the races here last Sunday there was an absolutely record crowd and more money bet than on any previous day in German racing history. The cheaper field and stands were so full of soldiers that the crowd seemed grey, which goes to show that the last man is not at the front.

State Socialism makes advances over here. A proposition is now discussed to compel the young men who are earning large wages to save a part thereof.

On the *Sussex* question, I got a colleague to ask about the punishment of the Commander and to say at the Foreign Office, after he had once been refused any information, that I had heard that the people at large in America believed the Commander has received "Pour le Mérite." Von Jagow said that he was sure that this was not so, but that he did not know the name of the Commander, and that it was not "usual" to tell what punishment had been given. So that I suppose the matter will rest, unless I get orders to ask formally about the punishment.

The German military people and ruling Junker class are furious at the settlement with America, and abuse America, the President and me indiscriminately.

Anything the President says about peace is prominently placed in the newspapers.

Yesterday in a debate in the Reichstag over the censorship, member Stresemann, National Liberal (the party which now holds the balance of power), violently abused President Wilson and said he was not wanted as a peace-maker. All applauded except the Socialists—so I think the President had better say nothing more about peace for the present. What he has said has done much good and has pleased the Government here, if not the Reichstag. Although von Jagow is a Junker of Junkers, the Junkers are against him and claim he is too weak. He may be bounced.

The crops are very fine.

Undoubtedly we shall have another crisis when the extremists here demand a "reckless" U-boat war because we are doing nothing to England.

Germany will last through on the food question.

I have heard reports that the Turks are tired of German rule and almost ready to flop.

I am to meet Prince Buelow, ex-Chancellor, to-morrow and may fish up something interesting.

The Kaiser has gone to the front, probably Russian. Next war loan will be 12 milliards.

Helfferich lunched here last Sunday. He speaks English fairly well. Zimmermann is laid up with the gout.

In the Reichstag debate yesterday, Streseman, applauded by all except Socialists, said that Germany threw away Wilson as a peace-maker. However, the Government is pleased with President's peace talk, as it keeps the people from thinking of food and U-boat crises.

U-boat question will come up again, when Pan-Germanists and Conservatives demand a reckless U-boat war because we have done nothing against England.

Harden's paper has been confiscated again.

June, 1916. I am sorry to lose Ruddock, who is sent to Belgium, but it is a good appointment, as his knowledge of German and relations here will help matters.

The debates in the Reichstag have been quite interesting yesterday and the day before. The Chancellor, irritated by the anonymous attacks on him in pamphlets, etc., made a fine defence. In the course of the debate allusions were made to President Wilson and the U-boat question. The U-boat question may break loose again any day.

I do not think that either Austria or Germany wishes President Wilson to lay down any peace conditions. There may possibly be a Congress after the Peace Congress, but meanwhile all parties here feel that America has nothing to do with peace conditions. America can bring the parties together, but that is all. The speech about the rights of small peoples has, I hear, made the Austrians furious, as Austria is made up of many nationalities and the Germans say that if the rights of small peoples and peoples choosing their own sovereignty is to be discussed, the Irish question, the Indian question and the Boer question, the Egyptian question and many others involving the Entente Allies must be discussed. I think that generally there is a big change in public opinion and the Germans are beginning to realise that the President is for peace with Germany.

The Germans expect that by September preparations will be finished and that the Suez Canal will be cannonaded, bombed and mined so that it will dry up, and then the Indian-Afghan troubles will begin.

June, 1916. The President's peace talks carried over the dangerous moment after the submarine submission. Von Jagow told me that because of debates in Reichstag the President must not think he is not welcome as mediator.

Crops look well.

The break on Austro-Russian front is reported to have been caused by wholesale desertions of Ruthenian troops to Russians.

The editor of the *National Zeitung,* responsible for the fake interview with me, has been "fired" from that paper which has published a notice to that effect.

Grand Admiral von Koester made a speech implying that reckless submarine war should be taken up and England thus defeated. He is retired, but is head of the Navy League, a concern backed by the Government, possessing a million members and much political influence.

Apropos of hyphenated Americans, a friend tells me that when he was secretary here some years ago, a certain Congressman tried for six years to get presented at Court, insisting that he be presented as a "German-American." The Kaiser turned him down, saying he knew no such thing as a "German-American," and the Congressman finally consented to be presented as an American.

The U-boat question will come up again, say in three months, unless we get in serious trouble in Mexico, when it will come up sooner.

Edwin Emerson has been sent out of the country, I think to serve in the Turkish Army in some capacity, perhaps paymaster or some such job.

The Foreign Office continues to protect these American mud-slingers—such as the "League of Truth" which is run by a German named Marten, posing as an American and a dentist (American citizen) named Mueller—these circulate a pamphlet entitled, "What Shall We Do With Wilson," etc., and are the gang who insulted the American flag by putting it wrapped in mourning on a wreath on

What shall we do with Wilson?

by

John L. Stoddard.

Meran. Tyrol. 1916.

Printing-office F. Pleticha, Meran, Tyrol.

COVER OF THE PAMPHLET FEROCIOUSLY ABUSIVE
OF PRESIDENT WILSON. ISSUED BY THE EX-TRAVEL
LECTURER, JOHN L. STODDARD

the statue of Frederick the Great with a placard, "Wilson and his Press do not represent America."

Letters, codes, etc., for Bernstorff and individuals are sent to America as follows: the letters are photographed on a reduced scale so that a letter a foot square appears as an inch and a half square. These little prints are put in the layers of a shoe heel of a travelling American or elsewhere, book cover, hat band, etc., and then rephotographed and enlarged in America. Also messengers travel steerage and put things in the mattress of a fellow passenger and go back to the ship after landing in New York and collect the stuff.

A German friend, just returned from Austria, says the feeling there against America is very strong on account of the Dumba incident.

Yesterday I was told by a German that the German army had aeroplanes which develop 300 H. P., and would soon have some of 1000 H. P.

July, 1916. Every one in this Embassy is getting to the breaking point. Nerves do not last forever, and the strain of living in a hostile country is great. The Germans, too, are on edge. They are going to take away our privilege of speaking to prisoners alone; this because they think I learned of the shooting of the second Irishman at Limburg from prisoners. As a matter of fact I did not, but cannot, of course, say how I did learn.

The Russian prisoners are being slowly starved, the French and English get packages from home.

There are rumors that a Bavarian regiment which was ordered a second time to take a position, which the Prussians lost at Verdun, refused and was ordered to be decimated, and that then the Crown Prince of Bavaria threatened to march all the Bavarian troops home unless the order to decimate was rescinded. I do not believe the rumour, but its circulation and other events such as the refusal of the Bavarians lately to adopt a common postage stamp, shows there is a little irritation growing between Prussia and Bavaria. For years before the war the Bavarian Comic papers cartooned the Prussians, common and royal, but like every other movement nothing will result.

There is much underground work for the resumption of reckless submarine war going on, all part of a campaign to upset the Chancellor. Von Bülow, Ex-Chancellor, is working hard. He, however, since his row with the Emperor over the "Telegraph" interview, which he passed as correct, will never be accepted by His Majesty. Nevertheless, he is becoming a focal point for opposition.

The Chancellor and his party are very timid about attacks. For instance, they will do nothing against Emerson, Mueller and that crew, which insults indiscriminately our flag, our President, the Chancellor, Zimmermann and me, because, as Zimmermann frankly told me, they are afraid of attacks. Mueller on the 4th of July hung out the American flag in mourning and circulated copies of the Declaration of Independence charged with a bloody hand and a black cross. I have filed in vain affidavits with the Foreign Office, by people who say he has threatened to shoot me at sight.

The Germans seem to fear the Russian attacks more than the English and French. They claim to have the measure of the English, and not to fear their offensive.

Dr. John R. Mott has been here. He made a great impression. I had him at lunch with the Chancellor, Zimmermann, and officials of the prisoner department and War Ministry.

Mass feeding of the people has begun. They pay a few pfennigs per meal.

I have heard rumours lately of actual dissatisfaction among soldiers at front and of many being transferred, but this unrest also will have no definite result.

Constant rain lately will damage the harvest and rot the potatoes to some extent. Nevertheless, as I have often said, the Germans will last. Holland has allowed more food in lately.

The long confinement will make many prisoners insane. Many old men at Ruhleben, living six in a horse's stall or in dim hay lofts, simply turn their faces to the wall and refuse even to complain.

The statement in the American papers that our National Guard could not mobilise for Mexico because of lack of sleeping cars caused much ridicule here, where they go to the front in cattle cars.

July, 1916. A committee called the National Committee for an Honourable Peace has been formed. Prince Wedel is at the head. Most of the people are friends of the Chancellor. One is an editor of the *Frankfurter Zeitung* which is the Chancellor's organ. On August 1st, fifty speakers of this Committee will begin to speak, probably the opposition will come into their meetings and try to speak or break up the meetings.

The *Lokal Anzeiger,* also a government organ, prints an editorial to the effect that Germany may take up ruthless submarine war again. Great numbers of U-boats are being built and in September operations will be on a big scale, though the Chancellor will try to keep them to cruiser warfare.

The prisoner question on all sides is growing acute. The Germans sent me a note to-day threatening stern reprisals if the alleged bad treatment of their prisoners in Russia does not stop.

We can no longer talk to prisoners alone. Von Jagow told me that after the visit of Madam Sasenoff, or Samsenoff, to a Russian prisoners' camp, there was a riot, but the real reason is that the Germans have much to conceal. The prison food now is a starvation ration.

The Alliance of the Six, really an organization fostered by big iron business in Westphalia, is very active for annexation. This wants to get the French iron mines and coal, and so control the iron business of the Continent and perhaps Europe.

A man from Syria passed through here recently and gave me most interesting accounts of the state of affairs there. The Turks are oppressing the Arabians and the revolt of the Grand Sheriff of Mecca may have great effects in this war. This man says that the English are building two railroads from Suez into the desert and the Germo-Turks are building toward the canal from the North. For the Canal attack there are, at present, principally Austrian troops assembled. The Turks are beginning to take Greeks from the Coast cities into the interior of Asia Minor and are oppressing the Syrian Arabian cities, such as Beirut, where thousands are dying of starvation. At the Islahje-Aleppo R. R., 30 Turkish soldiers a day die from cholera. The Germans, by their precautions, escape. He passed 147 German auto trucks in the Cilician mountains bound for Bagdad. Also saw the British prisoners from Kut el Amara, who are dying of dysentery, being compelled to walk in the hot sun from Kut. He thinks the English and the Grand Sheriff will transfer the title of head of the religion from the Sultan at Constantinople to either the Sultan of Egypt or some new Sultan to be established as an Arabian Sultan, perhaps at Bagdad if the Russians and English take it, or at Mecca, and he considers this movement of Arabians against Turks may assume great proportions.

There is still talk here of a resumption of reckless submarine war which question is complicated and involved in the eternal efforts of the Conservatives to get the Chancellor out.

The recognition of the "merchant submarine" has made a very good impression here.

The plain people are eager for peace but those interested in carrying on the war have the upper hand.

The harvest is good, and is now being gathered.

A number of navy and (which is significant) army officers visited von Tirpitz, lately in his Black Forest Retreat and gave him a testimonial.

There is prospect that what is called here a "Burg Frieden" (Peace of the City) will be declared between the Chancellor and the principal Conservative newspapers.

One of the American correspondents back from Verdun says that a corps commander said his corps took no prisoners.

I think many of the Hungarians are for peace. I get this from Andrassy's son-in-law who is also a member of the lower house. Tisza, however, is still in full control.

Prince Leopold's (he is a brother-in-law of the Kaiser) stags have destroyed vegetables of the plain people (as in the days of William Rufus) and people dare write letters, and Liberal papers dare publish them complaining of these depredations.

CHAPTER VIII

GERMANY'S EARLY PLOTS IN MEXICO

The Diary Concluded

*A*UGUST, *1916*. Count Andrassy, leader of the opposition to Tisza in Hungary, has been here for some time. He lunched with us one day and I had a talk with him in German. Andrassy is rather old and tired. Andrassy's father, the Prime Minister, was originally a great friend of Germany.

It is possible that Andrassy through German influence may be made Minister of Foreign Affairs instead of Burian. This is to be the first step in a German coup d'état to take place on the death of Francis Joseph—the throne successor to be given Austria alone, and Prince Eitel Fritz, the Kaiser's favourite son, to be King of Hungary with possibly a Czech kingdom in Bohemia.

Andrassy had an audience with the Kaiser here. Andrassy is apparently friendly with America and is also for peace.

Von Tirpitz is out with a statement practically demanding war with America. I am surprised that the newspapers are allowed to publish it. Very likely it will not be permitted to go out but it ought to be known in America.

Germany probably will come out with a strong note about Poland, refusing help and saying harvest is sufficient. This is not true as to food for babies who cannot live on rye and wheat, but need condensed milk.

The treatment of prisoners is going from bad to worse. The Chancellor and Foreign Office can do nothing against the military party.

Hoover, Professor Kellog, and I are all very much discouraged about Polish and other relief questions. The Germans are getting more and more disagreeable about these matters, even though they are for the benefit of Germany. Warwick Greene, of the Rockefeller Foundation, being a new arrival is more hopeful, but that will soon wear off.

The Germans are getting a blacklist of their own. One Barthmann, an American, who sells American shoes in Germany, wanted to get his pass stamped to go to America, and permission to come back, and was told that would only be done if the Chamber of Commerce (Handels-Kammer) consents; you see the connection—no American goods for Germany.

The Jews here are almost on the edge of being "pogrommed." There is a great prejudice against them, especially in naval and military circles, because they have been industrious and have made money. Officers openly talk of repudiating the War Loan which they say would only mean a loss for the Jews.

The Germans say they have new and horrible inventions which will end the war soon.

I supposed that because I had some acquaintance with German watering places and German-Americans I knew a little about Germany. I was wrong. No casual traveller ever gets to know the military caste nor do the members of that caste travel except on "business."

The members of the military caste live like Spartans and are consoled by the fact that they rule the country and look down on the merchant class. They feel that they have created modern industrial Germany. The military caste (of which the naval and all government bureaus are branches) has organised the nation for war with the efficiency of the managers of a great American corporation. The government is an absolutism. No Jew can become an officer. Officers of crack regiments do not go to the homes of persons in any kind of business. A business man is called a "Kaufmann," as we speak of a house painter. Some tame professors are paid by the State to give an impression of "Kultur."

This war is now a war for conquest or money. All people tell me that we must have "pay for so much blood." "If we don't keep Belgium there will be a revolution. Who is to pay for the War?" A Socialist who referred yesterday in the Reichstag to the Kaiser's speech of the beginning of the war which stated this was not a war to get

territory, was well sat upon. Even the Socialists
are all for war against Italy.

None of the German colonies is fit for Euro-
peans. *Germany last year proposed joint intervention in Mexico to England.* If successful Germany will try to get a foothold in the Western
Hemisphere. The Monroe Doctrine is like a red
rag to a bull to every German.

Relations with members of the Government here
are quite agreeable but there is not an effective
government at present. The Chancellor will take
no decisive action and leaves matters to department heads who fight with other department heads.
The Emperor saw fit to follow the traditions of
1870 and go to the field taking the Chancellor and
heads of many departments with him, hence great
governmental confusion, but this does not affect
military organisation. He is bored by the Chancellor, a good man, but of no action or decision. Von
Falkenhayn is the Emperor's favourite. He is the
chief of the General Staff. Von Tirpitz and von
Mueller (also naval) have great weight. The
Kaiser is thus surrounded by military influences.

Saw summaries of the news published by the
General Staff and given to the Emperor to read.
He gets only German-American news from America and no bad news from anywhere. On the *Lusitania* case there is a disposition to think, because
we were not warlike over Mexico, we will stand

anything. *The Kaiser will not see me because of the delivery of arms by Americans to the Allies and has so stated.*

There is no shortage of food supply. I was told yesterday they did not need our Polish Relief Committee for German Poland as Germany can take care of this alone. The hate of Americans is intense. But this hate can be turned off and on by the Government. The people believe everything they see in the papers. The monetary situation is not bad. All the money for war supplies has been spent in Germany, except perhaps for a few horses, etc., from Scandinavia.

The Chancellor and von Jagow have been in Vienna. Von Jagow told me only on current business, but this was a diplomatic statement. I believe they went to settle the fate of Poland. I hear Prussia wants an independent Poland and Austria wants to make it part of the Austrian Empire. In any event I think Prussia will secure the organising of the army which will soon be raised. A prominent Pole told me two days ago that the peasants were coddled by Russia, whose motto in Poland was "divide et impera," and that they will violently resent being drafted into the Prussian army.

The bitter attacks on the Chancellor continue. At a recent meeting in Bavaria resolutions were passed that the first objective of the war was to get rid of the Chancellor and the second to "clean out the Anglophile Foreign Office," which prevented Germany from resorting to "reckless" methods for the swift winning of the war.

As a son-in-law of a high official told me to-day, the break between the military and navy on one side and the Civil Government on the other has widened almost into civil war. The same man told me that the Kaiser has lately become quite apathetic and lets events take their course.

One of my attachés has broken down completely, cries when spoken to; living in a fiercely hostile atmosphere is not agreeable and I wonder how long the rest of us can hold out.

The harvest is very good, but does not provide fat, and as yet, meat. But the starving out business I have always said was an "iridescent" dream.

New men, 80,000 in this vicinity alone, are being called to the colours.

Every one here is getting more on razor edge, prisoners are treated more roughly and get worse food. Bavaria is getting restless and dissatisfied, this will not amount to anything definite but is a sign of the times.

I went to Herringsdorff for a few days of swimming. At a concert in the evening a man recited a poem he said he had written about "having bled enough." He was vehemently applauded. Quite a contrast to the days when the best actors in Germany were not ashamed to spout the "HYMN OF HATE"!

The military people use the censorship even

against papers friendly to the Chancellor and Germans certainly can hate each other as thoroughly and scientifically as they do most other nations. Dr. Alonzo Taylor thinks that in peace times some one fed this nation too much meat.

The newspapers are preparing the people for the entry of Roumania.

Professor ———, a school friend of Tisza's and Burian's who was recently in Austria, saw Burian and says Burian is ready and even anxious to make an arbitration treaty with America and also send an Ambassador in Dumba's place to Washington. This is out of my jurisdiction. He says that tomorrow or next day there will be an interpellation in the Hungarian Chamber about sending an Ambassador to America.

The National Liberals probably will unite with the Conservatives and demand a strong hold on Belgium, if not actual possession of that country, as one of the objects of the war.

This Union of National Liberals and Conservatives is dangerous and may mean a resumption of unrestricted submarine warfare.

The entry of Roumania took every one by surprise. Beldiman, the Roumanian Minister here, was visiting the reigning Prince of Hohenzollern Sigmaringen, brother of the Roumanian King, and apparently knew nothing of the danger of a break.

To-day Hindenburg is named Chief of the General Staff, and his Chief of Staff, Ludendorff, is made Quartermaster General, Falkenhayn, former Chief of Staff is bounced without even the excuse of a diplomatic illness. This is all a great concession to popular opinion. I do not know where Hindenburg stands with reference to America, but have heard that he is a reasonable man. Of course, here the Army has as much to say in foreign affairs as the Foreign Office, if not more. When I was at the Great General Headquarters, Falkenhayn, although I knew him, did not call on me, and dodged me. He did not even appear at the Kaiser's table when I lunched there. From all this I judge he was against America on the submarine question. I also have heard that when Helfferich was talking before the Kaiser, in favour of peace with America, Falkenhayn interrupted him, but was told by the Kaiser to "stick to his last" or words to that effect.

These people here are now nervous and unstrung and actually believe that America will now enter the war against them. It is impossible to conceive of the general breakdown of nerves among this people.

I have heard lately of men as old as 47 being taken for the Army.

Zimmermann has now gone on a vacation, his place being temporarily filled by von Treutler, Prussian Minister to Bavaria, who since the commencement of the war has been with the Kaiser. I judge this means the Kaiser is looking personally

into matters at the Foreign Office. Von Treutler
is, I think, against the resumption of reckless submarine war. He is lunching with me to-day. He
is rather the type of intelligent-man-of-the-world
and sportsman, and has little of the Prussian desire to "imponieren" by putting his voice two oc-
taves lower and glaring at one like an enraged bull-
frog.

Dr. William Bayard Hale, of Mexican fame, who
is in Berlin representing the Hearst papers, has
become very thick with officials here. Von Jagow
and Zimmermann are much impressed by him.

The Germans may hate the President, but there
are in America hundreds of thousands of Czechs
from Bohemia, Poles from Poland, Slovaks, Ruthenians, Croatians and Slavs from Hungary, Roumanians, Italians, Greeks, Russians, Scotch, Belgians, and French who HATE the Germans.

I believe the Germans want an excuse to resume
reckless submarine war and an American correspondent has taken the job of making bad feeling
to justify such a course.

September, 1916. As these people get desperate
the submarine question gets deeper and deeper
under their skin. I really think that it is only a
question of time.

Of course, from what I learn here Greece is sure
to come in and this is expected here.

As the Consul General at Hamburg has reported,

serious riots have occurred there, two by the poor classes, mostly women, and one by students. The crowd shouted "Down with the Kaiser," called for an end of the war, calling for unlimited submarine war against England.

The hate of Americans grows daily, if indeed it is possible to be greater.

Ira Nelson Morris, American Minister to Sweden, was here. He and his wife are charming people. He is very popular in Sweden. Elkus is also here on his way to Constantinople. If any one can "get away" with that difficult post he can. I took Elkus to see von Jagow and had him at lunch with von Treutler, the man in Zimmermann's place. I talked with Elkus to von Jagow about Syrian Relief. A Syrian, whose name I cannot give away, says the Turkish Government reported to our Embassy in Turkey that the harvest in Syria was the best in years, whereas, in truth this year's harvest, on account of drought and last year's on account of locusts, are the worst in 35 years. Missionaries have told me that Syrians are starving.

A fact for the Russian born—Germany does not recognise the American citizenship or naturalisation of a person born in Russia.

Yesterday there was a conference of all party leaders at the Chancellor's. I understand nothing was said about America or submarine question. I doubt this. The Press here and certain other agencies are trying to convince America that all is peaceful, but Baron Mumm two days ago told Elkus, in this house, that the ruthless submarine war undoubtedly would be resumed.

In general conversation with von Jagow, recently, he said that the offensive on the Somme could not continue without the great supply of shells from America. He also said that recently a German submarine submerged in the Channel had to allow 41 ships to pass, and that he was sure that each ship was full of ammunition and soldiers but probably had some protecting American angels on board, and, therefore, the submarine did not torpedo without warning. He seemed quite bitter.

The wife of an American newspaper correspondent was recently attacked in the street. Of course, the husband will not cable this to America. Two stenographers from this Embassy were recently slapped on coming out of a theatre because they were speaking English.

Reventlow's paper was recently suppressed and Reventlow forbidden to write without special permission. This is a good sign from the Chancellor.
Dr. Hale was recently given a special trip to the West front, and allowed to talk to the Crown Prince, etc.

December, 1916. The Germans are simply delighted with the President's peace note. Only a few cranks or conservative papers are against it.

I saw Zimmermann the day after my arrival. He was most friendly and said he hoped he and I would be able, as usual, to settle everything in a friendly manner.

Yesterday he lunched here and gave me the German reply after lunch. He told me at the first talk that he, the Chancellor, Hindenburg and Ludendorff were all working together. Most people here say that Hindenburg and Ludendorff are at present the real rulers of Germany. Zimmermann remarked that there was no danger from "reckless" submarine war.

Zimmermann said he regretted the sending of the Belgians to Germany but it was hard now to go back on what they had done. I have some hope that a retreat may be arranged—possibly by sending the Belgians back gradually and saying nothing about it.

The American Chamber of Commerce are to give a big dinner January sixth to welcome me back. Zimmermann and von Gwinner, head of Deutsche Bank, have agreed to speak and many prominent Germans have accepted.

The Press department of the Foreign Office has been reorganised by Zimmermann, and Hammann, the former head, fired. The new head is Major Deutelmoser, formerly of the General Staff, a personal friend of mine.

The Emperor is at Potsdam and consulted with Zimmermann, General von Kessel, etc., as to the reply to the President's peace note.

Berlin is much more melancholy than when I left. General von Kessel came to our American Colony Christmas tree for poor Berlin children. It was very pathetic. One little kid got up and prayed for peace and every one wept. I hope to get to see Ludendorff and Hindenburg soon and see how they feel toward America.

I went to Ruhleben, the British civilian camp, yesterday to tell the prisoners that all over 45 go home. It was quite a Christmas gift as 700 there are over that age. (Note: don't think this agreement of Germany and England ever went into effect!)

January, 1917. Germany wants a peace conference in order to make a separate peace on good terms to them with France and Russia, then hopes to finish England by submarines, then later take the scalp of Japan, Russia and France separately. The Allies ought to remember what Ben Franklin said about hanging together or separately. I get the above scheme from very good authority.

The weather is most depressing; dark, and rain every day. All hands seem cross. Zimmermann, I think, finds it much more difficult to be the responsible first than the criticising second. It is not as easy as it looked to him.

The Kaiser stated the other day that he did not expect peace now, that the English would try a great offensive in the spring and would fail.

Herbert Hoover writes me that the Germans are violating all their pledges in Belgium. He expects a year of great difficulties. I hear this confirmed on best authority and that even the German official who is supposed to see that food is not sent from Belgium to Germany in violation of Germany's pledges sends out butter to his family; that there is an absolute reign of terror in Belgium, sudden and arbitrary arrests, etc. I think the Germans want to see all foreign diplomats out of Bucharest and Brussels and the charges against Voypicka should be considered in that light.

The greatest danger from submarine war is that unthinking persons in the U. S. may start a crusade against the President's policy, encourage the Germans in the belief that we are divided and lead them to resume reckless acts in that belief. The continuance of a strong front is the very best way to keep the peace.

Both Zimmermann and the Chancellor asked me about Bernstorff, and returning good for evil, I said that he was O. K., on very good terms with the Government, well liked (*sic*) and that no one could do better!

A friend just returned from a week's visit in Hungary reports a great desire for peace. Persons who, a year ago, said that the President could have nothing to do with peace or negotiations, now say he is the only possible mediator. This comes from high government circles there.

The historic crown of St. Stephen was much too

large for the King, but the little crown prince made a great hit with the populace.

An Armenian woman came through here the other day. Her husband had been captured or killed and her tale of the treatment of the Armenians by the Turks was heartrending.

Everything points to a coming crisis in the matter of food, how serious it will be even the officials themselves do not know, as there is much concealed food and much smuggling over the various frontiers.

In some parts of Germany, the country police or gendarmes are searching the farm houses thrice weekly.

I have secured permission to visit and inspect the enslaved Belgians, have named as inspectors all members of our staff speaking French, but as yet have not received passes.

Here is a copy of a letter I have just received from a German:

"The hypocrisy of the German Government is really disgusting! It is a well-known matter of fact, that by hints and approbation, nay even by express orders of the German military authorities the troops in France and Belgium have been stimulated to give no quarter at all in the case of British adversaries, and that in Russia even whole regiments and brigades have been annihilated by grapeshot, although the poor wretches delivered themselves on mercy and raised their hands, to prove their submission. Both the Prussian and the Bavarian crown-prince have expressly ordered to make no prisoners, to spare ammunition and to despatch the surviving by steel and bayonet. Has the order been forgotten, issued by the Kaiser in the beginning of the German China-Expedition, to deal with the Chinese like the Huns, to destroy and annihilate every human creature both men and women and even innocent children!

Quis Aulerit Gracchos de seditione quaerentes?

Unus pro multis.

P. S.

The war would be decided and peace restored as soon as the U. S. A. Government would intervene in favour of humanity, liberty and civilisation. Down with the Prussian Tyranny!"

The Germans will do nothing about Belgium. The deportations were a military measure, demanded by Ludendorff, who constantly fears a British landing on the Belgian coast.

A man who called on von Tirpitz recently was told by von Tirpitz that he, von Tirpitz, was watched like a spy and all his letters opened. Von Tirpitz said that Hindenburg was the real ruler of Germany, that anything Bethmann said was censored by Hindenburg and that Hindenburg was now against reckless submarine war but that any substantial defeats in the field would make him change his mind. Von Tirpitz said that the Kaiser was losing his mind and spent all his time praying, and learning Hebrew.

PHOTOGRAPH TAKEN IN COURTYARD OF EMBASSY, AUGUST, 1916

Left to right—Lanier Winslow; Albert B. Ruddock; Percival Dodge; Grafton Minot; von Gwinner, head of the great Deutsche Bank; Surgeon Onnesorg, U. S. N.; Ernest Bicknell of Red Cross; Ambassador Gerard; Mr. Wilmeth of Treas. Dept.; Assistant Secretary of War Breckenridge; Roland Harvey; Charles Russell; Hugo Ballin, head of Hamburg-American Line; Major Ryan and First Secretary Grew.

The food situation grows worse. Potato cards must now be presented in restaurants and hotels. I doubt if potatoes can last beyond April. There is food in Roumania but much will go to the troops; Austrians and Turks: the railways are so used by troops, etc., that it is doubtful if any food from there can reach Germany for months.

All apartment houses in Berlin are closed at nine, and lights in halls extinguished. Theatres close at ten and movies also. There is want of coal due to lack of transportation.

The President's address to the Senate yesterday (Jan. 22, 1917) is splendid. I don't know yet how it will be taken here. If it is published it will give the German people something to consider.

Postcards showing Zeppelins in the act of murdering the sleeping babies of an enemy city are distributed here with pride.

All Germans of my acquaintance have impressed on me lately the renewed danger of submarine warfare. The American correspondents are not allowed to send out the hate of America speeches and articles. Cyril Brown of the *World* says that last week fifty per cent of the matter he sent was cut out by censor here.

The new U-boat campaign will go along the armed merchantman lines and an endeavour will be made to force or get us in some way to recognise that an armed merchantman is the same as a war-

ship and, therefore, may be fired on without notice.
It is the old story, but more subtly presented.

Food situation more and more serious, riots lately in two markets in Berlin.

Have not yet received passes to see the Belgians.

Undoubtedly Ludendorff is the real dictator of
Germany to-day. What he thinks about America
may be judged from the circumstances before Colonel Kuhn's recall.

The nearer I get to the situation the more I consider the President's peace note an exceedingly
wise move. It has made it very difficult for the ter-
rorists here to start anything which will bring Germany into conflict with the U. S.

*The Chancellor, Zimmermann, Stumm, have all
ridiculed the idea that Germany will go back on
her "Sussex" pledges; but if she does, then the
peace note makes it easier for America to enter the
war on the Allies' side with a clear conscience and
the knowledge on the part of the people at home
that the President did everything possible to keep
us out of the mess.*

CHAPTER IX

THE older I grow the more it seems to me that all men are alike and that they have been alike at all periods of history, capable of the same development and differing only because of environment.

I do not believe, for example, that any mystery is concealed behind the faces of the peoples of the East. Once I asked Soughimoura, my colleague in Berlin, Ambassador of Japan, whether the Japanese were as much subject to nerves as western peoples. He answered in the affirmative but said they were taught from infancy to control their nerves. I asked him how, and he said the principle of the system was deep abdominal breathing with a slow release of the breath as soon as nervousness came on. Japanese wrestlers practised this, he added, and when a man took deep breaths it was almost impossible to throw him.

Of course, social life and customs change with climate. But education is the most powerful factor of all. The Aztecs of Mexico offered human sacrifices, but the letter of the Aztec mother to her daughter, giving advice and counsel, mentioned by Prescott in his history, might have been written

by a New England mother to-day. Somewhere in
the world is a savage eating human flesh, persuaded that in so doing he is acting in accordance with
the tenets of his religion.

These are the extremes.

But the German or rather the Prussian, has been
moulded into the extraordinary person that he is
to-day by a slow process of education extending
through several generations. At Marienburg, on
the Baltic shore of Germany, stands the ancient
castle of the Teutonic Knights recently restored
by the German Kaiser. The Knights at one time
conquered and occupied much of the territory that
is now modern Prussia. A military religious order,
they attracted adventurers from all lands and their
descendants constitute many of the noble families
of Prussia. It is this tradition of conquest for gain
that still animates the ruling class of Prussia and
therefore all Germany.

Later through the middle ages and as the central
power of the Emperor grew weaker and weaker,
what is to-day Germany became a nest of dukedoms
and principalities. Before the French Revolution
these numbered hundreds. After the Thirty Years'
War which ravaged Germany from 1615 to 1645
extreme poverty was often conspicuous at these
petty courts. War was an industry and the poor
German peasants were frequently bartered as
slaves to the war-god, as the Hessians were sold
by their ruler to the British in our War of the
Revolution. The Germans were then the mercenaries of Europe, savages skilled in war, without

mercy towards the towns unfortunate enough to be given to their pillage. There is no more horrible event in all history than that of the sack of Rome by the German mercenaries in the year 1527. Under General George von Frundsberg, who joined forces with the recreant constable Bourbon of France and the Spaniards, these lawless Germans invaded the fertile plains of Italy and took Rome by assault.

The most awful outrages were perpetrated. Prelates were tortured after being paraded through the streets of the Eternal City, dressed in their sacred pontificals and mounted on donkeys. Altars were defiled, sacred images broken, vestments and services and works of art taken from the plundered churches and sacred relics insulted, broken and scattered. For nine months the orgy continued, the inhabitants being tortured by these German soldiers in their effort to find hidden treasure. In fact conditions in Belgium to-day had their counterpart centuries ago in the treatment of Roman Catholic Priests and the people of Rome.

The great change in the feeling of the country towards Prussia since the latter's conquest of the rest of Germany in 1866, is still exemplified by one quotation from Goethe. He said, "The Prussian was born a brute and civilisation will make him ferocious." We all have seen how prophetic was this sentence. Skilled in chemistry, in science, well educated, made rich by manufacturing and foreign commerce, the Prussians of to-day have shown themselves far more bloody, far more cruel than the German lansquenet of the middle ages who sold himself, his two handed sword, his military experience and his long lance to the highest bidder.

Tacitus tells of how the ancient Germans when drawn up in battle array used to sing a sort of war song to terrify their enemies.

It was Goethe incidentally who remarked "Amerika, du hast es besser." (America, you are better off.) The poet who died in 1832 foresaw, indeed, the coming power of the free democracy across the seas.

It was interesting to note the psychological development of the Germans during the war. For the very short time while war hung in the balance there was a period almost of rejoicing, among the singing crowds in the streets—a universal release of tension after forty years' preparation for war.

Next came the busy period of mobilisation and then, as the German armies swept through Belgium and France, stronghold and fortress falling before them, there came a period of intense exaltation, a period when the most reasonable Germans, the light of success and conquest in their eyes, declared German Kultur would now be imposed on the whole world.

The battle of the Marne ended this period of rejoicing and, through the winter of 1914-1915, when it became apparent that Germany would not win by a sudden assault, the temper of the people began to change to an attitude of depression.

It has been at all times the policy of the German

autocracy to keep the people of Germany from amusing themselves. I know of no class in Germany which really enjoys life. The Counts and Junkers have their country estates. Life on these estates, which are administered solely for profit, is not like country life in England or America. The houses are plain and, for the most part, without the conveniences of bath rooms and heating to which we are accustomed in America. Very few automobiles are owned in Germany. There are practically no small country houses or bungalows, although at a few of the sea places rich Jews have villas.

The wealthy merchant takes his vacation in summer at Carlsbad or Kissingen or in some other resort where his physical constitution, disorganised by over-eating and over-drinking, can be regulated somewhat. Many Germans take their families to Switzerland where the German of all ages with knapsack and Alpine stick is a familiar sight.

Earnestness is the watchword. For should the people once get a taste of pleasure they might decide that the earth offered fairer possibilities than life in the barracks or the admiring contemplation of fat and complacent grand dukes and princes.

Much of this sycophancy is due to the poverty of the educated classes. Salaries paid to officials are ridiculously small. The German workingmen both in wages and living are on a lower scale than those of other western nations with the possible exception of Russia, Italy and the Balkan States. The professional and business classes earn very little. The reason for the superiority of the German in the chemical industry is because a chemist, a graduate of the university, can be hired for less than the salary of an American chauffeur.

And this earnestness of life was insisted upon even to a greater degree by the autocracy with the opening of war. The playing of dance music brought a visit from the police. The theatres at first were closed but later opened. Only plays of a serious or patriotic nature were originally permitted. Dancing was tabooed, but in the winter of 1915-16 Reinhardt was allowed to produce a ballet of a severely classical nature and at the opera performances the ponderous ballet girls were permitted to cavort as usual.

I saw no signs of any great religious revival, no greater attendance at the churches. Perhaps this was because I was in the Protestant part of Germany where the church is under the direct control of the government and where the people feel that in attending church they are only attending an extra drill, a drill where they will be told of the glories of the autocracy and the necessity of obedience. In fact, religion may be said to have failed in Germany and many state-paid preachers launched sermons of hate from their state-owned pulpits.

Always fond of the drama and opera I was a constant attendant at theatres in Berlin. The best known manager in Berlin is Reinhardt, who has under his control the Deutsches Theatre with its annex, the Kammerspiel and also the People's

Theatre on the Bülow Platz. I made the acquaintance of Mr. Reinhardt and his charming wife who takes part in many of his productions. I dined with them in their picturesque house on the Kupfer Graben. In the Deutsches Theatre the great revolving stage makes change of scene easy so that Reinhardt is enabled to present Shakespeare, a great favourite in Germany, in a most picturesque manner. He manages to lend even to the most solemn tragedy little touches that add greatly to the interest and keep the attention fixed.

For instance in his production of "Macbeth," when Lady Macbeth comes in, in the sleep-walking scene, rubbing her hands and saying, "What, will these hands ne'er be clean?" the actress taking this part in Berlin gave a very distinct and loud snore between every three or four words: thus most effectively reminding the audience that she was asleep.

As the war continued the taste of the Germans turned to sombre, tragical and almost sinister plays. Only a death on the stage seemed to bring a ray of animation to the stolid bovine faces of the audience. In my last winter in Berlin the hit of the season was "Erdgeist," a play by Wedekind, whose "Spring's Awakening," given in New York in the spring of 1917, horrified and disgusted the most hardened Broadway theatregoers. The principal female rôle was played by a Servian actress, Maria Orska—very much on the type of Nazimova. In this play, presented to crowded audiences, only one of the four acts was without a death.

Another favourite during war-time, played at

Reinhardt's theatre, was "Maria Magdalena." The characters were the father, mother, son and daughter of a German family in a small town and two young men in love with the daughter. In the first act the police arrest the son for theft, giving the mother such a shock that she dies of apoplexy on the stage. In the second act, the two lovers have a duel and one is killed. In the third act, the surviving lover commits suicide, and, in the fourth act, the daughter jumps down the well. The curtain descends leaving only the old man and the cat alive and the impression is given that if the curtain were ten seconds later either the cat would get the old man or the old man would get the cat!

The mysterious play of Peer Gynt was given in two theatres during each winter of the war. All of Ibsen's dramas played to crowded houses. Reinhardt, during the last winter I was in Berlin, produced Strindberg's "Ghost Sonata," in quite a wonderful way. The play was horrible and grewsome enough, but as produced by him, it gave a strong man nightmare for days afterwards.

The German soul, indeed, seems to turn not towards light and gay and graceful things, but towards bloodshed and grewsomeness, ghosts and mystery—effect doubtless of the long, dark, bitter nights and gray days that overshadow these northern lands.

I think the only time I lost my temper in Germany was when a seemingly reasonable and polite gentleman from the Foreign Office sitting by my desk one day, in 1916, remarked how splendid it was that Germany had nearly two million prisoners of war and that these would go back to their homes imbued with an intense admiration of German Kultur.

I said that I believed that the two million prisoners of war who had been insulted and underfed and beaten and forced to work as slaves in factories and mines and on farms would go back to their homes with such a hatred of all things German that it would not be safe for Germans to travel in countries from which these prisoners came, that other nations had their own Kultur with which they were perfectly satisfied and which they did not wish to change for any made-in-Germany brand!

Certain Germans have prated much of German "Kultur," have boasted of imposing this "Kultur" on the world by force of arms. What is this German "Kultur"? A certain efficiency of government obtained by keeping the majority of the people out of all voice in governmental affairs, a certain low cost of manufactured products or of carrying charges in the shipping trades made possible by enslaving the workmen who toil long hours for small wages—a certain superiority in chemical production because trained chemists, willing to work at one semi-mechanical task, can be hired for less than a Fifth Avenue butler is paid in America, and a certain pre-eminence in military affairs reached by subjecting the mass of the people to the brutal, boorish, non-commissioned officers and the galling yoke of a militaristic system.

Subtract the German Jews and in the lines of real

culture there would be little of the real thing left
in Germany. Gutman, Bleichroeder, von Swabach,
Friedlander-Fuld, Rathenau, Simon, Warburg in
finance; Borchardt and others in surgery, and almost the whole medical profession; the Meyers, the
Ehrlichs, Bamberger, Hugo Schiff, Newburger,
Bertheim, Paul Jacobson, in chemistry and research; Mendelssohn, and others, in music; Harden, Theodor Wolf, Georg Bernhard and Professor
Stein in journalism.

But why continue—about the only men not Jews
prominent in the intellectual, artistic, financial, or
commercial life of Germany are the pastors of the
Lutheran Churches. And the Jews have won their
way to the front in almost a generation. Still refused commissions in the standing army (except
for about 114 since the war), still compelled to re-
nounce their religion before being eligible for nobility or a court function, still practically excluded
from university professorships, considered socially
inferior, the Jews of Germany until a few years ago
lived under disabilities that had survived from the
Middle Ages. They were not allowed to bear Christian names. The marriages of Jews and Christians
were forbidden. Jews could not own houses and
lands. They were not permitted to engage in agriculture and could not become members of the guilds
or unions of handicraftsmen. When a Jew travelled he was compelled to pay a tax in each province
through which he passed. Jews attending the fair
at Frankfort on the Oder were compelled to pay a
head tax, and were admitted to Leipzig and Dres-

den on condition that they might be expelled at any time. Berlin Jews were compelled to buy annually a certain quantity of porcelain, derisively called "Jew's porcelain" from the Royal manufactory and to sell it abroad. When a Jew married he had to get permission and an annual impost was paid on each member of the family, while only one son could remain at home, and the others were forced to seek their fortune abroad. The Jews could worship in their own way, in some states, provided they used only two small rooms and made no noise.

The reproach that the Jew is not a producer, but is a mere middleman, taking a profit as goods pass from hand to hand, is handed down from the time when Jews were forbidden by law to become producers and, therefore, were compelled to become traders and middlemen, barred from the guilds and from engaging in the cultivation of the soil.

The German newspaper in size is much smaller than ours. If you take an ordinary American newspaper and fold it in half, the fold appearing horizontally across the middle of the page and then turn it so that the longer sides are upright, you get an idea of the size. There are no editorials in German newspapers, but articles, usually only one a day, on some political or scientific subject, one contributed by a professor or some one else supposedly not connected with the newspaper.

The editor of the German newspaper in his desire to poison and colour the news to suit his own views does not rely upon an editorial, but inserts little paragraphs and sentences in the news columns. For instance, a note of President Wilson's might be printed and after a paragraph of that, a statement something like this will be inserted in parentheses. "This statement comes well from the old hyprocrite whose country has been supplying arms and ammunition to the enemies of Germany. The Editor." A few sentences more or a paragraph of the note and another interlineation of this kind. Small newspapers have a news service furnished free by the government, thus enabling the latter to colour the news to suit itself. It is characteristic of Germany and shows how void of amusement the life of an average citizen is and how the country is divided into castes, that there is no so-called society or personal news in the columns of the daily newspaper.

You never see in a German newspaper accounts common even to our small town newspapers, of how Mrs. Snooks gave a tea or how Mrs. Jones, of Toledo, is visiting Mrs. Judge Bascom for Thanksgiving. If a prince or duke comes to a German town a simple statement is printed that he is staying at such and such a hotel.

German newspapers, as a rule, are very pronounced in their views, either distinctly Conservative or Liberal or Socialist or Roman Catholic. The *Berliner Tageblatt* is nearest our idea of a great independent, metropolitan, daily newspaper. Other newspapers represent a class and many of them are owned by particular interests such as the

Krupps and other manufacturers or munition makers.

There is little that is sensational in the German newspaper. I remember on one occasion that two women murderers were beheaded in accordance with German law. Imagine how such an occurrence would have been "played up" in the American newspapers, with pictures, perhaps, of the executioner and his sword, with articles from poets and women's organisations, with appeals for pardon and talk of brainstorms and the other hysterical concomitants of murder trials in the United States. But in the German newspapers a little paragraph, not exceeding ten lines, simply related the fact that these two women, condemned for murdering such and such a person, had been executed in the strangely medieval manner—their heads cut off on the scaffold by a public executioner.

The German newspapers in reporting police court and other judicial proceedings often omit names and it is possible in Berlin for a man to prosecute a blackmailer without having his own name in print.

When a German victory was announced flags were displayed, but as the war progressed so many victories announced turned out to be nothing wonderful or decisive that little attention was paid to the vainglorious flaunting of German triumphs. Following an old custom ten or fifteen trumpeters climbed the tower of Rathhaus or City Hall and there quite characteristically blew to the four quarters of Heaven; but again as these official and brazen blowings were not always followed by the confirmation in fact, trumpetings were gradually discontinued.

The Germans cleverly kept back the announcement of certain successes in order to offset reverses. For instance, on a day when it was necessary to tell the people of a German retreat the newspapers would have great headlines across the front of the first page announcing the sinking of a British cruiser (sunk, perhaps, a month before) and then hidden in a corner would be a minimised announcement of a German defeat.

To us in Germany there was at the time no battle of the Marne. So gradually was the news of the retreat of the German forces broken to the people that to-day the masses do not realise that the fate of the world was settled at the Marne!

CHAPTER X

AS the king idea seems inseparably connected with war there is no country in the world where kings and princes have been held in such great account as in the Central Empires.

I believe there are only two Christian kings in the world—the kings of Italy and of Montenegro—who are not by blood related to some German or Austrian royalty.

For remember that while we think of Germany as ruled by the Kaiser and while it is his will that is certainly imposed upon the whole of that territory which does not exist politically or even geographically but which we call Germany, there are houses of royalty in it almost as numerous as our big corporations. There are the three kings of Bavaria, Würtemburg and Saxony, grand dukes and dukes, and princes, all of them taking themselves very seriously and all of them residing in their own domains; jealously keeping away from the Emperor's court and jealously guarding every remnant of rule which the constitution of the German Empire has bequeathed to them.

Once I asked one of these princelings what his older brother, the reigning prince, did with his time in the small provincial town which is the capital of the principality. The brother looked at me with real surprise in his eyes and answered, "Why he reigns!"

Before the constitution of the German Empire, many of these poverty-stricken little courts were centres of kindly amusement, even of intellectual life.

The court of the Grand Duke Charles-Augustus, of Saxe-Weimar-Eisenach at Weimar where Goethe resided and where he was entrusted with responsible state duties, was renowned in Europe as a literary centre.

Many of these princelings, however ridiculous their courts may have seemed, exercised despotic power. To-day the inhabitants of the two Mecklenburg duchies are protected by neither constitution nor bill of rights. The grand duke's power is absolute and he can behead at will any one of his subjects in the market-place or torture him to death in the dungeons of the castle and is responsible to God alone.

Here is an example from history. George Louis, Duke of Brunswick-Luneburg-Celle, married his mistress, a Huguenot girl called Eleanore d'Olbreuze. They had one daughter, Sophia Dorothea, who married the Elector of Hanover, who was also George I of England. Sophia Dorothea was supposed to have been involved in a love affair with a Swedish Count, Philip Konigsmarck. Konigsmarck was murdered by order of George I, and Sophia Dorothea incarcerated in Ahlden where she died in 1726. Konigsmarck's sister went to Saxony to beg the aid of the Saxon King, Augustus the Strong. She failed to get news of her brother, but became one of the mistresses of Augustus the Strong and the mother of the celebrated Marshal Saxe. I say one of the "mistresses" of Augustus the Strong because he boasted that he was the father of 365 illegitimate children!

The daughter of Sophia Dorothea was the mother of Frederick the Great and his brothers, and therefore, an ancestor of the present German Kaiser. Any one writing about her in a disparaging manner is subject to be imprisoned, under the decisions of the Imperial Supreme Court, for "lèse-majesté" or injuring the person of the present monarch in daring to slander his ancestors. And, I suppose, any one referring to Augustus the Strong may be shut up in Dresden for insulting a predecessor of the present King.

Every year the nobles of the Central Empires hold a convention at Frankfort, where the means are discussed by which their privileges may be preserved. No newspaper prints an account of this Convention of the highest Caste.

The German peasants, as far as I have seen, are not so much under the dominion of feudal tradition as are the peasants in Austria and Hungary.

I was shooting once with a Hungarian Count who stationed me in one corner of a field to await the partridges, which driven by the beaters were expected to fly over my head and as I stood waiting for the beaters to take up their positions two peasant girls walked past me. One of them, to my surprise, caught hold of my hand, which she kissed with true feudal devotion. As a guest of the Count I was presumably of the noble class and therefore entitled by custom and right to this mark of subjugation. And it became quite a task in walking through the halls of the castle to dodge the servants, all of whom seemed anxious to imprint on me the kiss of homage.

Thackeray in the "Fitzboodle Confessions" gives a most amusing account of life in one of these small, sleepy, German courts and relates how he left Pumpernickel hurriedly, by night, after the court ball where he had discovered not only that his German fiancée had eaten too much, but that she had a taste for bad oysters.

All of these small kings and princes are jealous of the King of Prussia and of his position of German Emperor and show their jealousy by avoiding Berlin.

In October, 1913, when in London on my way to Germany, I met the young Grand Duke of Mecklenberg Strelitz in the Ritz Hotel where he was dining with an English earl and his beautiful wife. As I happened to have a box for the Gaiety Theatre, we all went there together and paid a visit to George Grossmith behind the scenes and talked with Emmy Wehlen, the Austrian actress, who was appearing in the comic opera then running. But in all the time that I was in Germany I never once saw or heard of the young Grand Duke who rules the subjects of his duchy with autocratic rule without even the semblance of a constitution.

Formerly our minister used to be accredited to some of these courts and, on inquiring informally through a friend, I learned that the American Minister is still accredited to Bavaria on the records of the Bavarian Foreign Office, no letters of recall ever having been presented. The fact that the American Ambassador is accredited to none of these courts is a distinct disadvantage because without letters of credence he does not come into contact with any of the twenty-four rulers of Germany who control the Bundesrat in which their representatives sit, voting as they are told by the kings, grand dukes and princes. A number of these kings and princelings, combining in the Bundesrat, can outvote the powerful king of Prussia. But they don't dare!

CHAPTER XI

I HAD a shooting estate about twenty miles from Berlin, one that I could reach by automobile in forty-five minutes from the door of the Embassy. Because of the strict German game laws I had better shooting there than within two hundred miles of large cities in America.

There seemed to be something to shoot there almost every day of the year. On the sixteenth of May the season opened for male roe—a very small deer. About the first of August the ducks, which breed in northern Germany, can be shot. These were mallards and there were about two thousand or more on a lake on my preserve. We usually shot them by digging blinds in the oat fields, shooting them after sunset as they flew from the lake to feed in the newly harvested grain. The season for Hungarian partridge opened on August 20th. These were shot over dogs in the stubble and in the potato fields. After a few weeks partridges became very wild and we then shot them with a kite. When we had put up a covey out of range and marked where they went down in a potato patch or field, perhaps of lucern or clover, a small boy would fly a kite made in the form of a hawk over the field. This kept the partridges from flying and they would lie while the dogs pointed until we put them up.

By October 1st pheasants could be shot; English pheasants become wild. These roosted in the trees at night and so escaped the plentiful foxes. Later on came shooting at long ranges, after they had collected in bands, of the female roedeer and also the hare shooting. Rabbits were shot at all times, and in November and December and January on foggy days it was not difficult to get a wild goose.

The hares were shot in cold weather, after the snow was on the ground, by walking in line of ten or fifteen beaters with two or three guns at intervals along the line and later, when the hares were very wild and the weather very cold, by what is called by the Germans "kessel-jagd" or kettle-hunt. For this hunt the head keeper would collect a number of beaters, as many as a hundred, from the neighboring towns and villages, mostly small boys and old men. On the great, flat plain the keeper would send out his beaters to the right and the left, walking in a straight line at about twenty-yard intervals. After each side had gone perhaps half a mile they would then turn at right angles, walk a mile, and then turn at right angles until the two lines met, so that perhaps a square mile of territory would be enclosed by the beaters with the ten to fifteen men with guns at intervals in the line. When the square had been formed the head keeper blew a blast on his bugle and all turned and walked

149

slowly towards the centre and the hares were shot as they attempted to break through the line.

On one day just before I left Germany, I and members of the Embassy shot more than two hundred hares on one of these hunts. The German hare is an enormous animal with dark meat, almost impossible to distinguish from venison.

After these hare drives, besides, of course, paying the beaters their regular wages, I used to hold a lottery, giving a number of these hares as prizes or distributing hares to the magnates of the village, such as the pastor, the school teacher, the policeman and the postmaster.

When we were shooting in the summer and autumn the peasants were working in the fields and one had to be very careful in shooting roebuck with a high-powered rifle. It is customary to hunt roebuck on these flat plains from a carriage. In this way a bullet, travelling at a downward angle, if the buck is missed, strikes the ground within a short distance. If one were to shoot lying down, kneeling or standing, the danger to peasants in the fields would be very great. The pheasants were sometimes shot over dogs, but usually as the beaters drove small woods. A pheasant driven and flying high makes a difficult mark. One getting up before the dogs is almost too easy a shot.

We shot the rabbits by using ferrets, little animals like weasels wearing little muzzles and bells upon their necks. In the woods where the rabbits had their holes four or five ferrets would be put in the rabbits' holes and it was quite difficult to shoot rabbits as they came out like lightning, dodging among the trees. In the early spring the "birk-hahns" were shot, a variety of black and white grouse. There were some blinds or little huts of twigs erected near places where the ground was beaten hard and on these open, beaten spots early in the morning the "birkhahns" waltz, doing a peculiar backward and forward dance in some way connected with their marriage ceremonies. There were also on this estate numbers, at times, of a curious bird found only in Spain, Roumania, Asia Minor, and these plains of the Mark of Branden-burg, a large bustard called by the Germans "trappe." These birds were very shy and hard to approach. Although I had several shots at them with a rifle at four or five hundred yards I did not succeed in getting one.

In talking with the Chancellor he almost always opened the conversation by asking if I had yet killed a "trappe." As a rule the German uses for shooting deer and roebuck a German Mauser mili-tary rifle, but with the barrel cut down and a sport-ing stock with pistol grip added. On this there is a powerful telescope. Many Germans carry a "ziel-stock," a long walking stick from the bottom of which a tripod can be protruded and near the top a sort of handle piece of metal about as big as a little finger. When the German sportsman has sighted a roebuck he plants his aiming stick in the ground, rests the rifle on the side projection, care-fully adjusts his telescope, sets the hair trigger on his rifle and finally touches the trigger.

At the commencement of the war the Duke of Ratibor collected all these sporting rifles with telescopes and sent them to the front. These were of the same calibre as the military rifles and took the military cartridge, so they proved enormously useful for sniping purposes.

Going one day to a proof establishment to try a gun I opened by mistake a door which led to a great room where thousands of German military rifles were being fitted with telescopes. These telescopes have crossed wires, like those in a surveyor's instrument, and it is only necessary in aiming to fix the centre of the crossed wires on the game and pull the trigger. A clever arrangement enables the wires to be elevated for distant shooting.

So great is the discipline of the German people that game on these estates is seldom, if ever, touched by the peasants. There is no free shooting in Germany. The shooting rights of every inch of land are in possession of some one and the tens of thousands of game keepers constantly killing the crows, hawks, foxes and other birds and animals that destroy eggs and game make the game plentiful. The keeper has the right by law to shoot any stray dog or cat found a hundred yards from a village. I paid the head keeper a certain sum per month and in addition he received a premium called "shot money" for each bird or roebuck shot. He also received a premium for each fox or crow or hawk he destroyed, bringing, on the first of the month, the beaks and claws of the hawks, etc., to prove his claim. Foxes are very plentiful in Ger-

EXAMPLE OF THE COMMEMORATIVE MEDAL OFFERED FOR SALE. ON THE OBVERSE IS THE PORTRAIT OF THE CROWN PRINCE. ON THE REVERSE IS "YOUNG SIEGFRIED" ATTACKING A CHIMERA-LIKE MONSTER WITH FOUR HEADS: A BEAR FOR RUSSIA, A UNICORN FOR ENGLAND, A LION FOR BELGIUM, AND A COCK FOR FRANCE.

many and in one winter on this estate, only twenty miles from Berlin, the keeper trapped or killed twelve foxes.

The Emperor is very fond of fox shooting. Foxes are driven out of the forest past his shooting stand by beaters and one of the reasons why Prince Furstenberg was such a favourite of the Emperor was that he provided him with splendid fox shooting, although it is whispered that he bought foxes in boxes in all parts of Germany and had them turned loose for the Emperor's benefit.

In the more thickly forested portions of Germany deer as well as roedeer are shot and in many districts wild boar. In Poland and in a few estates in Germany on the eastern border, moose, called elk (elch in German), are to be had. These, however, have very poor horns.

Talking to the keepers and beaters on this shooting estate gave me a very good idea of the hardships suffered in rural Germany, of the way in which the people in the farming districts are kept down by the lords of the manor and by the government, and it was from this village and the neighbouring town that I got some idea of the number of men called to arms in Germany.

By a custom dating from the devastating wars of the Middle Ages there are practically no farms in Germany, but inhabitants of the agricultural districts are collected in villages and the few farms have, characteristically, a military name. They are called "vorwerk" or outposts. In the village on my estate there are almost exactly six hundred inhabitants, men, women and children, and of these at the time I left Germany one hundred and ten had been called to the Colours. In the neighbouring town of Mittenwalde, of almost three thousand inhabitants, over five hundred had joined the army. At the commencement of the war the population of the German Empire was about 72,000,000, or something over, and applying these same proportions it will be seen what a vast army was created.

In the industrial districts where men are required for munition work perhaps not as great a proportion has been called. The name of the village on my estate was Gross Machnow, the road from Berlin to Dresden ran through it and only a few miles east was the shooting place of Wusterhausen where the favourite shooting box of the father of Frederick the Great was and where he was accustomed to hold his so-called tobacco parliament, when, with his cronies, over beer and long pipes, the affairs of the nation were discussed with great freedom.

The horse races in Germany are excellent. There are several tracks about Berlin. The Hoppegarten, devoted almost exclusively to flat racing; the Grunewald, the large popular track nearest to Berlin where both steeplechases and other races are held; and Karlshorst, devoted exclusively to steeplechasing and hurdle racing.

The jockey club of Berlin is the Union Club, which owns the Hoppegarten track. Its officers are men of the highest honour and in no country in the world are the races run more honestly, more "on the level," than in Germany.

Nothing makes for mutual international under-standing more than sport. Even during the most bitter crises between Germany and America I felt that I could go absolutely alone to the crowded race tracks and, while I know the Germans differed em-phatically with the American views of the war, the gentlemen in charge of the races and the members of the Union Club treated me with the kindest con-sideration and the most graceful courtesy.

I am sorry that I never attended any of the Court hunts which took place in the vicinity of Potsdam. A pack of hounds is kept there and boars hunted. The etiquette is very strict and no one, not present-ed at court, can appear at these hunts. As I did not have an opportunity to present my letters of cre-dence until a month or more after my arrival in Berlin in the autumn of 1913, the winter rains had set in before I was eligible for the hunts and in ad-dition I had not taken the precaution to order the necessary costumes.

The first time that a man appears at one of these hunts he must wear a tall silk hat, a double-breasted red coat, with tails like a dress coat, white breeches and top boots. After he has once made his appearance in this costume he may, thereafter, substitute for it a red frock hunting coat, white breeches and top boots and a velvet hunting cap, the same shape as the caps worn by the jockies.

There are no jumps on these hunts. When the boar has been brought to bay by the dogs, the right to despatch him with a long hunting knife is reserved for the most distinguished man present. If a royalty is present at one of these hunts he distributes small sprigs of oak leaves to every one at the hunt, cherished ever after as valued souvenirs.

When I first arrived at Berlin, having brought horses with me from America, I used to ride every morning in the Tiergarten. Because so many Germans are in the army, riding is a very favourite sport and in peace times the Tiergarten is crowded with Berliners. Most of the riding was done between seven and ten in the morning. The early rising is compensated for, however, by the siesta after lunch, a universal custom.

Shooting is almost more of a ceremony than a sport. The letters exchanged between Emperor William and Czar Nicholas, lately discovered in the Winter Palace, show what a large part shooting played in their correspondence. One or the other is continually wishing the other "Weidmanns-Heil," which is the German expression for "good luck" as applied to shooting. All royalties must ride and keep in practice, especially because of military service. Indeed, all the sports of the Kaiser and his people converge toward a common object—military efficiency and war.

CHAPTER XII

E VEN the women, many of whom are honorary
colonels to regiments, must keep in trim for
the great parade days of autumn and spring.
Many of these female colonels appear in uniform,
riding at the head of their regiments. They sit on
side saddles, however, and wear skirts corresponding somewhat in colour with the uniform coat and
helmet of the regiment of which they are the honorary proprietors.

German female royalties are rather inclined to
set an example of quietness in dress. They seldom
wear the latest fashion and never follow the exag-
gerated modes of Paris. Even their figures are of
the old-fashioned variety—pinched at the waist.
While in the Tiergarten in the morning I saw many
good horses, but only one fashionably cut riding
habit. Many of the others must have been at least
twenty years old, as the sleeves were of the Leg of
Mutton style, fashionable, I believe, about that
number of years ago.

Many German noblewomen shoot and are quite
as good shots as their husbands. I was quite surprised once on a shooting party to meet an elderly
princess whose grey hair was in short curls and

who wore a coat and waistcoat like a man's. She shot with great skill and smoked long Havana cigars!

When German women get out of the country they very quickly imitate foreign fashions and extravagances of dress. The Czarina of Russia, for example, a German Princess, is very fond of fashions, and a friend of mine who had three audiences with her during the war tells me that on the occasion of his first audience she was dressed in black and received him in a room where yellow flowers were massed. On the second occasion she was in grey and the flowers were pink. At the third audience her dress was purple and the flowers were of lilac and white.

There is one good thing about the king and aristocratic system. The position of women in the social scale is fixed by the husband's rank. There is, therefore, none of that striving, that vying with each other, which so often exhausts the nerves of the American woman and the purse of the husband. The German women give their time and attention to the "Four K's" that, in a German's eyes, should bound a woman's world, "Kaiser, Kinder, Kirche, Kuche" (Emperor, children, church and kitchen).

The successful business man of New York or Chicago or San Francisco is surprised to find how docile and domestic the German woman is—no foolish extravagance, but a real devotion to husband and home, a real mother to her many children. She matches that short epitaph of the Roman matron—"She spun wool; she kept the house."

158

When I came to Germany I found, on studying the language, that there was no word in German corresponding to "efficient." I soon learned that this is because everything done in Germany is done efficiently, and there is no need to differentiate one act from another in terms of efficiency. But the German man could not be as efficient as he undoubtedly is, without the whole-hearted devotion of the German woman.

German girls are given a good, strong, sound education. They learn languages, not smatterings of them. They are accomplished musicians. Domestic science they learn from their mothers. They are splendid swimmers, hockey players, riders and skaters.

During our first winter in Berlin we spent many afternoons at the Ice Palace in the Lutherstrasse, an indoor ice rink much larger than the one in the Freidrichstrasse, the Admirals Palast, where the ice ballets are given and the graceful Charlotte used to appear. The skating club of the Lutherstrasse was under the patronage of the Crown Prince and was one of the very few meeting places of Berlin society. The women were taught to waltz by male instructors and the men by several young women —blonde skaters from East Prussia. I tried to improve my skating and spent many hours making painful "Bogens" or circles under the efficient eyes of a little East Prussia instructress. Afternoon tea was served during the interval of skating and one afternoon a week was specially reserved for the Club members.

One of my young secretaries used to go occasionally to Wannsee, near Berlin, to play hockey
with a German friend; as the young men were
nearly all in the war, girls made up the majority
of each team. My secretary reported that those
German girls were as strong, as enduring and as
skilful as the average young man.

Girls of the working classes, instead of flirting
or turkey trotting at night, make a practice of going
to the Turnvereins, to exercise in the gymnasiums
there. If the members of the German lower classes
only had the opportunity to rise in life what would
they not accomplish! So many of them are very
ambitious, persistent, earnest and thrifty.

Of course, female suffrage in Germany or anything approaching it is very distant. First of all,
the men must win a real ballot for themselves in
Prussia, a real representation in the Reichstag. In
the Germany of to-day, a woman with feminist
aspirations is looked on as the men of the official
class look on a Social Democrat, something hardly
to be endured. And this is in spite of the fact that
the nations to the North, in Scandinavia, freed
women even before America did.

The most beautiful woman in Berlin society is
Countess Oppersdorff—the mother of thirteen chil-
dren. She is not German, but was born a Polish
Princess Radziwill.

The chief lady of the Imperial Court is Countess
Brockdorff. She is rather stern in appearance and
manner, and rumour has it that she was appointed to keep the good-natured, easy-going Empress

to the strict line of German court etiquette, to see that the Empress, rather democratic in inclination, did not stray away from the traditional rigidity of the Prussian royal house.

Countess Brockdorff is a most able woman. I grew to have not only a great respect, but almost an affection for her. At court functions she usually wears a mantilla as a distinguished mark and several orders and decorations. We had three women friends from America with us in Berlin whom we presented at Court. All were married, but only the husband of one of them could leave his work and visit Germany. The two other husbands, in accordance with the good American custom, were at work in America. Countess Brockdorff spoke to the lady whose husband was with her, saying to her, "I am glad to see that your husband is with you," an implied rebuke to the other ladies and an exhibition of that failure to understand other nations so characteristic of highly placed Germans. With us, of course, a good-natured American husband, wedded as much to his business as to his wife, permits his wife to travel abroad without him and neither he nor she is reproved in America because of this.

Among the other ladies attendant on the Empress are Fräulein von Gersdorff, whose cousin is a lawyer practising in New York, and Countess Keller. There are other ladies and a number of maids of honour and all of them are overworked, acting as secretaries, answering letters and attending various charitable and other functions, either

with the Empress or representing her. One of the
charming maids of honour, Countess Bassewitz,
was married during the war to Prince Oscar, the
Kaiser's fifth son. This marriage was morganatic,
that is, the lady does not take the name, rank and
title of her husband. In this case another title was
given her, that of Countess Ruppin, and her sons
will be known as Counts Ruppin, but will not be
Princes of Prussia.

There is much misunderstanding in America as
to these morganatic marriages. By the rules of
many royal and princely houses, a member of the
house cannot marry a woman not of equal rank
and give her his name, titles and rank. But the
marriage is in all other respects perfectly legal.
The ceremony is performed in accordance with
Prussian law, before a civil magistrate and also in
a church, and should the husband attempt to marry
again he would be guilty of bigamy.

I gave away the bride at one of these morganatic marriages, when Prince Christian of Hesse
married Miss Elizabeth Reid-Rogers, a daughter
of Richard Reid Rogers, a lawyer of New York.
Prince Christian has an extremely remote chance
of ever coming to the throne of the Grand Duchy
of Hesse, but nevertheless and because of the rules
of the House of Hesse-Barchfeld, he cannot give
his rank and title to a wife, not of equal birth. The
head of the House, therefore, the Grand Duke of
Hesse, conferred the title of Baroness Barchfeld
in her own right on the bride, and her children will
be known as Barons and Baronesses Barchfeld.

When Prince Christian and his wife go out to
dinner in Berlin, he is given his rank at the table
as a member of a royal house, but his wife is treated
on a parity with the wives of all officers holding
commissions of equal grade with her husband in
the army.   As her husband is a Lieutenant, she
ranks merely as a Lieutenant's wife.   On the same
day that Miss Rogers and Prince Christian were
wedded, Miss Cecilia May of Baltimore married
Lieutenant Vom Rath.   I acted as one of Miss
May's witnesses at the Standesamt, where the civil
marriage was performed, while the religious marriage took place in our Embassy.   Lieutenant Vom
Rath is the son of one of the proprietors of the
great dye works manufactories known as Lucius-
Meister-Farbewerke at Hoehst, near Frankfurt
a. M., where salvarsan and many other medicines
used in America are manufactured, as well as dyestuffs and chemicals.

In my earlier book I described presentations at
the Royal Prussian Court in Berlin, especially
the great court called the "Schleppencour," because of the long trains or Schleppe worn by
the women.   All the little kingdoms and principalities of the German Empire have somewhat
the same ceremonies.   In Dresden, the capital of
Saxony, a peculiar custom is followed.   The King
and Queen sit at a table at one end of the room
playing cards and the members of the court and
distinguished strangers file into the room, pass by
the card table in single file and drop deep cour-
tesies and make bows to the seated royalties, who,

as a rule, do not even take the trouble to glance at those engaged in this servile tribute to small royalty. I suppose that the excuse for this is that it is an old custom. But so is serfdom!

There are in Germany many so-called mediatised families, so-called because at one time they possessed royal rank and rights over small bits of territory before Napoleon changed the map of Europe and wiped out so many small principalities.

At the Congress of Vienna these families who lost their right of rule, in part compensation, were given the right to marry either royalties or commoners; so that the marriage of a Prince of Prussia with a daughter of one of these mediatised houses would not be morganatic. The girl would take the full rank of her husband and the children would inherit any rights, including the rights to the throne possessed by him.

Thus the beautiful young Countess Platen, shortly before we left Berlin, was married to von Stumm, the very able Under Secretary of State for Foreign Affairs. While she became on her marriage Baroness von Stumm, nevertheless, if she had married the son of the Kaiser, she would have taken his rank and her children would have inherited all rights and titles possessed by their father. This is because the Platens, although bearing only the title of Counts, are a mediatised family.

It is noteworthy that in Berlin women of that blonde type with regular features, which we believe is the German type, are very rare. This type is to be found perfected in Scandinavia, although

164

a few specimens exist in Germany. Looking over a Berlin theatre I have often noticed the predominance of brown and black hair.

There is always some one higher up to whom German women must curtsy. All women, whatever their husband's rank, must curtsy to a Royal Prince. Unmarried girls curtsy to married women and kiss their hands. Men, on meeting women, always kiss their hands.

Berlin is certainly the gossip headquarters of the world. Some years ago the whole town was invaded by a mania for anonymous letter writing, and when the smoke had cleared away few were left with unriddled reputations.

It is the fashion of the present court, however, to be very puritanical. No such little affairs are going on publicly, as have occurred in the annals of the Hohenzollern family. For even the old Emperor William, grandfather of the present Kaiser, had numerous love affairs. The tree is still pointed out near the Tiergarten where he met Princess Radziwill every day.

And the Chancellor's palace was once the home of another royal "friend."

The Foreign Office was at one time the home of the Italian dancer, La Barberini, the only woman who ever for a time enslaved Frederick the Great. I discussed affairs of state with von Jagow and Zimmermann in the very room where she gave her supper parties.

CHAPTER XIII

HOME LIFE AND "BRUTALITY" OF THE PEOPLE

THE apartments of Berlin are designed for outward show for which the Berliners have a weakness. They have great reception and dining-rooms called "representation rooms," but very little comfort or space in the sleeping quarters.

It is impossible to think of dropping in suddenly on a Berliner for a meal. The dinners are always for as many people as the rooms will hold and are served by a caterer.

Only two very distinguished guests may be invited. The host and hostess sit opposite each other at the sides of the table, with the guests tapering off in rank to right and left of them, the ends of the tables being filled up with aides and secretaries. When a great man is invited his aide or secretary must be asked also. These come usually without their wives.

After dinner men and women leave the table together and smoke in the other rooms of the house, going from group to group. And, although perhaps ten kinds of wine are served during dinner, as soon as the guests leave the dining-room, servants make their appearance with trays of glasses of light and dark beer and continue to offer beer during the remainder of the evening.

The Germans talk much of food and spend a greater part of their income on food than any other nation. They take much interest in table furnishings, china, etc., and invariably turn over the plates to see the marks on the under side.

Whipped cream is an essential to many German dishes, and in the season a Berliner will commit any crime to obtain some plover's eggs.

The weiss bier of Berlin, served in wide goblets, is rather going out of fashion. It often is drunk mixed with raspberry juice.

The restaurants of Berlin are not gay, like those of Paris. There is, however, a rather rough night life created for foreign consumption. I did not take in any of these night restaurants and dancing cabarets, warned by the case of an Ambassador from —— who was reproved by von Jagow for visiting the "Palais de Danse."

In peace time few automobiles are to be seen on the Berlin streets. There are many millionaires in the city, but the old habits of German thrift persist.

The modern architecture of Germany is repulsive. The man who builds a new house seems to want to get something resembling as nearly as possible a family vault. Ihne, court architect and Imperial favourite, has produced, however, some beautiful buildings, notably the new library in Berlin.

Munich pretends to be more of a centre of art and music than Berlin. Artists have their headquarters there, but the disciples of the awful "art nouveau" and kindred "arts" have produced many horrors in striving for new effects.

The opera in Munich is better than in Berlin. One of the Bavarian Princes plays a fiddle in the orchestra in the Royal Opera House.

The Berlin hospitals are better than ours, except for the caste system which prevails even there, and there are first, second and third class wards.

The underground road is built at about the same depth as the New York subway. There are two classes, second and third; there are no guards on the trains, only the motorman in the first car. The passengers open the side doors themselves and these are shut either by passengers or station guards. Accidents are rare, all showing the innate discipline of the people. The charge is by distance. You buy a ticket for five or eight stations and give up the ticket as you go out of the station. If you have travelled farther than the distance called for by your ticket you must make the additional payment. This requires that each ticket be inspected separately when taken up.

The tramways have different routes. These routes are shown by signs and by numbers displayed on the car. Women motormen in the war period caused many accidents.

For those Germans who cannot afford to ride or shoot, walking is the principal recreation. There are a few golf courses in the German Empire, mostly patronised by foreigners and American dentists.

Military training is always in view and the use of the knapsack on walking tours is universal, even school children carry their books to school in knapsacks and so become accustomed, at an early age, to carry this part of the soldier's burden.

Occasionally, in summer, bands of girls or boys are to be seen on walking tours. In addition to the usual knapsack, they carry guitars or mandolins. These young people are known as "Wander vogel" (wandering birds), and sing as they walk. But they don't sing very loud. They might break some regulation.

Outside of the large cities and even in the cities vacant lots are occupied by "arbour colonies" (lauben colonie)—tiny little houses of wood erected by city workingmen and surrounded by little gardens of vegetables and flowers. Here the city workman spends Sunday and often the twilight hours and the night in summer time. Of course, these are possible only in a country where the workingman is in a distinct social class and where he is compelled to be content with the amusements and occupations of that class alone.

There is no baseball or substitute for it—the clerks get their diversion in a country excursion or at the free bath on the Wann or Muggel Lake.

These "free baths," so-called, are stretches of sandy lake shore where the populace resort in hot weather, undressing with the indifference of animals on the beach, men and women all mixed together, the men wearing only little bathing trunks and the women scanty one-piece bathing suits.

There is a bathing tent where two cents is charged for the privilege of undressing, but most prefer the open beach. Few swim or go in the water, but the majority lie about the beach, often sleeping in affectionate embrace, all without exciting any comment or ridicule.

The boy scout movement was taken up enthusiastically in Germany with the cheerful support of the military caste, who look on the activity as a welcome adjunct to military training. The boys certainly are given a dose of real drill. On one occasion I saw a boy company at drill march straight into the Havel river, no command to halt having been given at the river bank!

The workingmen of Germany are more brutal than those of England, France and America, but this is because of the low wages they receive, and because they feel the weight of the caste system.

In a speech in December, 1917, I said that a revolution in Germany would come after the war and that a fellow Ambassador in Berlin had said to me that because of the great brutality of the workingmen in Germany this uprising would make the French Revolution look like a Methodist Sunday School picnic. A newspaper reported me as saying this on my own authority and added that I had said the Germans were the most "bestial" people on earth.

I only want to be responsible for what I actually say. I did not call the Germans "bestial," although unfortunately it is a fact that many officers of the army and others have been guilty of a brutality which has helped turn the face of the world from the whole German people.

Not all the Germans are brutal. I received many letters revealing evidence to the contrary.

Here is the protest of a German soldier, an eye-witness of the slaughter of Russian soldiers in the Masurian lakes and swamps:

"It was frightful, heart-rending, as these masses of human beings were driven to destruction. Above the terrible thunder of the cannon could be heard the heart-rending cries of the Russians: 'Oh, Prussians! Oh, Prussians!' But there was no mercy. Our Captain had ordered: 'The whole lot must die; so rapid fire.'

"As I have heard, five men and one officer on our side went mad from those heart-rending cries. But most of my comrades and the officers joked as the unarmed and helpless Russians shrieked for mercy when they were being suffocated in the swamps and shot down. The order was: 'Close up and at it harder!'

"For days afterward those heart-rending yells followed me, and I dare not think of them or I shall go mad. There is no God, there is no morality and no ethics any more. There are no human beings any more, but only beasts. Down with militarism!"

This was the experience of a Prussian soldier. At present wounded; Berlin, October 22, 1914.

"If you are a truth-loving man, please receive these lines from a common Prussian soldier."

Here is the testimony of another German soldier on the East Front:

171

"Russian Poland, Dec. 18, 1914.

"In the name of Christianity I send you these words. My conscience forces me as a Christian German soldier to inform you of these lines.

"Wounded Russians are killed with the bayonet according to orders, and Russians who have surrendered are often shot down in masses according to orders in spite of their heart-rending prayers.

"In the hope that you, as the representative of a Christian State, will protest against this, I sign myself, '*A German Soldier and Christian.*'

"I would give my name and regiment, but these words could get me court-martialed for divulging military secrets."

The following letter is from a soldier on the Western Front:

"To the American Government, Washington, U. S. A.:

"Englishmen who have surrendered are shot down in small groups. With the French one is more considerate. I ask whether men let themselves be taken prisoner in order to be disarmed and shot down afterward? Is that chivalry in battle?

"It is no longer a secret among the people; one hears everywhere that few prisoners are taken; they are shot down in small groups. They say naïvely, 'We don't want any unnecessary mouths to feed. Where there is no one to enter complaint, there is no judge.' Is there, then, no power in the world which can put an end to these murders and rescue the victims? Where is Christianity? Where is right? Might is right.

"A Soldier and Man Who Is No Barbarian."

The first two letters refer to the battle of the Masurian Lakes, when the troops of Hindenburg, in checking the invading Russians, indulged in a needless slaughter of prisoners.

I heard in Berlin of many cases of insanity of both German officers and men who were driven insane by the scenes of slaughter at this battle and especially by the great cry of horror and despair uttered by the poor Russians as they were shot down in cold blood or driven to a living death in the lakes and marshes.

An American newspaper said this could not be true, asking why did I not publish the letters in my first book. But my first book did not contain all I have to relate, and the letters in question were sent by me to the State Department early in the war, and were not at hand on the publication of my other series.

But speaking of anonymous letters, shortly before I left Germany I received a package containing a necklace of diamonds and pearls with a letter, which, translated, reads as follows:

"The enclosed jewelry was found in the fully destroyed house of Monsieur Guesnet of 36 Rue de Bassano, Paris. It is requested that this jewelry, which is his property, be returned to him."

The package was addressed to the Embassy of the United States. I took it with me on leaving Germany and restored it to the family of the owner in Paris. The Guesnet country house lay within the German lines and the sending of the jewelry to me shows conscience somewhere in the German army.

CHAPTER XIV

AIMS OF THE AUTOCRACY

I HAVE shown how the Kaiser is imbued with a desire of conquest, how, as he himself states, he dreamed a dream of world empire in which his mailed fist should be imposed upon all the countries of the earth.

But the Kaiser alone could not have driven Germany into war. His system could.

The head of one of the great banks of Germany told me in the first few weeks of the war that the Kaiser, when called upon at the last moment to sign the order for mobilisation by the General Staff, hesitated and did so only after the officers of the General Staff had threatened to break their swords over their knees.

If this story is true, what a pity that the Kaiser did not allow the officers to break their swords! What would have happened? Would the military have seized the power and deposed the Kaiser, putting the Crown Prince in his place? I believe it might have happened had he refused to sign the order. The Kaiser, after leaving Kiel, attended a council at Potsdam where war was decided upon, and I really doubt whether at the last moment he did not shrink before the awful responsibility or hesitate to sign the mobilisation order.

The immediate cause of Germany's going to war was the feeling on the part of the autocracy that the people would not much longer bear the yoke of militarism. That this fear had justification was shown by the enormous vote of lack of confidence in the Reichstag after the Zabern affair. At all costs the autocracy must be preserved, and if in addition the world could be conquered, so much the better.

With modern improvements on the outside the heart of the government of Germany is that of the Middle Ages. The nobles as a rule are poor, the returns from their landed estates small, and, in peace times, the army general, the Prussian noble, and the Prussian official is overshadowed in display and expenditure by the rich merchant.

Army officers, nobles and governing class felt this and believed that war would restore what they regarded as the natural equilibrium of the country, the officers, the officials and the nobles at the top and the merchant class back in its place below.

With war, retired generals living on small pensions in dingy towns once more became personages, rushing about the country in automobiles attended by brilliant staffs and holding almost the power of life and death. His lands worked by prisoners at six cents a day, and their products sold at five times the original price with no new taxes on either land or incomes, the Prussian Junker is enjoying the war.

And this autocracy can make no peace which is not a "German peace," which does not mean that the Emperor and the generals can ride through the Brandenburger Thor to celebrate the conclusion of what may be thought a victorious war.

For the plain people of Germany, while they can make no revolution now, on returning to their homes maimed and broken after four years in the trenches, will revolt at last, if a peace has been concluded which does not spell success for Germany. They will say to their government,—to the autocracy,— "We had no political power. We left everything in your hands. We had nothing to say either about the declaration of this war or its conduct. In return for our submission you promised efficiency and you promised us more, the conquest of the world. You have failed and we are going to overthrow you."

It is the knowledge of this that makes the Emperor and the autocracy ready to take any chance, anxious to continue the war in the hope that some lucky stroke, either of arms or of propaganda, will turn the scale in their favour, because they know that any peace that is not a German peace will mean the end of autocracy and probably of the Hohenzollerns.

And all the while the people are told that the war is a defensive war, although the German armies fight far in enemy territory in France, in Russia, in Italy, in Serbia, and in Roumania. They always are told, too, that it is Germany who is desirous of making peace and that the Allies refuse.

Last summer (1917) when an interview I had with the Chancellor in which he named the peace terms of the autocracy was published, the interview was repudiated by the Chancellor, who stated that these terms were not his. I am sure that they are not his and were not his, but I am equally sure that they are the terms and were the terms of the autocracy of Prussia as stated by him. Shortly after this the newspapers confirmed part of these terms, telling of the talk in Germany of the guarantees to be exacted in case Belgium was surrendered by the Germans, which guarantees amounted to the absolute control of that unfortunate country and "rectification of the frontiers" demanded by Germany on the Eastern Front.

Outside of Germany the propagandist and the pacifist and other agents of the Central Empires have proclaimed that this war is not a war of conquest or aggression.

But the evidence is to the contrary.

Kaiser and pastors, Reichstag members and generals, orators and journalists, have all at different times during the war declared themselves in favour of conquest.

And it is extraordinary as showing the masterful manner in which the poor German people are led astray that most of the men making these declarations for annexation are able at the same time to cry that Germany is fighting a defensive war and is prevented from making peace only by the wicked Allies.

The King of Bavaria, speaking early in 1915 at

177

a banquet, said, "I rejoice because we can at last have a reckoning with our enemies and because at last we can obtain a direct outlet from the Rhine to the sea. Ten months have gone by. Much blood has been poured out. But it shall not be poured in vain, for the fruit of the war shall be a strengthening of the German Empire and *the extension of its boundaries,* so far as this is necessary in order that we may be assured against future attacks."

Duke John Albert of Mecklenburg, who is the gentleman who slapped his chest and cried out to me on one occasion that Germany would never forget the export of arms and ammunition to her enemies by America and that some day Germany would have her revenge, declared also in 1915 that the war would give Germany not only a mighty African Colonial Empire but a sufficiency of strongholds on earth for their navy, commerce, coaling and wireless stations.

The Kaiser, himself, speaking in July, 1915, in his call to the German people issued from the Great General Headquarters, said "that Germany would fight until peace came, a peace which offered the necessary military, political and commercial guarantees for the future."

Vice-President Paasche of the Reichstag, in April at Kreuznach, said, "We are not allowed to speak about conditions of peace. But the wish must be given expression that lives in the heart of every German that we will not give up enemy land conquered with so much German blood."

A sentiment also expressed in April, 1915, by the

178

National Liberal Reichstag member, Wachhorst de Wente, was to this effect: "Our fatherland must be larger. We must not allow it to be taken from us. Otherwise we will have obtained nothing except victory. We desire also to have the reward of victory. We will not give back all."

Von Heydebrandt, the Conservative Leader, the uncrowned King of Prussia, as he is called, demanded as a condition of peace "a stronger and larger Germany."

Naturally, the Conservative leaders are for conquest and annexation. Numerous articles in the Centrist Cologne *Volkzeitung* were published protesting against giving Belgium her independence again. In April, 1916, this newspaper approved the statement of Leader Spahn of the Centrum party that the war must not end without "tangible results," and also the statement of Stresemann, another member of the Reichstag: "We demand and expect a larger Germany." In February, 1916, *Germania,* the Berlin organ of the Catholic party, demanded also a tangible prize of war as one of the conditions of peace.

Countless examples can be given from speeches in the Reichstag and from leaders and newspapers of virtually all parties in Germany, showing this desire for conquest, showing that Germany will not be content to go back to the situation before the war. Even Maximilian Harden, who is respected all over the world because of his fearlessness and reason, has written since the war in favour of a greater Germany, thus:

179

"We wage the war from the rock of conviction that Germany after its deeds has a right to demand broader room on the earth and greater possibilities of action and these things we must attain."

Dr. Spahn, to-day the leader of the Centrum party, answering in December, 1915, Scheidemann, who had argued against annexation, and speaking in the name of 254 members of the Reichstag representing the citizens' parties said:

"We wait in complete union, with calm determination, and let me add, with trust in God, the hour which makes possible peace negotiations, in which forever the military, commercial, financial and political interests of Germany must, in all circumstances and by all means, be protected, including the widening of territories necessary to this end."

Ludendorff is now perhaps the man of most weight and influence, barring no one, in all Germany. When only Chief of Staff of the East Army he wrote: "The Power of Middle Europe will be strengthened, that of the Great Russians pushed back towards the East, from whence it came, at a time not very distant."

These quotations simply show that the great majority of Germans—those outside the social democratic party—of the Germans, indeed, who rule the country, conduct its commerce, and officer its army and navy—all have been infected with a dangerous microbe of Pan-Germanism and of world-conquest.

Every one who professes a knowledge of German life and character, every one who writes of the origin of the war, talks of Treitschke, Nietzsche and Bernhardi.

Nothing made the Germans angrier than to find in foreign newspapers that on this triumvirate was placed the burden of the responsibility for the war. And I agree with the complaining Germans. Bernhardi, who, during the war, was given a command behind the fighting front at Posen, was not considered a skilful general by the military or a great or even popular writer by the people.

How many people in our country or in France or in England are influenced by the lectures or writings of one college professor? And yet, according to many out of Germany, Treitschke, the deaf professor of Heidelberg, is the one man who transmuted the soul of Germany and incited the Empire to a cruel war.

In America you can find any brand of professor, from a professor in a Virginia College who recently boasted that he would not subscribe to American Liberty war bonds, but would send the money to the Socialist, pacifist candidate for Mayor of New York, to the Professor in the University of Chicago who based his claim to fame on the fact that he had never been kissed. What professor of history has had any great political influence beyond his own college?

And it is equally absurd to think of a Prussian Junker, sitting by the fire in the evening, deeply absorbed in the philosophy of Nietzsche. All Germans, as a matter of fact, through pride of conquest in 1864, 1866 and 1870 and great industrial

success, had come to believe themselves to be super-
men delegated by Heaven to win the world.
Treitschke and Nietzsche were simply affected in
their writings by this universal poison of overweening vanity. They but reflected the fashion of the
day in thinking; they did not lead the nation's
thought. Nietzsche himself wrote in one of his letters shortly before his death which occurred in 1900,
"Although I am in my forty-fifth year and have
written fifteen books, I am alone in Germany. There
has not been a single moderately respectful review
of one of my books."

I never found a German of the ruling class who
had read anything written by Treitschke, Nietzsche
or Bernhardi.

Tannenberg had more readers and a greater following, although he, of course, expresses only the
aspirations of the Pan-Germans. But he presents
concrete positions which any one can understand.

For instance, the German merchant looking at
Tannenberg's book and seeing the map of South
America coloured with almost universal German
domination, smiles and approves, for he thinks
German trade will swallow that rich continent and
clever laws and regulations will exclude the imports
of all other nations.

In some aspects Tannenberg foresaw what is
happening to-day when he says, "The Finns have
been waiting a long time to detach themselves from
the Great Russians, their hereditary enemies."

But in the main, in his sketch of the war to which
he looked forward, he failed to predict accurately

the attitude of the world. His predictions represent many of the dead hopes of the Pan-Germans, those Germans who believe it is the right and duty of Germany to conquer all.

Prophesying war between Germany on one side and France and Russia on the other, Tannenberg believed that more confusion and resistance to war than actually occurred would come in Bohemia and Poland following the order for mobilisation in the Slav parts of the Austro-Hungarian Empire. He mistakenly wrote also that Japan would declare war on Russia, a belief shared by the torchlight paraders of Berlin in August, 1914.

Tannenberg thought Italy would declare war on France. He was wrong in his confidence that France was decadent, wrong in believing that England and the United States would only talk but would not fight, yet right in his belief that revolution would break out in Russia. In fact, I think that for years after the Franco-Russian Alliance, Germany was preparing a Russian revolution to break out on whatever day the Russian troops were ordered to their colours. He says that France will be so thoroughly defeated that the "war ought not to leave her more than eyes to cry with."

I am afraid that while many eyes will cry in France, through the breadth of Germany there will be but few homes where eyes will not weep over the casualties of war, for which cruel, crazy dreamers of world empire, like Tannenberg, are largely responsible.

For Tannenberg's dream, the dream of the autocracy and of the Pan-Germanists, is to give to Germany most of South America, a great part of Africa, of Asia, the great islands north of Australia, including those of the Dutch; with Holland and Belgium part of the German Empire as well as the Baltic provinces, and a share of the French colonies to be divided with England.

The share of the United States for standing by and agreeing to the robbery was to be, according to Tannenberg, a protectorate over Mexico and Central America.

Mexicans who were offered Texas and New Mexico by Zimmermann should read this Pan-Germanistic book in which all of Mexico is generously bestowed on us.

And I wish that Tannenberg's book could be read by every public man in South America—that South America in which the Argentine, Chile, Paraguay, Uruguay, the southern parts of Brazil and Bolivia are, according to Tannenberg, to come under the protectorate of Germany. Latin-American publicists should inquire from the inhabitants of Bosnia and Herzegovina how long it is before a "protectorate" is transmuted into a conquered country. Tannenberg does speak for a great party in Germany. The children's school books show German "colonies" in Southern Brazil.

As Sainte Beuve said, there is a fashion in intellect. The German to-day is essentially practical, cold, cynical, and calculating. The poetry and the Christmas trees, the sentiment and sentimentality, remain like the architectural monuments of a vanished race, mere reminders of the kindlier Germany that once was, the Germany of our first impressions, the Gemany that many once loved. But that Germany has long since disappeared, buried beneath the spiked helmets of Prussianism, and another intellect is in vogue.

That older, kindlier Germany was the nation tempered and softened by the suffering of the Napoleonic wars. After the battle of Jena, where Napoleon rubbed the face of Prussia in the mud of defeat, there came on Germany that period of privation which left its impress so deeply on the German as to make thrift his first characteristic. A spirit of lofty, self-sacrificing patriotism imbued the whole people. Young girls cut off their long golden hair to be sold for the Fatherland. Jewels were given by all who possessed them. "Gold gab ich für Eisen" (I gave gold for iron) became a saying based on the readiness with which the rich made sacrifices to the cause of country. And with this patriotism, and with this penury, came into every home a more intimate family life, a greater earnestness, a deeper religious sentiment, a turning towards the idealistic side of life; but all was changed by the successful wars of Prussia that gave Prussia the leadership, the right to rule Germany. Then, with the end of the Franco-Prussian war, came a period of material prosperity, the rush of the population to the cities, and the building of great manufactories, of enormous shipping interests, of powerful banking institutions, of trusts and combinations which marked the Germany of 1914.

The fashion in intellect had changed, and the grasping, successful Prussian of 1914 was far removed from the ruined, chastened Prussian of 1810.

Nations, like individuals, change in character with the stress of life. From 1810, the period of a sorrowing Germany, to 1914 is one hundred and four years. The same number of years subtracted from the year 1796, when our new Republic was firmly established, and when George Washington made his noble farewell address, brings us to 1692, when nineteen persons were legally hanged, charged with witchcraft in Massachusetts, and when in that State Giles Cory perished under the awful torture, judicially applied, known as the "peine forte et dure."

It is quite true that weak voices against annexations have been heard.

Dernburg and Professor Hans Delbrück (the latter not to be confused with the disgraced, pig-slaughtering, ex-Vice-Chancellor), in their petition against the annexation of Belgium, showed a most reasonable spirit, and signing this petition with them were many of the great men and great minds of Germany. But their movement was a failure in Germany itself. Their campaign of reason could make no headway against the "League of Six"— the six great iron and steel companies of the West, who, with their paid lansquenets of the press and hired accelerators of public opinion, clamour for annexation so that they may rivet the chains of their industrial monopoly on the whole continent of Europe.

The Conservatives and Junkers, on the other hand, favour annexations to the East; especially do they eye greedily the Baltic provinces where great estates are in the hands of landowners of German blood. What a reinforcement to the conservative cause would these Junkers of the Baltic be and, in the Conservative view, if there are to be annexations in the West which would increase the number of industrial subjects and, undoubtedly social democrats, there must be a balancing accession of agricultural interest on the Eastern frontier.

The only cloud in the serene blue sky of Junker hopes is the fact that annexations in Poland would add to the number of Roman Catholics and, therefore, to the power of the Centrum or Roman Catholic party. Hence the desire to make of Poland an independent kingdom, but one controlled by the Central Empires.

The Poles are more at ease, having been given more liberty, under Austrian than under Prussian rule, and hence the tendency is to put Poland under Austrian rule. The Prussians do not object to this because it does not matter whether Prussia controls Poland directly or through Prussia's control of Austria, now, alas, only too apparent.

But the principal aim of the nobles and the landed aristocracy of Germany, followed by their host of office-holders and dependents, is to keep the "graft," to hold the offices, civil and military, filled so long by these old Prussian families.

The von Lachnows, to imagine a typical Junker family, hold one thousand acres of land in Bran-

denburg. The head of the house, Baron von Lachnow, was Minister to Sweden. After having held
as a young man a position of Secretary of Legation,
he left the diplomatic service to fight with his old
regiment, the Gleiwitz Hussars, through the
Franco-Prussian War. He then returned to the
diplomatic service in which he finally attained the
rank of Minister to Sweden. He now lives on his
estate of Lachnow, with a pension as ex-minister.
On great occasions he appears at the Royal Palace,
resplendent in uniform, wearing the Orders of the
Red Eagle and Prussian Crown with the Cross of
the Johannis Order. His total income from pensions
and estate is about ten thousand dollars a year.
The oldest son, Baron Karl Friederich, after serving
in his father's regiment, resigned and entered the
diplomatic service and is now second secretary of
the legation in Buenos Aires. He married there the
daughter of a rich cattle owner. The second son,
Baron Johann, is now Police President of the city
of Schelsau, after having been district attorney in
an industrial district where he distinguishes himself by his prosecution of the social democrats. He
married the daughter of the rich manufacturing
proprietor Schulz, who sells, wholesale, little stat-
uettes on the Ritterstrasse in Berlin. Baron August
is in the army, detailed to the General Staff and with
a great future before him. Baron Max is now out
of a job. While on his vacation the colony, in which
he was secretary to the Governor, was captured by
the British, and so at the outbreak of the war he
assumed his old uniform of First Lieutenant in the

VIEWS OF A TYPICAL HOLSTEIN COUNTRY HOME
OWNED BY A JUNKER COUNTRY NOBLEMAN

Gleiwitz Hussars and was given command of the prison camp at Schluttenberg, where he has won distinction for his severity with British prisoners. Baron Ernst is in the navy. This is considered rather a come-down by the family, as the navy, unlike the army, is not aristocratic. He has great hopes of marrying the only daughter of Von Blitz, who owns a splendid estate in Silesia. One of the daughters, Hilda, is married to Count Wenharp, owner of a beautiful estate in Pomerania, and the other to Hochlst, who is judge of the law court in Holstein and who owns the Rittergut (or manor) of Klein Spassberg, near Kiel.

The estate of Lachnow is perfectly flat ground. The road to Brandenburg runs through the estate and village, the houses of which front directly on the road. This road in the village is paved with rough cobblestones. The house of the von Lachnows almost touches the road, from which it is separated by an old stone wall. One side is on a square, cobblestoned courtyard, formed by the great barns, stables and sheds which surround the other three sides of the square. The house and all the barns are built of rough stone. The house is built on the plan of a piece of Castile soap, walls and roof and nothing more. Inside there are a dining-room, two parlours and an office-den for the master, upstairs bedrooms, opening on a long hall; no bathrooms, no conveniences, even the water is brought in by the maids from the well in the centre of the court. The furniture is old and plain. The family does not keep an automobile, but two horses draw a dog cart to the station and take the family on visits to the neighbouring aristocracy. The driver is the sexton of the village church on these occasions. On the two sides of the house away from the main road and the square of barns there is a park of about ten acres. Here are a few evergreens and gravel paths and a pond where some enormous carp excite the wonder of the village children.

Baroness Lachnow is renowned for her devotion to the four K's. No one has a better stock of household linen, all made by her, her daughters and her maids, in the whole Mark. She superintends every household detail and holds the keys to closets and wine cellar.

Of course, the family does not associate with the schoolmaster and the Lutheran minister of the village, but they speak very kindly to them and the Baron once interested himself in obtaining a long service decoration for the schoolmaster.

The von Lachnows live on their estate the year round, except for two weeks in February when they go to Berlin to a cheap hotel and attend one of the court balls. The Baroness never spends more than three hundred and fifty dollars a year on her clothes, although when in Sweden, as a Minister's wife she spent more. The Baron and Baroness sometimes condescend to dine with the father-in-law of their son, a manufactory proprietor, at his handsome apartment on the Kurfuerstendamm in Berlin, but Schultz, in spite of his four million marks and growing business, is made to feel the wide gulf that separates him from the nobility.

Baron Lachnow farms his own estate. His farm superintendent is von Treslow, once an officer in the Gleiwitz Hussars, who was compelled to resign because of a crippled arm, badly broken in a steeplechase. This taciturn, soured individual, on the outbreak of war, was given a place as commander of a village way station near the West Front, where his cruelties to the French inhabitants will long be remembered.

Food is very simple. The family drink beer except on great occasions, but the Baron drinks Moselle at the midday meal and a red wine in the evening. The recreation is shooting and visits to the neighbours.

Such a visit is a great event, arranged by letter beforehand. The von Lachnows drive to visit the von Seltows eighteen miles away. They arrive in time for lunch, when much wine is drunk. After this the women gossip over their fancy work and the men visit the stable, discuss crop prices and inspect the host's collection of horse flesh. The family photographs are inspected and Count Reventlow's latest article abusing the Americans is discussed and the belief suggested that a democratic people without King or Kaiser or nobility cannot be organised for war. The Social Democrats are condemned and the story gleefully told of how the son of von Seltow cut down a Social Democrat who was slow in getting out of his way.

I can understand the feelings of the von Lachnows, the imaginary, typical Prussian family of

the ruling class which I have pictured for you. If
Germany should be democratised, what place would
be left for them? The offices of the government
thrown open to all classes in fair elections, places in
the army and navy and diplomacy open to competition in great academies like West Point and Annapolis. Deprived of the aroma of power given
now by diplomatic or military place and noble birth
in the caste system, the sons and daughters could
no longer make rich marriages with the sons and
daughters of the rich business men and manufacturers. No more would the civil offices of Prussia
be open only to appointments among the noble or
Junker class.

I do not blame the von Lachnows because they
fight tooth and nail for the retention of their old
privileges—because they endeavour to hold the
common people in a serfdom almost as complete as
that of the Dark Ages. The dawn of constitutional government will be their twilight, the twilight of the Gods of militarism, of privilege, and
of caste. Prussian autocracy made the war in a
last desperate endeavour to bribe the people into
continued submission.

The only excuse for the existence of the Prussian ruling class to-day, as much out of place as
chain armour or robber barons, is its supposed hon-
esty and efficiency; but no class which has brought
this war on the German people can be described as
competent; no sane governing class would have
plunged into disastrous war a country that by
peaceful penetration, by thrift and manufacture,

192

and financial and commercial ability was in process of acquiring much of the wealth of the world.

The *first* aim of German autocracy is to keep its own political position at home.

Second—To obtain as much of the territory of other nations, as great an influence in unconquered lands, as possible.

Third—To make peace now, but only if that peace is a German peace, a peace which can be called and advertised and proclaimed as a German victory.

More particularly, Germany now looks to the East. In the so-called Baltic provinces of Russia the lands to a great extent are owned by Russian subjects of German blood. The peasants are poor, servile, without education or property, an ideal field for the advance of autocracy. It is hoped to either annex these provinces boldly or to establish protectorates, which, sooner or later, at an opportune moment, will fall into German hands—just as Austria gained the consent of Europe to a protectorate over Bosnia and Herzegovina and then suddenly added them to the domains of the Hapsburgs.

The German propagandists have long been working on the people of that part of Russia known as the Ukraine. If the Ukraine can be made a separate protectorate or a semi-independent state, some day it will be easily absorbed. The autocracy has the same hope about Lithuania, at one time semi-independent. There, too, the propagandists have worked on Lithuania—all these provinces, of course, differing slightly from the races surrounding and all with a semi-independent history, as, for instance, Courland.

But all these races should think twice before they accept a momentary independence, if that autonomy is to lead them under the Prussian yoke. Whether that yoke is easy to bear or not is best answered by the Danes, Alsatians, Poles and Lorrainers who have been forcibly incorporated in the Kingdom of Prussia.

But greatest prize of all is the commercial control of Russia which the autocracy hopes to win for its merchant class. Time and again I was told in Germany that a separate peace with Russia was near and that the exploitation of Russia by the enterprising German merchants, in a short time, would repay Germany for all the losses of the war.

Would it not seem extraordinary if the language of business and commerce of the United States were French? But to-day in Russia and for years back the language of commercial business intercourse has been German. A great beginning, a great foundation it is for the eventual control, not only of the business, but the political structure of Russia. If the Germans at war with Russia have been able to split, revolutionise and divide it and put their representatives in control, what will they not be able to accomplish when peace shall bring them full liberty to circulate freely in that rich but ignorant country.

In the end, all classes in Russia will demand a strong government, and if no military dictator, no Russian Napoleon has taken in his hands the reins of government, then the German Kaiser will stand by ready to whisper to the torn people of Russia, as Napoleon III did to the French, "My Empire is Peace!"

But even if Germany evacuates France and restores the complete independence of Belgium, even if no territories are gained to the East, or protectorates or independent states carved from the body of Russia to be a later prey of Germany, Germany will have won—if from Bremen to Bagdad German influence or actual German rule is predominant in Middle Europe, the Great Central State, where the cotton of Mesopotamia, and the coal and iron of Westphalia, the copper of Servia, the oil and grain of Roumania all will contribute to the manufacturer of Germany, who, in turn, will sell his goods in that vast territory. And best of all in autocratic view, the man power of the Central Empires will be so increased that at a propitious moment, in a characteristic sudden assault, the armies of the Central Empires will invade and conquer Palestine, Egypt and India, and take what they will in Africa and Asia, while British, Japanese, and American and French navies impotently rage in useless control of the high seas.

CHAPTER XV

FEW people in America perhaps realise how completely Austria-Hungary is under the domination of Germany and Kaiserism. There are those who think that the hand of the Vienna Government was forced by Berlin when the ultimatum to Serbia was answered so reasonably by the little country to the south, but there can be no doubt that Austria has been ever since under the yoke of the German General Staff.

And because the first break, the first glimpse of reasonable peace will in turn be forced on Germany by sorely tried Austria-Hungary, bent by war and bowed by debt, it is well to study a little the races and assess the influences of that unfortunate land.

My wife's sister married a Hungarian Count, a member of the Hungarian House of Lords, and I have met many of the political leaders and magnates of that country on my trips there.

The Germans of Austria are handsomer, more attractive but far less efficient than their bloody brethren from the cold, wind-swept plains of Prussia. They have acquired a slight touch of the Oriental and something of the mañana (to-morrow) of the Spaniards, a heritage, perhaps, of the days when Spain and Austria were so closely connected by Hapsburg rule.

In the presence of an Austrian one feels his charm instead of the aggressive personality which is Prussian. Undoubtedly the Prussians counted on the good nature of the southern Germans, Hungarians, Poles and Slavs in their insidious campaign to make these peoples, practically, if not in name, subject and tributary to Prussian rule. The Prussian propagandist has brought them face to face with a new Kaiserism.

Shortly after the war a great number of Austrian professors of German blood issued a manifesto demanding closer union with Germany—a prelude to the plots being hatched in Berlin against Hapsburg rule.

The Court of Austria is quite different from that of Berlin; no modern ideas during the reign of Francis Joseph disturbed his medieval outlook.

The beautiful Empress of Austria, who was assassinated by an anarchist in Switzerland, was probably insane. At any rate, for many years she lived apart from the Emperor, devoted to hunting and horses, going often as far as Ireland for her favourite sport and seldom appearing in Vienna. Francis Joseph, however, was consoled by an ex-actress, Frau Kathie Schratt, whom he visited daily and who occupied a position in Vienna almost as powerful as that of the mistresses of Louis XIV. Even in this very war when Frau Schratt established a hospital, she was photographed in the centre of a group of women all occupied at this hospital and all holding the highest rank at the Austrian Court. The instant the old Emperor died, however, her power, influence and prestige disappeared and I imagine that her titled and high born helpers were not long in deserting the hospital wards over which she had presided.

That extraordinary Empire known as the Austrian Hungarian Dual Monarchy is less an Empire or a Kingdom or a State than the personal property of the Hapsburgs, whose hereditary talent for the acquisition of land is recorded on the map of Europe to-day.

For centuries this royal family by treaty, by intrigue, by war, purchase and marriage has been adding to its dominions, bringing under its personal rule races who do not understand each other's language and who differ widely in customs, intellectual attainments and religion.

The last acquisition of territory by the house of Hapsburg was in the year 1908, when the Austro-Hungarian Foreign Office boldly declared that Bosnia and Herzegovina, placed under the protectorate of Austria-Hungary by the Treaty of Berlin in 1878, had been annexed to the Empire. The German Kaiser, standing by like a watching accomplice while the burglary was in progress, threatened a general European war if any nations protested.

At a time when Prussia was a struggling state, Austria was the dominant power in Central Europe, but the one battle of Sadowa in 1866 settled for

ever the question of supremacy and the German
States like Bavaria, Saxony, Würtemburg, etc.,
which stood with Austria in that war, after receiving a sound beating, ranged themselves on the
side of the victor and, in 1870, joined in acclaiming
the King of Prussia as the First German Emperor.

That event settled the question of leadership in
Central Europe and the dream of the Emperor
Frederick who died about the time of the discovery
of America. It was he who wrote the famous ana-
gram on the vowels A, E, I, O. U.

ustria st	mperare rbi		niverso
A	E	I	O	U
lles	rdreich st	esterreich	nterthan

"It is the fate of Austria to rule the world."

In upper and lower Austria, so-called, there are
about twelve million German Austrians. This territory is comparatively small and in it lies the city
of Vienna. To the north and northeast lie Bohemia
and Moravia, the country of the Tchechs or Szechs
of Slavic blood. These people together number
about six million. Prague is the capital of Bohemia, while in Moravia there is no great city. For
centuries these peoples have been oppressed by the
Austrians and in the Hussite rebellion the lands of
Bohemia and Moravia were parcelled out to the
Austrian nobles as well as to the warlike adventurers who had joined the Austrian armies.

With extraordinary obstinacy and patriotism
these peoples cling to their old language and cus-

toms. They have suffered much during this war and many tales are told of the shooting of all of the officers of Tchech regiments and the execution of every tenth man among the privates.

It is a bit of poetic justice that the town of Bethlehem in Pennsylvania, where my friend Schwab is making so much war material to be used against the Central Powers, was founded by fugitives, who, rebelling against oppression, left Moravia in search of liberty.

North of the Carpathians lies Galicia, a Polish country, with Lemberg and Krakow as its capitals, and in the eastern part the Ruthenians, a race identical with the Russians. These Ruthenians number upwards of four million.

It is a peculiar fact that in the curious Dual Monarchy each race oppresses some other. The Ruthenians complain that they are oppressed by the Poles. The kingdom of Hungary lies to the east of Austria containing in its twenty million inhabitants about ten million Magyars, who are the dominant race and who in turn rule over a population of one and one-half million Ruthenians, two and one-half million Slovacks or Tchecks, three million Roumanians in the southeastern portion and about three million of the race now known as Jugo-Slavs. Of these Jugo-Slavs about two million are in that part of the Dual Monarchy under Austrian rule. These are the principal divisions of peoples. A Slavish race differing somewhat from the others is in the mountains to the east of Hungary where much fighting has taken place in the last war known as Boukovina. In the south-eastern part of Hungary there is a German speaking country, known as Siebenburgen, where live the descendants of a German colony planted about two centuries ago.

In Styria, in the mountainous districts of Austria to the west of Hungary, lives a race differing again from all the others, a mountain race supposed to be eaters of arsenic, a drug which they believe gives them a good complexion and stamina for mountain climbing. It is said that the bodies of these arsenic eaters remain undecomposed for a long time. And from this part of the world comes the curious superstition of the existence of human vampires.

Slovenes, and Jews, Carinthians and inhabitants of Carniola, Serbs living like Moslems in Bosnia and Herzegovina and Italians in Trieste and the Trient—all make up the strange Austro-Hungarian monarchy.

The union between Austria and Hungary is a personal union. The Emperor of Austria is King of Hungary. Only in four particulars are the Empire and the Kingdom united, namely, a joint administration of the army and navy, of diplomatic affairs and of such finances as are connected with joint expenditures for these purposes.

In 1848 Hungary sought to break away from Austria. Kossuth heroically led the Hungarians against their Austrian masters, only to be beaten in the end because of the advent of the Russians, because one autocrat came to the aid of another.

Since then, by superior political talents and taste for intrigue, the Magyars have not only held the Slovaks, Roumanians, etc., of their own country in political subjection, but have held much of the power in the Dual Monarchy. Their danger lies, however, in the predominance of German influence; and some day the gay, easy-going, pleasant Hungarians may awake to find the Prussian Eitel Fritz seated on their throne and to learn what Prussian efficiency means when applied to those whom Germans consider an inferior people.

The twelve million Austrian Germans differ much in character from the Prussians. They are far more polite, far more agreeable, far more fond of amusement of all kinds. Indeed it is because of their pleasant personal characteristics that so many other nations have been content to remain under their rule. In no city of the world is the mass of the population as fond of pleasure as in Vienna. The best light operas come from that city. Vienna is the original home of the waltz. The "Blue Danube" was composed on the shores of the river which flows through the Austrian capital.

The dominant religion of the German Empire is Protestant, but in the Dual Monarchy it is Roman Catholic among the ruling Germans in Austria and Magyars in Hungary.

In Austria and in Hungary most of the land is held in great estates. The peasants, as in Germany, sometimes own a few strips of land near their miserable villages. Possession of land is necessary to the standing of any noble. In Hungary, for example, no noble sits in the house of Magnates or House of Lords unless he is the owner of a certain amount of land.

Once across the Hungarian border, one sees the people taking a certain delight in refusing to understand German. The names of the railway stations are in Hungarian, and the uniforms of station officials, conductors, etc., differ from those in Austria. Every effort is made by the population to emphasise the fact that Hungary is an independent kingdom, joined to Austria by personal rule alone.

There is no melting pot in this part of the world. In the Lower House of the Hungarian parliament sit forty-three Croatian delegates, Croatia being that part of southwestern Hungary near the Adriatic where the inhabitants are of Slav blood. By the Hungarian constitution those delegates have the right to speak in the Hungarian parliament in their own language and so from time to time a Croatian delegate arises in his place and delivers an ambitious harangue in Croatian, understood by no one except his fellow delegates who already know what he intends to talk about. This is only one example of how these peoples cling tenaciously to their language and national rights.

It is possible to find in Hungary an Hungarian village, a German village, a Slav village and a Roumanian village, all within a short distance of each other. Men from each of these villages after one month in the United States throw aside their national costume and buy their clothes in the same Bowery shop, eat the same food and send their children to the same public school not only without protest, but with eagerness, whereas, in Hungary, not one of the inhabitants of these different villages would think of abandoning his national traits to learn the language of his German neighbours.

Because commands are given in German in the armies of the Dual Monarchy all the male population, at least during the term of their military service, have been compelled to learn some German. But this they forget as soon as possible when they return from their period of military service.

Many members of these races go to America and after working there a short time amass enough money to return to Austria-Hungary and purchase a small piece of land,—the ambition of every one born of the soil.

One of the sons of Prince Lichtenstein told me that a friend who was running for the Hungarian Lower House in a district of Hungary largely inhabited by Slavs, spoke in Hungarian and, finding that his audience did not understand him, tried German. Finally, when matters had come to a standstill, some one in the back of the room called out to him, asking if he spoke English. The candidate answered that he did. Whereupon the crowd told him to speak English which nearly all understood, and so the Hungarian, a candidate for parliament in Hungary, was forced, in order to be understood, to address his Hungarian electors in the language which they had learned in America.

Franz Ferdinand, whose murder at Sarajevo was used by the Central Powers as a pretext for a war determined on long before that time, was the heir to the throne of the late Francis Joseph. He was a romantic character. He visited frequently at the house of Archduchess Isabella, where Countess Chotek, of a Bohemian noble family, was a lady in waiting. Franz Ferdinand fell violently in love with the fair Bohemian, and in his desire to marry, enlisted the aid of Koloman Szell, Premier of Hungary. Szell told friends how Franz Ferdinand loved mystery and how, when he wanted to talk to him about marriage plans, instead of meeting somewhere openly in Vienna, would arrange that Szell's train should stop in the open fields. Szell, on alighting and following directions, would find Franz Ferdinand hiding behind a designated haystack.

In a country where one royal family not only rules but owns the land, this attempt of Archduke Franz Ferdinand, then heir to the throne, and mad with love, to marry Countess Sophie Chotek, lady in waiting to Archduchess Isabella, caused a palace revolution. By the aid of Szell he at last succeeded in carrying out the marriage. But this was only after he and his wife had been required to submit to the most humiliating conditions and subscribe to a marriage contract or promise which was not only enacted thereafter as a statute in Hungary, but was formally put on record by the Austrian parliament.

In this declaration, Franz Ferdinand declared it to be "his firm and resolute resolve to marry Countess Sophie Chotek, that he had sought, in accordance with the laws of the house, to obtain consent of the Imperial and Royal Apostolic Majesty, the Emperor and King, Francis Joseph I, gloriously reigning, that the most serene, supreme head of the Arch house had deigned graciously to grant this permission and that Franz Ferdinand, however (describing himself as 'We'), recognise the house laws and declare them binding on Us particularly with regard to this marriage declaration, that our Marriage with Countess Chotek is not a marriage of equal birth, but a morganatic one and is to be considered as such for all time, and that in consequence neither our wife nor our issue or descendants is entitled to possess or claim those rights, titles, armorial bearings and privileges that belong to wives of equal birth and to children of archdukes or marriages of equal birth." Franz Ferdinand, further, recognised that his children from this marriage would have no right to succeed to the throne in the kingdoms and lands of Austria nor, consequently, to the lands of the Hungarian Crown and that they were excluded from the order of succession.

He further agreed and promised not only for himself but for his wife and children, that none of them would ever attempt to revoke this declaration.

The old Emperor gave the wife of Franz Ferdinand the title of Princess Hohenberg and later raised her to the rank of duchess which, in the Central Empires, is a higher rank than that of princess. She was also created a Serene Highness after the birth of her third child, Prince Ernest, in 1904. The first child, Princess Sophie, was born in 1901, and the second, Prince Maximilian Charles, in 1902.

In spite of the rank thus granted to her, the Duchess of Hohenberg was frequently slighted by Archdukes and Archduchesses of the House of Hapsburg, and when the present Emperor, the Archduke Charles Francis Joseph, married Princess Zita of Bourbon-Parma, in 1911, and this marriage was followed by the birth of a son, on November 20, 1912, it was plain to Franz Ferdinand and his wife that the hostility of the old Emperor and the other members of the House of Hapsburg, aided by events, had succeeded in definitely excluding his children by Countess Sophie from the throne.

These slights to his wife, so marked as to cause the publication of articles inspired by himself in a newspaper devoted to his interests, and the birth of the heir to Carl, must have had a profound influence on melancholy Franz Ferdinand.

In all Europe there was one monarch clever enough to take advantage of the situation, to win Franz Ferdinand to him by the honours he paid to the Duchess of Hohenberg,—the German Emperor. Kaiser Wilhelm invited the pair to Potsdam and there both were made to feel that in one court, at least, the honours due to a wife of equal birth were paid to the ex-Countess Sophie. This Potsdam visit was in 1909, and I believe that, thereafter, the German Emperor and Franz Ferdinand met on other occasions.

In the chapter on Emperor Wilhelm, I have stated the belief prevalent, even in Germany, that he intended as his first step towards his openly expressed ambition for world dominion, to make himself, on the death of Francis Joseph, Emperor of a Great Continental Empire in which the German Princes, his sons, should occupy the thrones of Hungary and Bohemia, the heir of the House of Austria to rule as king or grand duke of Austria with possibly another German ruled kingdom touching the sea on the south.

There are some who believe that when the Kaiser, accompanied by von Tirpitz, visited Franz Ferdinand at Konopisht in June, 1914, before the Kiel week, that a great conspiracy was entered into, in which it was arranged that a great Central Empire should be created with one of the sons of the Duchess of Hohenberg on the throne of Bohemia and the other provided for by some newly carved out kingdom made from Bosnia, or a portion of Serbia. And it may have been part of this plot that Eitel Fritz and other sons of the Kaiser should be provided with thrones derived from Balkan territory.

It will be remembered that as Franz Ferdinand and his wife fell under the assassin's bullet at Sarajevo he called out: "Sophie, live for our children!" His devotion to his wife and to their children was extraordinary. He was continually sparing from his income so that on his death his sons would have a large sum of money, saved from the income of estates which they could not inherit.

It is hard to believe that such a crime against the House of Hapsburg and against his own country was contemplated from the inside of royalty. But one event seems a confirmation of this theory. The dead Franz Ferdinand and his wife were buried with such lack of honour, almost with such contempt, as to lead to the belief that the head of the House of Hapsburg, Emperor Francis Joseph himself, without whose directions the Chamberlain, Count Montenuovo, would not have dared to act, discovered his heir in some act against the laws or fortunes of the Imperial House.

For the funeral arrangements were such, that the Austrian and Hungarian aristocracy were moved to protest and as a result a belated order was issued directing that the troops of the Vienna Garrison should take part in the funeral ceremonies. About one hundred and fifty members of the leading families of Hungary and Austria, without invitation, entered the funeral procession and followed the bodies to the railway station. The *London Times* correspondent called attention to this in cables to his newspaper at the time.

Personally, I do not incline to this view, but I do believe that at Konopisht the war of 1914 was finally agreed on. Too many bits of evidence point to this and from something said to me at Kiel by a very high personage, before the assassinations at Sarajevo, I would have guessed that war was coming, had it not been impossible for me to believe that the world was to be plunged into war simply because the German people were restless under the rule of the autocracy.

When the murders occurred at Sarajevo, all plans

had been laid for war and the death of Franz Ferdinand and the Duchess of Hohenberg merely gave another excuse to begin hostilities, after Austria, in the Council of Potsdam, had ratified all the arrangements made by the Emperor Wilhelm and Franz Ferdinand for the European war. Undoubtedly the German Emperor used his influence with Franz Ferdinand and his wife in order to secure the former's aid in dragging Austria into the war, —a war begun to win the dominion of the world.

How many in America have heard the name of Sophie Chotek? Yet the ambitions of this woman have done much to send to war the splendid youths who from all the ends of the earth gather in France to fight the fight of freedom.

The clever German Emperor, playing upon her ambitions, induced the gloomy, hated Franz Ferdinand to consent to the world war, and matters had gone so far that even the death of the Archduke Franz Ferdinand could not change the situation nor turn the war party of Hungary and Austria from their programme of blood. Eighty-four years of age, the old Francis Joseph could only offer a weak defence to the martial insistence of Tisza, Premier of Hungary, and his able understrapper, Forgotsch, who represented him in the Foreign Office at Vienna and who undoubtedly is the man who drafted the forty-eight hour ultimatum to Servia.

Berliners say that although the German Emperor gave the Duchess of Hohenberg all the honours due to the wife of an Austrian Archduke, heir to

MAIN STAIRWAY IN THE AMERICAN EMBASSY, BERLIN

the throne of the Austrian Empire, he was careful not to bring her claims in direct conflict with any Prussian female Royalty and that on the first visit of Franz Ferdinand and his wife to Potsdam, when the doors of the banquet room were thrown open, it was seen that the Kaiser had skilfully placed all the guests at small tables, sitting at one with the Empress and his two guests. In this way he prevented a conflict of precedence and a possible scene with some Prussian royal princess.

After one of these Potsdam visits, the Austrian government appropriated three hundred millions for new Skoda cannon and a great and unexpected increase of the navy was voted. In Austria itself it was seen that the German influence was dragging Austria-Hungary nearer and nearer to war.

Ferdinand disliked the Hungarians and in turn was hated by them. If he had attained the throne of the Empire, as his children could not inherit, he would have endeavoured first to remove that obstacle, but if he had not succeeded he intended, as I have said, either to restore the kingdom of Bohemia and place his son, child of a Bohemian mother, on the newly created throne, or create, possibly from conquered lands, another kingdom over which his heir could reign.

The Magyars, the real Hungarian ruling race, are most skilful politicians. Their elections often are corrupt and all the tricks of the politician are in use in Hungary.

In many families political talent seems hereditary. Tisza, the Premier of Hungary for the period for some time before the war, was the son of Tisza, who was Premier of Hungary about the year 1875. Kossuth, son of the great Kossuth, has been active in politics. The father of Count Julius Andrassy was Premier about 1866 and favoured Germany, a policy which has been inherited by his son. One of the sons-in-law of Count Andrassy's wife, Marquis Pallavicini, came to America to act as best man when my wife's sister married Count Sigray.

Andrassy came to Berlin during the war where I had several long talks with him. The one desire of Hungarians and Austrians alike is for peace, but surrounded by the armies of their German masters, they have lost their independence of action, a bitter blow to the Magyars, who are not fond of the Germans.

Count Stephen Tisza is an obstinate and able man, so many sided that it is related of him that he fought a duel, rode a steeplechase and made a great speech in Parliament, all in one day.

Duelling is still a custom in Hungary, Austria and Germany. Once when I was in Hungary I took supper with a Count who had been second in a duel that day. One young Magnate was at a restaurant with an actress who wore a wide brimmed hat. Another young Magnate of his acquaintance looked under the hat brim to see who the girl was. Result: a duel with sabres in a riding school. On this occasion, as the insult was not deadly, the use of sharp points was forbidden. The duel was stopped after one young Magnate received a cut on the forehead.

Stephen Tisza, on first taking office, was permitted by the old Emperor to obtain some apparent concessions for Hungary in order to make his premiership popular. It was arranged that Hungarian flags should be carried by Hungarian regiments, and that the officers of those regiments all should be Hungarians, but German was to be used as the military language and language of command even in the Hungarian regiments.

As soon as Tisza became premier for the first time, Count Apponyi left the Liberal party and lately Count Julius Andrassy and his wife's sons-in-law, Count Karoli and Marquis Pallavicini, have been in violent opposition to Tisza, Pallavicini even fighting a duel with the Prime Minister.

In a country where the majority of the inhabitants are Roman Catholics it is rather strange that Tisza and his father, both strong Protestants, should have attained the Premiership. The father of Count Stephen Tisza was even more obstinate than his son and greatly oppressed the Slovaks and Roumanians within the borders of Hungary.

A great responsibility lies at the door of Stephen Tisza. He allowed the Germans to use him in bringing on the world war. Doubtless he believed that Russia and the Powers would not move, that Austria-Hungary could seize or invade Serbia, while Germany terrorised the world as in 1908 when Bosnia and Herzegovina were added to the Imperial dominions. But his failure to read the intentions of Russia and the other Powers is no excuse for the calamity he brought on Hungary and the world, no excuse for the fact that his country is now overwhelmed by Kaiserism, its armies surrounded by the armies of Germany and its very independence threatened by the subtle influence and intrigues of the master intriguer of the world,—the German Kaiser.

The franchise in Austria and in Hungary is like that given grudgingly to the Prussian, a mere ghost of suffrage. Autocracy rules. In Hungary, particularly the Magyars, seeking to keep the political power in their hands, oppose a broadening of the franchise. Tisza has always been against any letting down of the bars, but when the young and brilliant Count Esterhazy was made Premier, many looked for a change—a change which has, however, not yet come.

The new Emperor Carl at first seemed to exhibit Liberal tendencies, but only for a moment.

The events in Russia will have a grave effect in Austria-Hungary. More than a million Russians are prisoners in the Dual Monarchy, nearly a million of whose subjects are in Russia—and of these at least fifty thousand Czechs are fighting the Austrians and Germans in the ranks of the Roumanian army. Many more will refuse to leave Russia, but the coming back of one-half, after having witnessed the winning of liberty by the Russians, will influence their countrymen in no small degree. Just as the French soldiers under Lafayette and Rochambeau, after helping us gain our independence, returned from the free fields of America to a France where the burdens of the plain people were almost unendurable and brought on the great French Revolution, the soldiers and prisoners who return to Prussia and to Austria-Hungary from the strange scenes of the Russian Revolution may, perhaps, leaven the inert slave masses of the Central Empires with a spirit of revolt for liberty.

We should institute a great propaganda from the Italian front. For instance, I have been told by a man who has been on that front, a man who should know, that if a few American troops were sent there and signs erected stating "Come over and surrender to the Americans, you will be taken to America well fed and paid a dollar per day when you volunteer to work," there would be a great rush of Austro-Hungarian troops eager to be taken prisoner.

The losses of Austria and Hungary have been enormous—men up to fifty-five have been drafted for the army, and the troops have often suffered defeat and the horrors of retreat at the hands of Russians, Serbians, and Italians.

And all the time the iron hand of the German Kaiser grasps more and more of the power. Cheerless prospect it is for the once gay Hungarians, the once happy Austrians, if to financial ruin and the killing of the flower of their youth is to be added the iron horror of Prussian domination.

Our citizens of Austrian and especially of Hungarian descent have been loyal to their new flag. And our great President with enlightened wisdom has eased the enemy alien regulations so as to favour those born in the Dual Monarchy. America will never forget the loyalty, ungrudgingly given by those of her people born under the double eagle of the Hapsburgs.

In my many visits to Hungary I grew to like and admire the Hungarians. Natural in manners, hospitable, polite, there is something in them that wins Americans. How different the open hospitality and friendliness in Budapest from the stern, cold formality of the Prussian capital!

And with all friends of Hungary I hope that that country will soon throw off the trance of Prussianism, which has led the Dual Monarchy into a Dance of Death.

CHAPTER XVI

JUST as I had the opportunity to study conditions in Austria, so also I came in contact with the politics and diplomacy of the nations contiguous to Germany on the north.

My grandfather, Benjamin F. Angel, was American Minister to Sweden and Norway and on leaving received from the King the Order of St. Olaf. I have always taken a deep interest in Scandinavian affairs and it behooves the American people to regard closely what is happening nowadays in Norway, Sweden and Denmark.

The outbreak of the European War in 1914 served to bring the three northern nations close together. Their Kings met in conference and a peace monument was erected on the boundary of Norway and Sweden as if to proclaim to the world that in spite of their recent separation, Norway and Sweden were sister countries.

The people of these three countries are of the same blood and their languages are somewhat similar. Norwegian and Danish written are practically the same. But there is quite a difference in pronunciation. Swedish is more like German and the pronunciation is not as difficult to learn as that

217

of Norwegian and Danish. In Norway, there are older dialects, differing from Danish, and there has lately been a great movement in favour of a more national language. Many Norwegians regard the official Danish-Norwegian as a reminder of old subjection to Denmark and not at all fitted for the new independent Norwegian kingdom. The new national language is called "Landsmaal."

Sweden and Norway were both under one king from 1814 to 1905. In that year after a peaceful secession, Prince Charles of Denmark, the son of the King of Denmark, was made the King of Norway, with the title of Haakon VII. Although both have kings, Denmark and Norway may be termed democratic countries.

Copenhagen is lively since the war. The population of Denmark is only 2,500,000 and the whole country is only 14,829 square miles, which means an area about the size of Maryland. The country was once larger but in 1864 Prussia went to war with Denmark and, finally, after the war with Austria in 1866, added to the Crown of Prussia the two Danish duchies of Schleswig and Holstein. As the city and port of Kiel were included in this territory annexed, it is easy to see why the Germans engaged in this enterprise against Denmark.

Denmark possesses the Faro Islands which lie far to north of Scotland, the great island of Iceland and Greenland, relics of the times when the Viking ships brought such terror to the other countries of Europe, that the Litany used to read: "From plague, pestilence and famine, from battle and murder, from sudden death and from the fury of the Northmen, good Lord deliver us."

In Christiania we saw on our trip out two graceful Viking ships dug out of the clay shores oi the coast in a state of fair preservation—one of them a Princess's ship on which it was easy to imagine some blonde princess of the North, her long braids of golden hair flying in the wind, urging on her Scandinavian oarsmen.

The Danes are a sturdy race, the women more independent than those of other countries. On the *Frederick VIII,* when we sailed from Denmark, September 28, 1916, for the United States, were two handsome girls, nineteen and twenty-one years of age, the daughters of the proprietor of the largest department store in Copenhagen. They were going to America to find employment in department stores in the different cities of the country, travelling entirely alone, and expected to return to Denmark after a year's experience in America with many new ideas of management and advertising for their father in Copenhagen. These girls were wonderfully educated, speaking in addition to Danish, French, German and English with hardly a trace of accent. They lived a short distance out of Copenhagen and told me that every morning of the year they jumped into the sea at six-thirty in the morning, something that I should not care to do even in August in that cold northern land.

Danish farmers learned early that in order to be prosperous they must practise intensive farming. I believe that Denmark, which even before the war

enjoyed a high degree of prosperity, is the only
country in the world where there are pig sties steam-
heated and electric lighted while the farmer himself does not have these luxuries.

Our farmers have much to learn from the farmers of Denmark both in agricultural methods and
in co-operation for the marketing of products. The
reclamation of the Danish moors in Jutland has
made surprising progress: it is in Jutland that a
park has been preserved in its primeval state—
the Danish-American Park, bought with money
subscribed by Danish emigrants to America who
prospered in their adopted land.

Ever since the conquest of Denmark by Germany, there has been a deep hatred of all things
German in Denmark on account of the treatment of
those Danes, numbering between one hundred and
two hundred thousand, who were living in Schleswig and Holstein and were unfortunate enough to
be turned over as property to the King of Prussia.

I found the Danes agreeable people. Of the
same race as the Germans, living like them in the
dark North, this difference in behaviour is perhaps
accounted for by the fact that the Danes are free,
while the Germans are oppressed by the weight of
an ever present autocracy.

While the Danish people hate the Germans, officially Denmark is careful to conceal this hate
and even, apparently, to lean towards the German
side, through fear of the German troops, which
could easily overrun Denmark in thirty hours.

Denmark, during the war, received oil cake from

220

America, which was fed to cattle later sold to Germany. A great tonnage of fish has also been sent from Denmark to Germany while salt and potash have been imported. There is no question but that supplies of all kinds and in great quantities have found their way across the Danish border.

And the Danes have prospered enormously since the war. Many people have become millionaires through the sale of food and other supplies to the Germans. A great deal of this food supply was sent in the form of canned meat, popularly known as goulash, and so to-day whenever an automobile passes on a Danish road, the small boys call out "goulash Baron," in the belief that the occupant is a new-made millionaire, enriched by trade with Germany.

It is hard for us to realise how far north the Scandinavian countries lie. Christiania, the capital of Norway and in its southern part, is in the same latitude as the south point of Greenland; and is it not difficult to imagine a modern city situated in Greenland?

In Christiania it is not fairly daylight in December until ten in the morning and dark early in the afternoon. The ample water power of Norway and Sweden furnishes electric light, a godsend in the short dreary winter days.

Norway, in many respects, is one of the most advanced countries in the world. Having been ruled by Denmark for four hundred years, it was united to Sweden by the Treaty of Kiel, in 1814, with the approval of all the Powers, but against the inclinations of the Norwegians, who knew that they were given to Sweden to compensate that country for the loss of Finland, annexed to Russia.

The ambitious Bernadotte arranged to govern Norway as king of that country, which was theoretically to retain its independence and be united to Sweden only through the personal rule of the one monarch.

At this time, the Norwegian Constitution provided that no more personal privileges should be granted and since then the progress of Norway towards a real democracy has been rapid. It was the conflict over the right demanded by the Norwegians to establish a separate consular service that led to the dissolution of the union between Norway and Sweden in 1905, Norway voting for separation 368,211 to 184.

There are now no nobles in Norway. Shortly after the union it was decided that those who had titles of nobility could hold them for life, but that their descendants could not inherit.

Legislation for the protection of child workers, women, for insurance, etc., is of an advanced character. For instance, no child under fourteen is permitted to work and no woman for six weeks after her confinement—women receiving full sick benefit pay during this period. Many of the railways are state owned.

Norway is a land of little farms, the shipping and fishing industries occupy many men, but with the exception of the water power driven nitrate plants, on the coast, and the wood-pulp factories, there is little manufacturing.

The mass of the people are with the Allies. Last winter, when it was proposed that a German concert troupe should play and sing in Christiania, the people threatened to burn the theatre if the performance was permitted.

But, as in Sweden, the German propagandists are at work in Norway. Here again, unless we present our case, the people may be turned from the Allies.

King Gustavus V, who occupies to-day the throne of Sweden, has a German wife. All the sympathies of the court, which copies the little courts of Germany, of the aristocracy and of the army are strongly with Germany.

In Sweden, although the king has not much more power than the kings of Denmark and Norway, there is an aristocracy which inclines to imitate the manners of the German aristocracy and to seize, if possible, the privileges enjoyed by that body. The officers in the army in Sweden are devoted to German ideals and, since the war, great bodies of them have been invited to Germany, where there has been much ado over them.

The people, however, do not sympathise with Germany, knowing what the triumph of Germany means for them and how the court and the army and the aristocracy would be thereby encouraged to put the Swedish people in what the Germans would call "their place."

The Swedes fear the domination of Germany

and the domination of an aristocracy and army imbued with German ideas. They know that if Germany wins, the king business will take on a new lease of life. The ground was ripe for the Allies but the German propaganda, cleverly managed, spending money without stint, is gradually bringing the people to a point where, if the blockade is tightened, they may consent to Sweden's entering the war as an ally of the Central empires.

In spite of the dislike of the people for the German cause, I think that the aristocracy and the court and the army would have forced Sweden into the war but for one thing. After some months of war, an arrangement was made whereby the so-called "heavily wounded" were exchanged with prisoners between Russia and Germany. The German who was a prisoner of the Russians and had lost an arm or a leg, was sent home. These wounded prisoners on their way to their home countries, were compelled to travel the whole length of Sweden and it was the sight of these poor stumps of humanity, as the trains stopped at the various stations in Sweden, that kept the Swedish people out of war. Many pictures of them printed in the Swedish papers caused profound dismay in Sweden and developed an inexpressible abhorrence of war.

Since hostilities commenced, on the other hand, the Government, army and aristocracy of Sweden not only have been consistently opposed to the Allies, but of the utmost service to Germany.

Swedish iron ore goes into German cannon and

makes the best steel for aeroplane engines, and the imports into Sweden from America of foods and fats from America increased one thousand per cent almost immediately. These imports, with great quantities of copper and other supplies, found their way to Germany to the great profit incidentally of Swedish business men. For the plain people of Sweden the cost of living increased without a corresponding increase in salaries and wages, so that the new prosperity was confined to the "goulash barons."

There is no question but that, just as in Argentina, the Swedish diplomatic pouch was in all countries at the service of Germany, and that the orders to the German spies in Russia were sent by this means. In fact, it is believed German prisoners in Russia found their way to Petrograd, there to participate in revolution and counter-revolution under orders sent through the Swedish officials.

Smuggling is winked at and at Lullia on the Swedish coast near the head of the Gulf of Bothnia great quantities of rubber, block tin and oil arrive from Russian Uleaborg across the gulf.

The French wanted to send a consul to Lullia, but their request was refused, doubtless because the Swedish authorities did not care to have any official foreigners see this traffic.

Cleverest of all has been the work of the German financial agents. Warburg, the Hamburg banker, is attached to the German legation in Stockholm. So skilfully has he managed his task, that Swedish firms and Swedish banks have been in-

duced to take German paper money, commercial
paper and securities instead of gold, in return for
copper, rubber, tin, food, fats, wool and supplies
and in this way the Swedish business men, by the
touch of self-interest, have been made to favour
Germany.

I confess that it is hard to bring about, but as
each nation has the right to choose with whom its
citizens shall do business, we must mercilessly
blacklist those firms which assist Germany by ac-
cepting, in lieu of the gold which would thus be
drained from Germany, what amounts to the promise of Germany to pay if successful in war.

The Queen of Sweden, herself a German and an
admirer of the German Emperor, has great influence over her husband and the Court.

At a time when she was visiting her family in
Karlsruhe (for she is a Princess of Baden) a re-
prisal attack made by Allied aeroplanes narrowly
missed the royal palace and, consequently, the
Queen. This has added to her prejudice against the
Allies. The Crown Princess of Sweden was a
Princess of Connaught, the sister of "Princess
Pat," but she does not dare take any stand against
the anti-ally propaganda.

I am sure that President Wilson appreciates the
gravity of the situation and that means are being
taken to place our position not only before the
Swedish people but those of Swedish birth and descent in the United States whose influence should be
brought to bear on their friends and relatives in
the old country.

The crew of every Swedish ship that lands here should be given our viewpoint; every Swede who returns to Sweden should go as a missionary—we must not permit Sweden, whose people are bound to us by ties of blood and friendship, by the hospitality which we offered to every Swedish immigrant, to be ranged among our enemies by the German-admiring aristocrats of Sweden who by birth, training and education are opposed to democracy, who hope, if Germany wins, to gain as great an ascendancy in the government as the Prussian Junkers possess in Germany.

The Finns who occupy that part of Russia nearest to Sweden have quite a sympathy for the Swedes, Finland having been at one time a part of Sweden. The races, however, are not the same. The Finns are a Mongolian race and certain similarities of language make it plain that the Finns and the Hungarians came from the same mysterious place of origin somewhere in the great mountains and highlands of Central Asia.

Three languages, three influences, fight for mastery in Finland. The official Russian, the language of the government; Finnish, now receiving a new lease of life; and Swedish, the language of those who once conquered and held Finland, and who so imposed their civilisation on the more ignorant Finns, that to-day Swedish is the language of the more prosperous classes and of most of the business men.

The women of Finland received the suffrage in

1906, all voting who are over twenty-four and who have been for five years citizens of Finland. Many women thereafter were elected to the Finnish parliament.

In two Scandinavian countries the women vote. Norway was the first sovereign state of Europe to give full citizenship rights to women. In 1913, all Norwegian women of twenty-five and citizens for five years were put on a voting equality with men, and the only positions under the national government for which women are not eligible are in the army and navy, the diplomatic and consular service and the Supreme Court.

The Danish women received the full franchise in 1915, but in aristocratic Sweden only the women paying income taxes have rights in the communal councils.

In 1908, in Norway, a law was passed providing that women doing the work of men shall receive equal pay.

Military service in all three northern nations is universal and compulsory.

Possibly on a "tip" from Berlin to a fellow autocrat, there occurred in February, 1914, an extraordinary political event, arranged and "accelerated" by the Government, when thirty thousand farmers, meeting in Stockholm for the purpose, marched in procession to the Royal Castle to address the King and tell him that they were ready to bear any extra taxes imposed for the purpose of providing for national defence.

Russia was the power particularly feared by

Sweden who thought she desired to annex a part of Northern Sweden and Norway in order to get an outlet to the sea on the Norwegian coast.

But recent events in Russia have ended this fear and the only question for the Swedes is the same, one with which the whole world is faced—Kaiserism or Democracy.

Sven Hedin, the explorer, who was the leader in this movement for national defence, has appeared as a German propagandist so violent as to have become popular with the Germans. It is hard to understand why so intelligent a man should range himself on the side of autocracy. Now that the Russian danger, if danger there was, is past it is to be hoped that this celebrated man will be found in the ranks of those opposed to the autocracy which ordered the murders of many Swedish seamen.

Norway, although it has often met the submarine of the Kaiser, which, defying all law, has sent to death so many Norwegian sailors and fishermen, suffers also from German propaganda and a certain self interest because of the forty-five million kronen sale of fish this last year to German buyers.

Germany works, too, in Denmark with the Socialists and deliveries of coal are used to obtain food from that country.

The jolly, free, brave Scandinavians are naturally opposed to all that Pan-Germanism and German rule means. It is necessary for us, especially our citizens of Scandinavian descent, not to lose this initial advantage.

CHAPTER XVII

SWITZERLAND—ANOTHER KIND OF NEUTRAL

FREE SWITZERLAND! You cannot imagine the feeling of relief I experienced as I passed from the lands of the Hohenzollerns and Hapsburgs to a free republic.

It was February 11, 1917. To go into the railroad station restaurant and order an omelette and fried potatoes without a food card and with chocolate on the side seemed in itself a return to liberty.

Our Minister, Mr. Stovall, gave us a dinner and evening reception so that we could meet all the notables and we lunched with the French Ambassador (for France maintains an Embassy in Switzerland) and dined with the British Minister, Sir Horace Rumbold, a very able gentleman who had been Chancellor of the British Embassy in Berlin before the war.

As war had not yet been declared between Germany and the United States the correspondents of German newspapers waylaid me. Some seemed to think that in spite of the insulting blow given us by Germany, we nevertheless, scared to whiteness by the U-boat ultimatum, would lend all our energies to bring about a German peace.

I received a letter from one of the editors of a

Swiss newspaper published in Berne, probably inspired by the German Legation there, asking me if President Wilson, in spite of the break in relations, would not continue his work for peace.

We all know that Switzerland is a republic but even those of us who have travelled there, probably because we were on a holiday, gave little thought to the Swiss political system. Indeed before this war we cared little about the government of any country except our own.

The present constitution of Switzerland was adopted in 1848 and in many particulars is modelled after that of the United States.

There are the same three great Federal powers, the Federal Assembly, representing the legislative branch, the Federal Council, representing the executive branch, and the Federal Court, representing the judicial branch.

The lower Chamber is made up of representatives elected directly by the people, and the other Chamber of members elected, as in our Senate, two by each canton or state. The Bundesrat or Federal Council which has all the executive powers, is elected by the Federal Assembly and it is the Chairman of this body who is known as the President of Switzerland. In reality he does not possess the powers of our President, but it is the Bundesrat as a whole which exercises the powers. Each member of this Council is minister or head of some separate department, such as Military, Justice and Police, Foreign Affairs, Posts and Railways, etc. The Swiss Cantons have much power, and there is a distinct jealousy by each canton of states' rights.

It is in Switzerland that we encounter two little friends, sponsored by William Jennings Bryan—the Initiative and Referendum—means by which the Swiss people are given a direct voice in their government. By the Initiative a certain number of voters may propose new legislation and when the requisite number sign a petition the proposed law must then be submitted to popular vote. This rule applies both in the separate cantons and in the Republic as a whole.

The Referendum, more often used, provides that if the requisite number of signers be obtained any law passed by a cantonal legislative body or by the Federal Assembly shall be submitted to the voters. In certain cantons the Referendum is obligatory and every law is thus submitted to the people. In practice the Referendum has acted as a check to advanced legislation.

The Swiss have reason to fear the designs of Prussia. As late as 1856, Prussia and Switzerland were on the edge of war. Prior to 1815 Neuchatel acknowledged the King of Prussia as its overlord; the Congress of Vienna, however, included this territory in the Swiss Confederation as one of the Swiss Cantons. But Prussia, in spite of this formal arrangement, with its usual disregard of treaties, continued to claim Neuchâtel.

In 1848 the revolutionary influence resulted in more democratic rule in Neuchâtel but the Prussian propagandist of that day was at work and, in 1856, Count Pourtales' plot was discovered and several hundred prisoners seized by the Swiss government. All but a score were released. Frederick William IV of Prussia demanded their instant pardon and release and ordered the mobilisation of his army but, finally, through the intervention of Napoleon III, the affair was settled, the prisoners released by way of France, and the Prussian King renounced all rights over Neuchâtel.

The Kulturkampf of Bismarck, his contest against the Roman Catholics, had its echoes in Switzerland and it probably was due also to German influence that until 1866 full freedom was withheld from the Jews.

The Red Cross had its origin in Switzerland and the Geneva Conventions have done much to bring about the adoption of better rules of war. The Geneva Cross is the badge of international charity and help.

Switzerland always has opened her doors to the politically oppressed. Over ten thousand revolutionists from Baden took refuge in Switzerland in 1848. Austria, in 1853, as a reprisal for the alleged actions of Italians in Switzerland in conspiring against Austria, drove thousands of Swiss citizens from that part of Italy occupied by Austria. Also in the Franco-Prussian war the French General Bourbaki and his army of nearly one hundred thousand men sought an asylum in Switzerland.

The army of Switzerland is a true citizen army —an army of universal service—and it is due to the existence of this force that Switzerland remains an independent state in the midst of Europe.

To stand apart in Europe is the very essence of life for Switzerland. It is regrettable therefore that German money and German propaganda and some sympathy for Germany among the officers of the army should have touched the fine flower of Swiss neutrality. A triumphant Prussia and a free Switzerland cannot exist in the same Europe.

In Switzerland, it is in the military that we find the greatest sympathy for Germany. In 1915, Swiss officers were discovered working out the ciphers of other nations for the benefit of the German armies and the punishment given, at the ensuing Court Martial, was not only incommensurate with the offence, but was a plain indication of the early sympathies of the Chiefs of the Swiss Staff.

The food question between the United States and Switzerland requires delicate handling. We like the Swiss and do not wish them to suffer, but the Swiss must understand that our food is our own and that we do not propose it shall go to nourish Germans or that it shall take the place, in Switzerland, of Swiss food sold by the Swiss to our enemies.

The President of Switzerland related to me the difficult position in which Switzerland found herself. Iron and coal, necessary to the industries of Switzerland, to keep the population warm and to cook the food, came, he said, from Germany, while food was shipped to the French Mediterranean port of Cette from America and the Argentine, and transported across part of France to Switzerland, so that since the war Switzerland, as the President explained, has been dancing about; first on one side, then on the other, in the attempt to get food through France and coal and iron through Germany.

Everything in the office of the President was the extreme of republican simplicity. He questioned me about the situation in Germany, especially from the food standpoint. And I learned of the difficulties of the Swiss. It must not be forgotten that in Switzerland about seventy per cent of the people speak German, twenty-three per cent, French, and seven per cent, Italian. Many of the German-speaking Swiss, of course, sympathise with Germany. They are the farmers, dairymen, etc., but in French-Switzerland, in the neighbourhood of Geneva and Lausanne, the industrial population sides with the Allies. Millions of the delicate fuses used on shells have been manufactured in that part of Switzerland for the Entente. In retaliation for this the Germans boycotted Swiss watches.

The usual German-paid propaganda newspapers operate in the principal towns. The army officers are the first to be influenced. It is the same in Switzerland as with the officers of many armies, solely because of the past reputation of the German military machine.

We and the civil authorities of South America must not forget that Japan copied German military methods, that the armies of Argentina and Chili have been trained, for years, by German officers sent there on temporary leave of absence from the German army.

Von Below, a German officer in Berlin who had been in the Argentine, used to make merry over the Argentine soldiers and said that they objected to drilling when it rained. I do not believe this officer, but I should like to have the brave Argentine officers hear his jokes and gibes.

We left, after three or four days in Berne, on the evening train, for the French frontier. In the train corridors, outside the compartments, spies stood staring at us, spies pretending to read newspapers came into each compartment; police spies, betrayed by heavy boots; general staff spies, betrayed by a military stiffness; women spies; spies assorted and special. And these gentry had followed me all over Berne—for in the neutral countries of Europe as well as the belligerents are we constantly reminded of the insidious methods of Kaiserism.

CHAPTER XVIII

A GLIMPSE OF FRANCE

A T Pontarlier, on the French frontier, a special
train was waiting for my party and into this
train a German-American inserted himself after
first mixing his baggage with mine. I went through
the train and this enterprising gentleman and another German-American were detained for some
days at Pontarlier. One of them, later, on reach-
ing Spain, reported immediately to the head of the
German secret service there, thus justifying my sus-
picions. Fortunately when he subsequently arrived
in Spain we had already sailed, so that if he bore
any sinister message from Berlin to the German
agents in Spain to hinder our voyage, he was too
late.

The night trip to Paris was uneventful. At the
Gare St. Lazare we were met by our Ambassador,
Mr. Sharp, with several of his staff and a repre-
sentative of the French Foreign Office.

Paris was indeed a changed Paris since I had
last seen it in October of 1913. The pavement in
the Place Vendôme, in front of the Hotel Ritz,
where we stopped, was full of holes, but taxicabs,
almost as extinct as the dodo in Berlin, rushed mer-
rily through the crowded streets. The boulevards

were lively, full of soldiers looking far more cheery, far more snappy, than the heavy footed German soldiers who so painfully tramped down Unter den Linden. Many soldiers were to be seen without an arm or leg, something impossible in Germany where, especially in Berlin, it has been the policy of the Government to conceal those maimed by war from the people at home. Although constantly walking the streets of Berlin I never saw a German soldier without an arm or leg. Once motoring near Berlin I came upon a lonely country house where, through the iron rails of the surrounding park, numbers of maimed soldiers peered out, prisoners of the autocratic government which dared not show its victims to the people.

At night in Paris the taxicabs and autos rushed dangerously through streets darkened to baffle the Zeppelins. In the hotel there was little heat, only wood fires in one's room. In the homes a single electric light bulb was permitted for each room; violation of this rule meant loss of electric light from that apartment for three weeks.

In the Ritz Restaurant there were lights on the table only. And the gloomy dining room, where a few Americans and British officers and their families conversed in whispers, resembled but little the gay resort so often filled, before the war, with American millionaires. Olivier, the head waiter, appeared only at night, absent during the day on war duties. No lights, no music, it is hard to think of Paris without these, Paris which calls itself the "Ville Lumière"—the City of Light.

On our first Sunday in Paris a grand concert was held in the Trocadero—a great government owned auditorium on the banks of the Seine,—under Canadian auspices. When Ambassador Sharp and I entered the centre box the vast audience rose and cheered—a new sensation for me to be so welcomed after my war-years in Berlin, where I had been harried and growled at, the representative of a hated people, of a people at once envied for their wealth, hated because they had dared to keep their rights and treaties and sell goods to the enemies of Germany, and despised because the Germans believed them too rich and cowardly, too fat and degenerate, to fight in the great war for the mastery of the world.

Lord Esher called on me at the hotel and invited me on behalf of Field Marshal Haig, to visit the British line. I am sorry that I did not have time to accept this invitation, especially as in Germany I had not even heard the distant firing of cannon.

The Great General Headquarters at Charleville-Mézières where I had visited Emperor William at the end of April, 1916, was only about seventy kilometres from the battle front near Rheims. I was naturally anxious to inspect, if not the front trenches, at least the vicinity of the front, but the army officers attached to the German Foreign Office, who had accompanied me, informed me that the Chancellor had telephoned all the Generals in the vicinity to ask permission for me to visit the lines but that not one of them would permit me to visit his sector. This was a fairly certain indication that sooner or later the hate for America must lead to war or that the U-boat settlement made at the time was only a stop gap until the increased number of submarines would enable Germany to commence ruthless U-boat war once more in defiance of law and humanity, and with a greater hope of military success.

Compared to Berlin, Paris seemed a land of abundance. In the restaurants, however, the customer was limited to two courses, but with the privilege of a second helping.

I called on Lord Bertie, the British Ambassador, to ask him to convey my acknowledgments to the Honourable Arthur James Balfour, from whom I had received a most complimentary communication. I found him in the beautiful home of the British Embassy on the Rue St. Honoré, a house so cold for want of coal that I was compelled to make my visit short for fear of pneumonia.

With Mrs. Gerard we lunched with our friends from Berlin, Jules Cambon, a former French Ambassador there, and his family, at the La Rue restaurant, opposite the Madelaine. Cambon seemed as game as ever, but fatigued.

Briand, who was then Premier, invited me to breakfast at the Minister of Foreign Affairs. The other guests included our Ambassador, Mr. Sharp, Cambon and the Ambassadors of Britain, Italy, Russia and Japan and several distinguished Frenchmen.

I did not sit next to Briand as I ranked after the Ambassadors accredited to France, but after

AMBASSADORS WILLIAM G. SHARP AND JAMES W. GERARD
FROM A PHOTOGRAPH TAKEN IN PARIS, FEBRUARY, 1917

lunch I sat alone with him before the fire in one of
the large and beautiful salons and there we had a
long talk, as, naturally, he wanted to know about
the situation in Germany. He impressed me as a
strong man, with the vigour of an orator, a man
of temperament, a man endowed by nature to become a leader of the French—as the French were
before the war.

Lord Esher, at the request of General Lyautey,
then at the head of the military force of France,
took me to see that General. I had to wait for him
some time, as he was appearing before a committee of the Chamber of the Senate. His inability to
agree with the Chamber caused his resignation not
long afterwards.

I was struck in France by the fact that the leaders, civil, military and naval, seemed older than
those in similar positions in other countries.

The present Premier, Clemenceau, is an example
of this fondness of the French for government by
old men. Clemenceau is seventy-six years old, but
is a vigorous fighter.

Mrs. Gerard and I lunched with Gabriel Hanotaux and his attractive wife at their home. Cambon was there, and Ribot, since become Premier of
France, a good old man; also the Secretary of the
Navy and several learned French philosophers and
members of the Academy and one of the heads of
the Credit Lyonnais, perhaps the greatest financial
institution of France.

War, war—who could talk of anything else?
Hanotaux said that in our time we had been un-

usually fortunate, unusually free from war, that there was underneath France, underneath even the fair city of Paris, under the smiling sunlit fields, another France, a France of caves and catacombs, excavated by the poor people, the plain people who, during the One Hundred Years' War, had sought in marching armies, the far-riding plunderers and the depths of the earth refuge from the harassing, camp followers, the roving bands of "White Companies," the robber barons who, English and French, Gascon and Norman, harried the lands of France.

I said that I had heard the statement made, and there seemed no reason to doubt it, that since the birth of Christ the world has only in one year out of every thirteen enjoyed a rest from war.

Mr. Fabre-Luce, Vice-President of the Credit Lyonnais, told us of an interesting book written by a Russian and published before the war which predicted much that has happened in this war with almost the foresight of a Cassandra. I was so impressed that I secured a copy.

This book, "The Future War," by Ivan Stanislavovich Bloch, counsellor of the Russian Empire, and published in 1892, had so great an effect on the Czar of Russia that it was the reading of it which impelled him to call the Peace Conference at The Hague. In the course of his book the author explains that it is impossible for the Powers to continue

242

longer in the path of armaments and that they
ought to look each other in the face and demand
where these great armaments and this extension of
forces are conducting them. He writes:

"How can one believe it possible to solve international
questions by means of the veritable cataclysm which will
constitute, with the present means of destruction, war
waged between the five great Powers, by ten millions of
soldiers? . . . In this war explosives so powerful will be
employed that every grouping of troops on the flat country or even under the protection of fortifications will become almost impossible and that, therefore, the preparations of this character made in expectation of the war
will become useless. . . .

"The future war will see the use of a great quantity of
new aids to war, bicycles, pigeons, telegraph, telephones,
optical instruments and photographic instruments for the
purpose of mapping from a great distance the positions
occupied by the enemy and means to observe the movements of the enemy such as observing ladders, balloons
and so on. . . .

"In the future war every body of troops holding itself
on the defensive or found taking the offensive, when it
is not the question of sudden assault, will have to fortify
itself in a chosen position and the war will be confined
principally to the form of a series of combats in which
the possession of fortified positions will be disputed, and
in which the assailant will have to meet the accessory de-
fensives in the neighbourhood of the fortifications such
as barricades, barbed wire, etc., the destruction of these
objects costing many victims. . . . The infantry, when
on the defensive, will dig itself in. The conduct of the
war will depend, in a large measure, on the artillery."

According to our author, who foresaw "No Man's Land" between the two opposing forces, "there will be formed a certain zone absolutely impassable in consequence of the terrible fire with which it will be inundated from a short distance from each side." Bloch adds: "This war will last a long time and entire nations will be seen in arms or rather the flower of each nation. Germany will begin the war by throwing itself on France and then, using the many German railroads, will turn against Russia. By virtue of its military force Germany will take the initiative of operations and will make the war on the two fronts."

His prophetic eye saw even the submarine war of the future. "It will happen, possibly, that the future war will produce engines of war completely unknown and unexpected up to the present time; in any event one can foresee the advent in a short time of submarines destined to carry below even ironclads, torpedoes powerful enough to wreck the strongest ships."

He quotes the opinions of Jomini, who says that future armies will not be composed of troops recruited voluntarily but of entire nations called by a law to arms and who will not fight for a change of frontier but for their existence. Jomini states "that this state of affairs will bring us back to the third and the fourth centuries, calling to our minds those shocks of immense peoples who disputed among themselves the European continent," and "that if a new legislation and a new international law do not come to put an end to these risings of whole peoples that it is impossible to foresee where the ravages of future war will stop. It will become a scourge more terrible than ever, because the population of civilised nations will be cut down, while in the interior of each nation the normal economic life will be arrested, communications interrupted and if the war is prolonged financial crises will come with a fearful rise in the price of everything and famine with all its consequences."

Bloch, in depicting the future war, says that "in 1870, the struggle was between two Powers, while in the war of the future at least five great nations will take part without speaking of the intervention of Turkey and England. . . . The comparing of the coming war with any war of the past is impossible because the increase in the effective fighting forces has been of a rapidity so unexampled and this increase brings with it so great an augmentation of expenditures and of victims that the future war will have the character of a struggle for the existence of nations. . . . It is true that the war of 1870 gave us something of an example of this character. That was a war without mercy, brought on by secular hate, a war of revenge on the part of the Germans because of the ancient victories of the French, a war where volunteers were shot and villages burned and where unheard of exactions were imposed on the conquered whom the conqueror sought to wrong and weaken for a long period of time. A new war in Central Europe will be a second edition of the same struggle but by how much will it not surpass the former wars by its magnitude

245

and by its length and by the means of destruction employed."

Does not Bloch give a better prediction of this war than the often quoted Bernhardi?

The table conversation at Hanotaux's was in French; few Frenchmen and hardly any public men in France speak English.

At this lunch, Ribot, since Premier, said to me, "In men, in fighting, we can hold out, but we must have help on the credit side."

How much more than credit have we sent since to help beloved, beleaguered France!

My interview with President Poincaré of France was set for five-thirty in the Elysée Palace. I had to wait some minutes in an ante-room, hung with splendid tapestries, where the secretary in charge introduced me to Deschanel, the Secrétaire perpétuel of the Academie Française, with whom I had a few minutes' talk.

The President sat in a small, beautifully decorated room in this historical Elysée Palace. A small fire burned in the grate, a bit of grateful warmth in almost coalless Paris. He, too, plied me with questions, but not as closely as others, about the land I had left behind. He spoke of a great gift of money made by James Stillman, a fund to help the families of members of the Legion of Honour.

Poincaré is a man of fifty-seven, wears a small beard growing grey, and is a little under medium height (of this country) and has much the manner of an American lawyer. What a contrast those polite, agreeable Frenchmen were to the stiff, formal, overbearing Germans. There are "well born" Germans with charming international manners and the lower classes in Germany have kindly, natural manners, but the manners of the minor members of the merchant class and of the lesser officials is rude to boorishness.

And here I want to say a word about the democracy of my own countrymen. Before the war and during it we entertained countless Americans in the Embassy; all sorts and under a variety of conditions, Jew and Gentile, business men and students, travellers and musicians. They carried themselves with ease, whatever the occasion. I was proud of them always and of our system of education that had given them such pleasant equality.

After my arrival in Berlin a magnificent darkey, named George Washington Bronson, called in search of a job. Over six feet four and well built, I thought he would make an impressive appearance opening carriage doors or taking hats in the hall. So I engaged him. But he did not get on well with the other servants, and his discharge followed. Great consternation was caused shortly afterwards at our Lincoln day reception when Mrs. Gerard and the ladies of the Embassy were receiving the American Colony, by the report that George Washington, dressed up to the nines, accompanied by a coloured friend, presenting the appearance of a new red buggy, was on his way up stairs. I decided that on Lincoln's birthday all were welcome; so George Washington and his friend, resplendent, received the same greeting accorded all Americans and the manners of George Washington excelled those of a Grand Duke. But although one could see his mouth water, he did not approach the table where our local Ruggles presided over the refreshments. There was "that" about Ruggles' eye which told George Washington he would have to "go to the mat" before his former superior officer would serve him with champagne.

The cold in Paris was bitter, biting into the very bones, and all classes of the population suffered intensely from the lack of coal. In the theatres, for instance, there was absolutely no heat. Theatrical performances were permitted in each theatre three times a week. Evening dress was prohibited. I went to the Folies Bergères, arriving so late that the crowded house had warmed itself and it was possible to stay until the end in spite of the want of ventilation.

At one of the theatres I arrived early, but the cold was so bitter that even sitting in fur overcoat and with my hat on I was so chilled I had to leave after twenty minutes. This play was a *revue,* the actresses appearing in the scanty costumes peculiar to that form of entertainment, but the cold was of such intensity that they had added their street furs, presenting a curiously comical effect.

I spoke to many of the soldiers in the streets. All were animated by a new spirit in France, an obstinate calm, a determination to see this thing through, to end forever the fear of Prussian invasion which for so many years had impended. If any sign of weakness was apparent it was among the financiers; not among the poor and the men of the trenches.

At the railway station I talked with a blue-clad French soldier, calm, witty, but determined. He said, "My family comes from the East of France, my great grandfather was killed by the Prussians in 1814, my grandfather was shot in his garden by the Prussians in 1870, my father died of grief, in 1916, because my two sisters in Lille fell into Prussian hands and were taken as their slaves with all that that means. I have decided that we must end this horror once and for all, so that my children can cultivate their little fields without this constant haunting fear of the invading Prussian."

We left Paris on the evening train for the Spanish border. Newspaper men taking flashlights and "poilus" in uniform crowded the station platform as the train with our still numerous party pulled out.

How France has disappointed German expectations! France to-day is not the France that calls out, "We are betrayed," and runs away after the failure of its first assault. France to-day is a calm France that seeks out its traitors, and deliberately punishes them, that organises with an efficiency we once thought a Prussian monopoly, a France that bleeds but fights on, a France that, standing with its back to its beloved, sunny fields, with many of her dearest sons dead, facing the Kaiser across No Man's Land, cries boldly, bravely to the world, the war cry of Verdun, "They shall not pass!"

But even while war goes on, even while the French poilus hold fast the long battle line, the French people are beset within by agents of the Kaiser. Face to face they are with the secret agents, the spies, the informers, the buyers of newspapers and of public men, the traffickers in honour who, behind French citizenship or neutral passports, seek to divide France, to make the soldier at the front feel that he is betrayed by traitors at home, to render the French distrustful and suspicious of each other and thus to strike as mortal a blow at the French defence as was attempted at Verdun.

Bolo Pasha and all his tribe slip past trench and barbed wire and do more damage than a German army corps to the cause of Liberty.

CHAPTER XIX

NEUTRALS—how obsolete the word seems! Yet there are some nations in Europe which will remain neutral no matter how great the hardship. How much this is due to inherent weaknesses of government, fears that the people may acquire too much of the infectious spirit of liberalism that war brings and thereby overthrow royalty, is hard to judge. But I must say that Kaiserism has omitted no word or act to impress upon the royalty of those countries, which might otherwise be inclined to aid the entente, the advantages to them of keeping out of the war unless they become allies of Germany.

You will meet Kaiserism in Spain and the other neutral countries of Europe as much as you will in Austria or Bulgaria or Turkey. I do not mean that Spain, for instance, is by any means an ally of Germany, but I do mean that the German propagandist has had free rein.

I shall never forget the fact that the King of Spain, during my talk with him, remarked: "Remember that while I am King of Spain, I am also an Austrian Archduke."

And not only is the King of Spain by descent and

251

in the right of his father an Archduke of Austria but his mother was an Austrian Princess of the House of Hapsburg. Study, for the moment, the genealogy of the King and Queen of Spain and you will see how royalty is inter-related in this war.

The Queen of Spain was brought up at the court of the late Queen Victoria of England and is a Battenberg princess. In 1823, Alexander, Prince of Hesse and the Rhine, took in morganatic marriage a Countess von Hauke. He made her Countess of Battenberg and in 1858 she was given the title by the ruler of Hesse, of Princess Battenberg, her children and their descendants to take the same title. One of these Battenbergs, descendants of Countess von Hauke, married Beatrice, daughter of Queen Victoria, and the daughter of the marriage is the present Queen of Spain, who just before her marriage to Alfonso was created a Royal Highness by King Edward VII. Queen Victoria Eugenia has become quite Spanish. With a mantilla on her head, she attends bull fights and is very popular.

The father of Alfonso XIII, Alfonso XII, was very intimate with the German Court. In 1883, he visited the old Emperor William I in Germany and accepted the colonelcy of a Uhlan regiment then in garrison in Strassburg, one of the towns taken from France in 1870. On his return journey he stopped in Paris and was the object of a popular demonstration so violent that the President of France and his ministers called in a body to apologise.

252

Shortly thereafter the Crown Prince (later Emperor) Friedrich paid a visit to Spain and an intimacy was maintained between the two courts.

It is the inclination of those in the king business to keep together and a tradition of Prussia that fellow Kings must be sustained and, if possible, maintained against democracy. That's why the Kaiser finds reciprocal sympathy in Spain.

Our popular Ambassador, Mr. Willard, and his staff, with a representative of the Spanish Foreign Office, met us at the station at Madrid on my arrival from Paris.

Madrid is a handsome city, comparatively modern. From its highest point the great Royal Palace dominates the capital and from the palace the royal park stretches unbroken to the Guadarrama mountains sixty miles away.

In many respects Spain seems a land upside down. We arrived at Madrid just at the close of the Carnival season. Masked balls began at three in the afternoon and many theatres not until ten or even eleven at night. Madrid sleeps late. The rich people get up only in time for lunch. The streets are full of noise and people until four in the morning, the sellers of lottery tickets making special efforts to swell the volume of night sounds.

My visit to the King of Spain was at eleven in the morning. Ambassador Willard went with me. As we entered the palace and waited at the foot of an elevator, the car descended and one of the little Princes of Spain, about eight years old, dressed in a sailor suit, stepped out. Evidently he had been trained in royal urbanity for he immediately came up to us, shook hands and said, "Buenos dias."

And as we strolled down a long corridor where Palace guards in high boots and cocked hats stood guard with halberds in their hands another little Prince, about eleven, also in a sailor suit, came out of a room and walked ahead of us; behind followed two nuns, walking side by side at a respectful distance. As he appeared in the corridor one of the guards stamped his halberd on the floor, calling out in Spanish, "Turn out the guard—the Infant of Spain." And in the guardroom at the end of the corridor the guards, forming in line, clashing their arms, did honour to the baby Prince.

Ambassador Willard and I waited in the great, splendid room of the Palace. Inside, priests and officers, ladies, officials, diplomats, were waiting to present petitions or pay homage to their King. Outside in the court yard, the guard was being changed, infantry, cavalry and artillery all being represented. A tuneful band played during the ceremony of guard mount, which was witnessed by crowds of poor folk who are permitted to enter the Palace precincts as spectators.

While waiting I was presented to the Archbishop of Toledo, head of the Spanish Church, resplendent in his gorgeous ecclesiastical robes. Finally a court official came and said that I was to go into the King alone; that Mr. Willard was to see him later.

I found King Alfonso in a small room about twenty by fourteen feet. He wore a brown business suit, a soft shirt and soft collar fastened by a gold safety pin—quite the style of dress of an American collegian. He is tall and well built.

The King speaks perfect English—without a trace of accent. After we had talked a few moments, I noted the difference between Teuton and Latin, the vast abyss which separates the polite and courteous Spaniard, thinking of others, anxious to be hospitable, and the rough, conceited, aggressive Junker of Germany. How often have I found that we ourselves, although good hearted and easy going, in comparison with our friends in South and Central America, do not measure up to the standards of Castilian courtesy.

Some one knocked at the door and King Alfonso rose and answered. He returned with odd looking implements in his hands which I soon discovered to be an enormous silver cocktail shaker and two goblets. After a dexterous shake, the King poured out two large cocktails, saying, "I understand that you American gentlemen always drink in the morning."

I had not had a cocktail for years and if I had endeavoured to assimilate the drink so royally prepared for me I should have been in no condition to continue the conversation. I think King Alfonso himself was quite relieved when, after a sip, I put my cocktail behind a statue. I noticed that he camouflaged his in a similar manner.

Unfortunately, as Maximilian Harden said, the Germans think of us as a land of dollars, trusts and corruption; and other nations think of us as devotees of the cocktail and of poker. Their school boys dream of fighting Indians in Pittsburg and hunting buffalo in the deserts of the Bronx.

The characteristic of Alfonso which impresses one immediately is that of extreme manliness. He has a sense of humour that will save him from many a mishap in his difficult post. He has a wide knowledge of men and affairs and, above all, as the Spaniards would put it, is *muy español* (very Spanish), not only in appearance but in his way of looking at things, a Spaniard of the best type, a Spaniard possessing industry and ambition and bravery, a Spaniard, in fact, of the days when Spain was supreme in the world. His favourite sport is polo, which he plays very well. Indeed, the game, which requires dash, quickness of thought, nerve and good riding, is particularly suited to the Spanish character. The King showed at the time of the anarchistic outbreaks, that he was a brave man. Yet he must be careful at all times to remember that he is a constitutional king, that in a country like Spain leadership is dangerous, that he should always rather stand aside, let the representatives of the nation decide, thus taking no definite position himself. A king who abandons the council table to shoot pigeons or play polo is often acting with far more wisdom than a constitutional ruler who attempts by the use of his strong personality and lofty position to force upon his councillors a course which the majority of them do not recommend.

The Spaniards are politically an exacting people.

But it is to be hoped that they will not turn the heavy artillery of their criticism upon a king who serves them so gracefully and well.

The king has a natural desire to take a prominent part in the negotiations for peace, but here again is dangerous ground for him. He should be given a part, if possible, in the preliminaries of peace, but while I believe that he sympathises with one of the Entente countries, the Allies are forced to recognise the fact of which he himself reminded me, that he is not only King of Spain, but Archduke of one of the Central Empires, the son of an Austrian Archduchess.

The king told me that he was most desirous that American capital should become interested in the development of Spain. He did not tell me the reason for this desire but perhaps he fears that if German capital should take a great part in the development of industrial Spain that the tentacles of the German propaganda and spy system which go hand in hand with her commercial invaders would wrap themselves around the commercial, social and political life of Spain.

Perhaps King Alfonso, when he wishes capital other than German to become interested in Spain, is thinking of the occurrences of 1885, when Spain and Germany so nearly clashed. In that year the crew of a German warship hoisted the flag of the German Empire on the island of Yap, one of the Carolina group, an island long claimed by Spain. The act so stirred the people of Spain that a great meeting was held in Madrid, attended by over one hundred thousand people. Later the mob attacked the German Embassy and Consulate, tore down the shield and flag staff of the Consulate and burned them in the principal square of Madrid. In the end, Spain was compelled to humbly apologise to Germany for the insult to the German Ambassador.

Some years before the war the King sent to this country a special emissary to interest American capital in Spain. Means of transportation are very meagre. Great mineral districts are as yet undeveloped and many other opportunities for foreign capital present themselves.

I asked the Spaniards why Spain was not developed by Spanish capital and they told me that the rich put all their money in government bonds and lived as gaily as possible on the interest.

Our own Government, whether Democratic or Republican, must always be careful to see that taxes are not so high as to prevent the naturally enterprising American from risking part of his capital in new ventures and such protection must be given to American citizens that they will continue to try their luck at business in foreign countries for the immediate benefit, of course, of themselves, but also for the commercial supremacy of the United States.

The American who goes to Mexico and there develops a railroad or a plantation, a commercial business, a bank or a mine, is not only adding to the wealth of Mexico, but any money which he makes after paying his due share of taxes there, is brought back by him to the United States, is subject to taxation, and by just so much not only lightens the tax burden of other Americans, but adds to the power in trade of the whole country.

A business man who is taxed too much on any profits that he makes will, like the Spaniard, invest his capital in Government bonds. He will stop taking up new enterprises because if he loses no one compensates him for his loss, while if he wins most of his profit is taken in taxes by the State.

I do not think that the Spanish harbour any spirit of revenge against us because of the events of the Spanish-American war. There was nothing in that war to arouse particular resentment. No one used poison gas, or enslaved women or cut off the hands of babies. On our side, at least, there was an intense admiration for the splendid, chivalrous bravery of our enemies. Spain was, in reality, benefited by the loss of Cuba and the Philippines; in fact, they were practically lost to her before we entered the war. Thinking Spaniards believe the war with America benefited Spain; and the lower classes rejoice because their sons and husbands are not forced to serve in the Spanish Army in the fever-laden swamps of the tropics.

On the war Spain is hopelessly divided: Conservative, against Conservative; Liberal, against Liberal. The usual German propaganda is furiously at work, all the paraphernalia, bought newspapers—bribes. Roman Catholic prejudice against former French Governments is a great stumbling block in the way of the Allies in Spain, for that country became the refuge of many orders and priests driven from France. Many of the Spanish Catholics still resent the action of previous French Governments towards the Catholic Church.

But whatever may be the faults of the French Government in this particular, whether it or the teaching orders went too far—the Roman Catholics of Spain sooner or later will realise that, after all, the bulk of the French and Italian and Belgian people are their co-religionists, and they will recall the attempts of Bismarck to master the Roman Catholics of Germany and to bind its priests to the will of the Imperial Government, attempts recent enough to keep the Catholics of Germany still organised in the political party which they created in the dark days of Bismarck's "war for Civilisation," as he dared call his contest with the great Roman Catholic Church.

Spanish and other Catholics throughout the world will remember this and will remember, too, that from every valley of the Protestant section of the German Empire the eye can see a "Bismarck Thurm," or Bismarck Memorial Tower, erected on some commanding height by the admirers of the dead Iron Chancellor.

I believe that after the war the Roman Catholic Church in France and Belgium will be on a healthier, sounder basis, that it will have more and more influence with the people, that it will be more popular and respected than before, unless some act on the part of the Pope should lead the French and Belgians to believe that he favours Germany. Priests are not exempt from military service in

France and these Abbés, fighting, dying, suffering wounds and privation, working cheek to cheek with the soldiers of France, will do much to bring about the change. I met a number of these priest-warriors in the prison camps of Germany. They are doing a great work and have earned the respect and love of their countrymen—their fellow prisoners.

Several of these soldier Abbés were prisoners in Dyrotz, near Berlin, and I remember how they were looked up to by all the soldiers. What a consolation were these noble warriors who fought a twofold winning fight—for their country and their faith.

Spain has suffered much from the war. In the northeast part called Catalonia are located the manufacturing industries of Spain, cloth weaving, cotton spinning, etc. In Barcelona, the principal industrial town, are many manufacturing industries. If these plants cannot obtain raw materials or a market for their finished products, then industrial depression ensues and thousands are thrown out of employment.

So in the north, where iron ore is produced, the submarine blockade of England, chief buyer of iron ore and the seller of coal, has made itself felt in every province; and in the south, the land of sun and gypsies, oranges and vines, the want of sea and land transportation, the diminished exports of wine and fruits to other countries have brought many of the inhabitants to the verge of ruin.

In the coast cities sailors and longshoremen are out of employment, and this condition—these hundreds of thousands without work through disturbance of industry,—has ripened the field for the German propagandist and agent who threatens the King with revolution, should he incline to the Allies.

In no country of the world has the German agent been so bold and no neutral government has been more forcibly reminded in its policy and conduct of the fact that it is always face to face with Kaiserism.

CHAPTER XX

GERMAN SPIES AND THEIR METHODS

GERMAN spies who looked like "movie" detectives hung about and followed us on the journey from Berlin to Switzerland, France and Spain. There were even suspicious characters among the Americans with German accent who came on our special train from Germany to Switzerland.

Berne is now the champion spy centre of the world. Switzerland, a neutral country, bordering on Germany, France, Italy and Austria, is the happy hunting ground and outfitting point for myriads of spies employed by the nations at war. The Germans, however, use more spies than all the other nations together.

Bismarck said that there are male nations and female nations, and that Germany was a male nation—certainly the German has less of that heaven-sent feminine quality of intuition than other peoples. The autocrat, never mingling with the plain people of all walks of life, finds the spy a necessity.

Spy spies on spy—autocracy produces bureaucracy where men rise and fall not by the votes of their fellow citizens but by back stairs intrigue. The German office-holder fears the spies of his rivals. I often said to Germans holding high office

263

during the war, "This strain is breaking you down, —all day in your office. Take an afternoon off and come shooting with me." The invariable answer was, "I cannot—the others would learn it from their spies and would spread the report that I neglect business!"

While in Spain I met the then Premier, Count Romanones, a man of great talent and impressive personality. He told me of the finding of a quantity of high explosives, marked by a little buoy, in one of the secluded bays of the coast. And that day a German had been arrested who had mysteriously appeared at a Spanish port dressed as a workman. The workman took a first class passage to Madrid, went to the best hotel and bought a complete outfit of fine clothes: Undoubtedly the high explosive as well as the mysterious German had been landed from a German submarine. Whether the explosive was destined as a depot for submarines or was to help overturn the Spanish government was hard to guess, but Count Romanones was worried over the activity of the German agents in Spain.

It has been very easy for German agents in America to communicate with Germany through this submarine post from Spain to Germany, the letters from America being sent to Cuba and thence on Spanish boats to Spain.

At all times since the war the Germans have had a submarine post running direct from Germany to Spain. Shortly after our arrival in Spain Mrs. Gerard received mysteriously a letter written by a friend of hers, a German Baroness, in Berlin. This letter had undoubtedly been sent through the very efficient German spy system.

Sometime in 1915 a German soldier, in uniform, speaking perfect English, called one day at the Embassy. He said that his name was Bode and that he had at one time worked for my father-in-law, the late Marcus Daly. Of course, we had no means of verifying his statements and Mrs. Gerard did not remember any one of that name or recall Bode personally. He said that he was fighting on the East front and that he had a temporary leave of absence, I gave him some money and later we sent him packages of food and tobacco to the front, but never received any acknowledgment.

In Madrid one of my assistants, Frank Hall, while walking through the street, ran across Bode, who was fashionably attired. His calling cards stated that he was a mining engineer from Los Angeles, California. He told Hall a most extraordinary fairy story, saying that he had been captured by the Russians on the East front and sent to Siberia, that from Siberia he had escaped to China and from there he had gradually worked his way back to America and thence to Spain.

Of course, without any definite information on the subject it is impossible to say exactly what he was doing in Spain. But I am sure that it is far more likely he had landed from a German submarine on the coast of Spain and that he was posing as an American mining engineer for a particular purpose.

I told certain people in Spain about Bode and of his intention to visit the mining districts of Spain where numbers of men are employed. Bode must have suspected that I had given information about him, for Hall and I received several postcards of a threatening character, evidently from him.

My cables to and from the State Department passed through our legation at Copenhagen, and, of course, if the Germans knew our cipher these messages were read by them. On special occasions I made use of a super-cipher the key to which I kept in a safe in my bedroom and which only one secretary could use. The files of cipher cables sent and received were kept in a large safe in the Embassy. But before leaving Germany, knowing the Germans as I did, and particularly what they had done in other countries and to other diplomats, knowing how easy it would be for them to burglarise the safe after we left, when the Spaniards and Dutch were out of the building at night, I tossed all these despatches as well as the code books into a big furnace fire. Commander Gherardi and Secretary Hugh Wilson stood by and personally saw that the last scrap was burned. Of course, copies of all the cables are in the State Department.

German spies are adepts at opening bags, steaming letters—all the old tricks. The easiest way to baffle them is to write nothing that cannot be published to the world.

For a long time after the beginning of war I was

266

too busy to write the weekly report of official gossip usually sent home by diplomats. I suppose the Germans searched our courier bags for such a report vainly. Anyway, its absence finally got on the nerves of Zimmermann so much that one day he blurted out, "Don't you ever write reports to your Government?"

Sealed letters are opened by spies as follows:

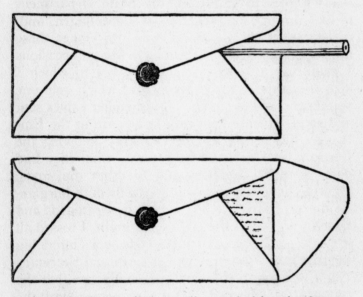

by inserting a pencil or small round object in the envelops, steamed a little, if necessary; the envelope is opened at the end flap and the contents pulled out without disturbing the seal, the contents are then read, put in their place again, the end flap re-inserted, a little gum used and the envelope is as intact as before.

The only safe way to seal an envelope is thus:

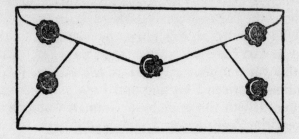

Even then a clever spy can open the letter, read the contents and seal it again. This is done by cutting through the seals with a hot razor—the divided seals are then united by pressing the hot razor against each side of the cut and then pressing the two parts of the cut seal together. This is, however, a very delicate operation and doesn't always work.

From the outbreak of war we sent and received our official mail through England, and couriers carried it between Berlin and London through Holland via Flushing and Tilbury.

On account of the great volume of correspondence between Ambassador Page and myself on the affairs of German prisoners in England and English prisoners in Germany, there were many pouches every week. These were leather mail bags opened only by duplicate keys kept in London and Berlin and, for the American mail, in Berlin and Washington. Our couriers did their best to keep the numerous bags in their sight during the long journey but on many occasions our couriers were separated,

I am sure with malicious purpose, from their bags by the German railway authorities and on some occasions the bags not recovered for days.

Undoubtedly at this time the Germans opened and looked over the contents of the bags. Later in the war our courier while on a Dutch mail boat, running between Flushing and England, was twice captured with the boat by a German warship and taken into Zeebrugge. Undoubtedly here, too, the bags were secretly opened and our uncoded despatches and letters read.

German spies were most annoying in Havana and one of them, a large dark man, followed me about at a distance of only six feet, with his eyes glued on the small bag which I carried from a thick strap hanging around my shoulder. I brought it from Germany in that way. I never let it out of my hands or sight.

What was in that bag? Among other things were the original telegrams written by the Kaiser in his own handwriting, facsimiles of which appear in my earlier book, "My Four Years in Germany," and the treaty which the Germans tried to get me to sign while they held me as a prisoner. Under the terms they proposed the German ships interned in America were to have the right in case of war, to sail for Germany under a safe conduct to be obtained from the Allies by the United States. Somewhat of a treaty! And quite a new, bright and original thought by some one in the Foreign Office or German Admiralty. There were also in this mysterious bag many other matters of interest that may some day see the light.

Poisonous propaganda and spying are the twin offspring of Kaiserism.

There is in Mexico, for instance, one force that never sleeps,—the German propaganda. It is the same method as that used by the Teutons in every country, the purchase or rental of newspaper properties, bribing public men and officers of the army and the insidious use of Germans who are engaged in commerce. This propaganda is backed by enormous sums of money appropriated by the German government which directs how all its officers and agents, high and low, shall participate in the campaign.

In the long run a paid propaganda always fails. It is like paying money to blackmailers. The blackmailer who has once received money becomes so insatiable that even the Bank of England will not satisfy him in the end. Sometimes the newspapers which are not bought, but are equally corrupt, become vehement in their denunciation of the country making the propaganda in the hope of being bought and in the hope that their bribe money will be in proportion to their hostility. Corrupted public men who are not bribed often become sternly virtuous and denunciatory with a similar hope. Those who have received the wages of shame, on the other hand, become more insistent in their demands, crying, "Give! Give!" like the daughter of the horse-leech.

The blows of war must be struck quickly. Delays are dangerous and the temporary paralysis of one country by propaganda may mean the loss of the war. The United States has been at a great disadvantage because our officials have not had the authority, the means or the money to fight the German propaganda with effective educational campaigns, both offensive and defensive.

Bernstorff in this country disposed of enormous sums for the purpose of moulding American public opinion. I, in Berlin, was without one cent with which to place America's side before the German people. It is a conflict of two systems. In Berlin I did not even have money to pay private detectives and on the rare occasions when I used them as, for instance to find out who was connected with the so-called American organisation, the League of Truth, which was engaged in a violent propaganda against America inside Germany, I was obliged to bear the expense personally.

South of the Rio Grande the Germans are working against us, doing their best to prejudice the Mexicans against the United States, playing upon old hatreds and creating new ones and, in the meantime, by their purchase of properties and of mines creating a situation that will constitute for us in the future a most difficult and dangerous problem.

The Germans cannot understand why we do not take advantage of conditions in Mexico in order to conquer and hold that unfortunate country. They could not believe that we were actuated by a spirit of idealism and that we were patiently suffering much in order really to help Mexico. They could not believe that we were waiting in order to convince not only Mexico but the other States of Central America and the great friendly republics of South America, that it was not our policy to use the dissensions and weakness of our neighbours to gain territory.

On one occasion before the war I and several other Ambassadors were dining with the Kaiser and after dinner the conversation turned to the strange sights to be seen in America. One of the Ambassadors, I think it was Cambon, said that he had seen in America whole houses being moved along the roads, something of a novelty to European eyes where the houses, constructed of brick and stone, cannot be transported from place to place like our wooden frame house. The Emperor jokingly remarked: "Yes, I am sure that the Americans are moving their houses. They are moving them down towards the Mexican border."

CHAPTER XXI

OUR party was so numerous that we were compelled to charter a special train to take us from Madrid to La Coruña, the port in the extreme northwestern corner of Spain from which the *Infanta Isabela* was to sail.

Just before the train started, a Spanish gentleman from the Foreign Office, who had courteously come to see us off, said to me, "Do you know you have a Duke as engineer?" "The Duke of Saragossa is going to take out your train." So we ran forward to the engine and I shook hands with the Duke who was in blue overalls.

This Duke of Saragossa, Grandee of Spain, often drives the engine of the King's train. Why he engineered our train I do not know, unless it was because of the rumours that German agents would try to stop my journey home.

At any rate the Duke proved a most competent engineer, guiding us with velvet touch through the steep inclines and sharp turns of the Guardarrama mountains. At Venta de Baños his turn at the engine ended and on my invitation he came to dine with us in the dining car. He proved a most charming gentleman, speaking English well. He said that

273

his great ambition was to visit America and see the big locomotives and the pretty girls. At dinner he was, of course, dressed in his overalls and carried out the professional touch by using clean cotton waste instead of a pocket handkerchief.

Arrived at La Coruña in the morning, carriages sent by the Spanish government met us and the Mayor and the other officials were most polite. The Mayor accompanied us on board ship next day, giving to Mrs. Gerard a beautiful basket of flowers entwined with ribbons of the colours of the City of La Coruña.

We found the *Infanta Isabela* a clean splendid ship—her Captain competent and kind. I cheerfully recommend her to any who wish a safe voyage across the Atlantic during the war.

My stay in Havana was brief and I was soon en route northward from Key West.

As our train came north through Florida there were crowds and bands at the stations and at St. Augustine my eyes were delighted by the sight of Frank Munsey and Ex-Senator Chauncey Depew.

At the station in Washington Secretary McAdoo met me. What a splendid record of achievement is his since the war, and now with the burden of all the railways in the country added to that of finance I suppose in no country at war has one man so successfully undertaken such gigantic tasks.

President Wilson was ill in bed but next day got up on purpose to hear my report. I was with him for over an hour.

The following day I arrived in New York, being

THE "INFANTA ISABELLA," ON WHICH AMBASSADOR GERARD
RETURNED FROM EUROPE.   FROM A PHOTOGRAPH TAKEN IN
HAVANA HARBOR, MARCH, 1917

met in Jersey City by a committee headed by the celebrated lawyer, John B. Stanchfield; Clarence Mackay, Herbert Swope (whose splendid articles in the *New York World* were the first warnings to America and other countries respecting the ruthless submarine warfare), United States Marshal Thomas D. McCarthy, State Senator Foley, James J. Hoey,—a faithful trio of good friends who saw me off for Denmark only a few months before. I was escorted to the City Hall where I was welcomed by the Mayor. In a speech on the steps of the City Hall I said:

"We are standing to-day very near the brink of war, but I want to assure you that if we should be drawn into the conflict it will be only after our President has exhausted every means consistent with upholding the honour and dignity of the United States to keep us from war. I left Berlin with a clear conscience, because I felt that during all my stay there I had omitted nothing to make for friendly relations and peace between the two nations.

"I am very glad to-day to see on the list of this Reception Committee the names of people of German descent. It is but natural that citizens of German descent in the beginning of the war should have had a sentimental feeling toward Germany, that they should have looked back through rose-coloured glasses on that land which, however, they left because they did not have equality of opportunity. We read to-day in the newspapers for the first time that there is a prospect that after the war the Germans will be given an equal share in their own government. I believe that in our hour of trial we can rely upon the loyalty of our citizens of German descent, and if they would follow me I would not be afraid to go out with a regiment of them and without any fear of being shot from behind.

．　　　．　　　．　　　．　　　．　　　．　　　．

"The nation that stands opposite to us to-day has probably no less than 12,000,000 men under arms. I have seen the Germans take more prisoners in one afternoon than there are men in the entire United States Army.

"Does it not seem to you ridiculous that the two States of New York and New Jersey should have more chauffeurs in them than there are soldiers in our army? My companions from the Twelfth Regiment that have honoured me by coming here to-day, and more men like them throughout the country, have done what they can. But they can't do it all. There must be a public sentiment if we are to maintain ourselves as a nation. If we had a million men under arms to-day we should not be near the edge of war.

"Gentlemen, I have tried in Berlin to be, as the Mayor has told you, an American Ambassador, and I thank you because you, an audience of patriotic Americans, by your presence here set your seal of approval upon my conduct during the last two and a half years."

I have never been able to understand why so many people did not sooner realise what Kaiserism meant for us. But now, at last, the nation understands that we must fight on until this menace of military autocracy has vanished and that not until then will the world enjoy a lasting peace.

Almost as soon as I was settled in New York I was drafted. Drafted by a public curiosity which insisted on knowing something about Germany and the war.

And so for me began a new life—that of a public speaker—I spoke first in New York at a lunch at the Chamber of Commerce—war had not then been declared and I was compelled to be careful—for even then there seemed a fear of Germany, a foolish desire to surrender all manhood to a fat neutrality.

On April 2nd came President Wilson's message demanding war. I was in the opera house that night. Between the acts extras appeared. I telephoned Swope of the *World* who confirmed the news. While I was receiving this information one of the directors of the Metropolitan Opera Company came in the room. I told him what had happened and asked if he was not going to do something—order the news read from the stage—for example, and the "Star Spangled Banner" played. He said, "No, the opera company is neutral."

I returned to the box where I was sitting and stepping to the front called on the house to cheer President Wilson. There was, for a moment, surprise at such unconventional action, but the whole house soon broke into cheers.

Conventionalism was gone.

The opera was DeKoven's "Canterbury Pilgrims" and a few minutes after the curtain rose on the last act Frau Ober, a German singer, who was taking one of the principal parts, keeled over in a faint,—rage, perhaps, that the Yankees were at last daring to cheer, to assert themselves against the Kaiser!

As I spoke in Albany, Buffalo, Harrisburg, Trenton and Boston, in Philadelphia, Providence and many times in New York and other places, I noted always an eagerness to learn about Germany, the war and foreign affairs. We Americans had travelled, but not with our eyes open—"seeing, we saw not."

The first great, great question we faced was that of universal service for the war—or the selective draft—again how farsighted our President then proved himself. What would be our situation now if we had tried to go to war under the volunteer system? This question once solved, our President led us with a breadth of vision, an efficiency, and on a scale commensurate with the size of the undertaking in which we at last had become partners.

Perhaps we are a little over indulgent, however, in the treatment of the German enemy alien within our gates. No American singer or musician could travel about Germany at will, unwatched by the police, collecting money from Americans to be used in propaganda, or things much worse, against America. Americans in Germany are compelled to report twice daily to the police and cannot leave their homes at night. November 17, 1917—seven months after we went to war with Germany—I met Hugo Schmidt, a director of the Deutsche Bank, riding in Central Park. He lived at the German Club, saw whom he liked and only reported to the police when he changed his residence. In January 1918, he was finally interned.

Long before our break with Germany, American consuls and officials were insulted in the street and in opera houses because they made use of their own language, not at all because they were taken for British for every one knew that all British had been interned.

The wife of our naval attaché attended a reception presided over by a German admiral's wife. She was presented to this high personage by the wife of a German naval officer, who, in making the presentation, spoke in English. The admiral's wife rebuked both the wife of our attaché and the officer's wife for daring to talk English. I am thankful to say that Mrs. Gherardi immediately left the house to receive later the officially ordered apologies of the admiral's wife.

And while Americans did not dare use their own language in Berlin in time of peace between the two countries yet after the outbreak of war, newspapers in the United States, printed in German, owned by Germans and German sympathisers, dared to attack America and her President.

The autocracy always hope to divide us, to make of us a Russia, torn by Maximalists and Minimalists, by Militarists and Bolsheviki and, consequently, impotent for war.

In travelling through the United States in August and September of 1917, although I was on private business, I made speeches in many cities, such as Minneapolis, and Helena, Billings, Butte and Missoula in Montana, Spokane, Seattle and Tacoma in Washington, Portland, Oregon, San Francisco and surrounding country, Los Angeles, San Diego and Pasadena and then Milwaukee, Chicago and Cleveland. In all this territory I found great enthusiasm, great patriotism and a sincere desire to learn about Germany and the war. But I found everywhere also the trail of Germany's poisonous propaganda.

The great majority of our citizens of German-American descent have been splendidly loyal to their country in this crisis of its history. But the fact must be faced that there are those who, for some unknown reason, still sympathise with the German Kaiser in his war of aggression.

More unfortunately there are politicians in America who seek the votes of those disaffected, and approach treason in doing so. In all the history of sordid politics, there is nothing more nauseating than the effort of these cheap politicians thus to gratify their personal ambitions.

Their shameful identity is known to all. A generation from now their own descendants will be applying to the courts for a change of name.

If, when the test comes, it is found that the votes of these disaffected citizens count for something in our elections, we must find some means to disenfranchise them rather than have our low politicians outbidding each other within the law in order to get these votes.

Have we not had examples enough from Russia

of what the slimy bribe and the snaky propaganda can do?

In Chicago, where one Thompson is Mayor, there is a censorship of moving picture films. The chief censor is Major Funkhouser. When I was in Los Angeles, at the end of September, like all strangers there, I visited movie-land to see the pictures made.

At the house of my college chum, Dr. Walter J. Barlow, I met the beautiful and celebrated Mary Pickford.

In conversation she told me about Major Funkhouser, and how he had refused an exhibition permit for one of her films called "The Little American." Curious to see the film rejected by Chicago officialdom, I asked Miss Pickford if she would have it run off for my benefit. I could see nothing in the film that could hurt the susceptibilities of any except the Germans with whom we are now engaged in war!

Later the Fox Film Company informed me that their film called "The Spy" and which deals with the adventures of an American who is supposed to go to Germany to get a list of German spies and agents in America, was refused the right of exhibition in Chicago by this same Major Funkhouser. In this case the Fox Company appealed in the courts and obtained from Judge Alschuler an injunction preventing any one from interfering with the exhibition of this film. The decision of Judge Alschuler was affirmed on appeal.

And yet the mass of the people in Chicago are

281

splendidly patriotic as the record of Chicago for enlistment and Red Cross and Liberty Loan shows.

When I spoke in the great Medinah Temple under the auspices of the Hamilton Club, on October twenty-second, I was able to show to the audience two German text-books used in the Chicago public schools, stamped with the royal arms of Prussia. The books had been approved by Ella Flagg Young, Superintendent of Schools, in 1914.

These books were furnished me by my friend, Anthony Czarnecki of the *Chicago Daily News* whom I first met in Berlin where he came to do most excellent work for his paper. In one of these books is printed the German patriotic song, The Watch on the Rhine ("Die Wacht am Rhein"). What a howl there would have been if some public school superintendent had selected for the schools under her jurisdiction a text-book of English literature with the royal arms of England stamped on the cover and "Rule Britannia" prominently displayed inside!

These text-books were cleverly compiled to impress children at a youthful age with a favourable idea of kings and emperors. In one of these was an anecdote about Frederick the Great and a miller, and in another, one about the Emperor Charlemagne and the scholar, of course, making Frederick and Charlemagne appear as good kindly people, and giving the impression that all kings and emperors are beneficent beings. But no word is there in these books quoting the present German Emperor's statement in which he puts Frederick in the same class as the four other bloody conquerors of history, Alexander, Julius Cæsar, Theodoric and Napoleon, and says that where they failed in their dreams of world conquest, his mailed fist will succeed. Why was not Frederick the Great's statement printed in these books, his admission that he engaged upon the Seven Years' War "in order to be talked about"?

These books contained quotations from Goethe. Why did they not contain Goethe's statement, "Amerika, du hast es besser."? (America, you are better off). Or his prophecy about the Prussians, "The Prussian was born a brute, and civilisation will make him ferocious."

The only foreign language taught in the grammar schools of Chicago is German. Parents are compelled to sign a statement in which they answer the question as to whether they wish their children to be taught German or not.

See how subtle this is! Doubtless if a Teuton parent answers that he does not desire to have his children taught German the paid agents of the German propaganda stir up feeling against these Germans who have dared to refuse to have their children taught the language of the fatherland.

And when a parent has once elected that his children shall be taught German, not the principal of the school, not the district superintendent, but only the head of all the Chicago school system, on the application of the parent, can excuse the child, during his or her school course, from further study of German.

Worst of all, however, is the Chicago official

school speller, a book printed under the direction and compiled by the school authorities of Chicago. In this speller there is just one piece of reading matter and that a fulsome eulogy of the present German Emperor.

This is an account of an alleged incident of the Kaiser's school days and the author concludes that the facts set forth (probably untrue) show that the Kaiser as a boy had the "root of a fine character in him," possessed "that chivalrous sense of fair play which is the nearest thing to a religion" in boys of that age and hated "meanness and favouritism." The Chicago Board of Education end the eulogy by stating, "There is in him a fundamental bent toward what is clean, manly and aboveboard."

"Chivalrous sense of fair play and hates meanness!" "Fundamental bent toward what is clean, manly and aboveboard!" How about the enslavement of women and girls in France, the use of poison gas, the deportations of the Belgians, the sinking of the *Lusitania* and the killing of women and babies by Zeppelins and submarines.—Sickening!

A number of the books used in the public schools of New York have so much in them favourable to kings and emperors, have so much of German patriotism and fatherland, that the hand of the propagandist must have had something to do with the adoption of these books.

Of course, it is only in the books of the advanced courses that propaganda appears. It is not possible, however clever the author, to incorporate much propaganda in simple exercises, or in such sentences as "Have you seen the sister of my cousin's wife?" or "The bird is waiting in the blacksmith shop on account of the rain."

But the following extracts from books used in the public schools of New York should not be without interest to those who know that the impressions given to persons under the age of sixteen or seventeen are the impressions that often persist through life.

For instance in the "Deutscher Lehrgang, First Year," by E. Prokosch of the University of Texas, "Die Wacht am Rhein" is printed with music.

I should be very much surprised to hear that the "Star Spangled Banner," with music, had ever been printed in any school book in Germany.

On page 109, of this book, there is an article in German entitled, "The German Constitution." It begins with the sentence, "The German Empire is a union State like the United States of America." How far the German Empire is from the United States of America in political liberty can be answered by any German immigrant or Jewish merchant who has voted under the circle system or been denied access to court because of his religion!

The second paragraph commences with the sentence, "The German Kaiser is not monarch of the Empire. He only is President of the Union." I am quite sure that if the Kaiser ever saw this sentence he would very soon convince the author that he was something more than the President. The article continues:

"He is the over-commander of the army.

Through him is war declared and peace made, but he can declare war only with the consent of the Bundesrath."

The Bundesrath had nothing to say about the commencement of this war. They never voted on the question. The German Constitution, as a matter of fact, gives the Kaiser the right to declare war himself, providing that the war is a defensive war. In 1914, the Kaiser first announced, without presenting any evidence, that Germany had been attacked, and then declared war on the strength of this statement, never since substantiated.

The text book writer adds: "The people are represented in the Reichstag as the American people are represented in Congress." If the American people were represented in Congress under the same unfair representation from which the German people suffer, there would soon be a revolution in this country. The districts which elect members to the Reichstag have not been changed since 1872, so that millions of Germans are not represented at all in the Reichstag.

"Professor" Prokosch remarks: "The Bundesrath is like the Senate of the United States. It is composed of representatives of the particular States."

Of course, the only *difference* is that our Senators are elected by the people and the members of the Bundesrath are appointed by the ruling kings and princes of the German states and vote exactly as they are told by these rulers.

This is only to show how carelessly, if not maliciously, Professor E. Prokosch of the University of Texas and his helper, C. M. Purin of the State Normal School at Milwaukee, have handled the German Constitution, doubtless to give the impression to school children in America that the German empire instead of being a despotic autocracy, is ruled in very much the same manner as our own republic.

Frederick the Great, who admitted that he went to war "in order to be talked about," who boasted that he had only one cook and a hundred spies, who was one of the most tyrannical kings of all history, has a whole book dedicated to him for use in the Public Schools of New York. Frederick Betz, head of the Department of Modern Languages in the East High School of Rochester, New York, is the author of a book called, "About a Great King and Others." The author in the preface states that the anecdotes which he prints do not narrate the story of the lives of these famous Germans, but, nevertheless, give glimpses of what they did and may help to show why the Germans held them in such high esteem. The book contains four anecdotes about King Frederick William I, the father of Frederick the Great, a villainous king who was prevented from executing his own son only by the protests of the other kings of Europe.

Then follow forty-nine anecdotes about Frederick the Great, all of them, of course, revealing him as a good king and a popular character; eight anecdotes about Beethoven, Mozart, Schiller, and Lessing, and the remainder of the book is made up of one anecdote about Queen Louise, one about Field Marshal Blücher, eighteen anecdotes about Bismarck, three about the Emperor William I, and three about the present Emperor.

The booklet entitled "German Poems for Memorizing," with music to some of the poems, edited by Oscar Burkhard, Assistant Professor of German in the University of Minnesota, contains a number of German patriotic poems and prints the "Wacht am Rhein" twice, once in the text and once with music. "Deutschland über Alles" is printed twice in the same way.

I should like to be present at the trial in the secret court in Germany of a schoolmaster who dared to teach his pupils to sing the "Star Spangled Banner" or the "Battle Hymn of the Republic." Prokosch and Purin seem to be popular with the Board of Education, for they are represented by another book called "Conversation and Reading Book," which is full of stories and patriotic anecdotes. Charlemagne, Barbarossa and Frederick the Great are all exhibited as great men to be emulated. There is a picture of the coronation of Charlemagne which represents the Pope about to place the iron crown on Charlemagne's head while the Deity, attended by seraphim and cherubim, floating on clouds overhead, lends his presence to the ceremony; only another example of how the Prussians believe that God is the tribal Deity of their nation who takes a personal interest in all their ceremonies and wars.

A long article appears in these books entitled, "The Germans in the United States." It implies that William Penn had no success until he called in Dr. Daniel Pastorius of Frankfort. Among the bits of history set forth the author alleges that, in 1760, there were more than a hundred thousand Germans in Pennsylvania, and that on account of their importance in this State it was proposed to make German the official language, the proposition being beaten by only one vote! The article says further: "The only reason why the contentious Puritans succeeded in making English the language of the country and in impressing their character on its politics was because the German immigrants were poor, downtrodden people."

But it is when we come to the description of the War of the Revolution and other wars that the authors really turn loose. We learn that Washington's bodyguard was composed of Germans and that Baron von Steuben apparently reorganised the American army, so that Washington moved Congress to name General von Steuben, Inspector General, and to make his position almost independent. The writers say that the siege of Yorktown and surrender of the English army was in a great part the work of Steuben.

I think that other historians might have something to say on this subject. The authors fail to tell that Baron von Steuben, a soldier of fortune, who sold his services to the highest bidder, was hired to join the American army by a Frenchman, Beaumarchais, who sympathised with the United States.

Attention is also called to the fact that 190,000

Germans fought against the South and the authors observe in conclusion:

"If to-day the United States of America is a power of world political importance, if its industry, agriculture and commerce betoken a powerful danger commercially over the old Europe, so have they to thank the political power and the methodical perseverance of the Anglo-Saxon immigrants from England as well as the industry, the bravery and the cheerfulness of the Germans who have placed themselves politically in the service of the Anglo Saxons."

It is noteworthy that of the four books I have set forth as examples, three apparently have been produced since the commencement of the World War.

Does not all this show the hand of the German propaganda—the same hand which sends from Berlin every year a large sum of money to the German colonists in the southern states of Brazil in order that the German schools may be maintained there, German ideas inculcated and the population prevented from losing its German identity?

From the time of the visit of Prince Henry to this country the German system of propaganda has been at work smoothing out traditional differences and feuds between Germans and doing its best to make Germans from Bavaria, Saxony and Hanover and Württemberg, and Hesse forget that their countries were conquered by the Prussians in 1866.

When Prince Henry was here on his trip through the country he spent very little time with Americans. He was chiefly occupied with German-Americans and German-American Societies.

Prince Henry's visit to the United States in 1902 was primarily to attend the christening of the racing yacht of the Emperor which was being built in this country. One of the members of his suite was von Tirpitz, then secretary of state of the German Navy. After having been officially received by President Roosevelt he visited Annapolis, Brooklyn Navy Yard and West Point and then toured the middle west stopping at twenty cities between New York and St. Louis. During the entire trip he continually asked questions of all the delegates sent with him by the U. S. Government, such as for instance facts about the shops at Altoona, the coal mines, farms, factories and handsome women!

At every station he was met by the Mayor of the city and the German Societies, and greeted with German music. The Deutscher Kriege Verein, a German Society consisting of military veterans, always had a place of honour in the celebrations. In many cities the German-American citizens gave the Prince albums or souvenirs in which were engraved pretty pledges of devotion to the Fatherland. For instance in Chicago, the German Roman Catholic Society presented the following address: "The German Roman Catholic Staats-Verband of Illinois begs your Royal Highness to permit it to express its great joy for your visit to the United States and to assure your Royal Highness of its respect and regard.'

"We extend to your Royal Highness our hearti-
est greeting as the illustrious guest of this country
and *the envoy of the wise and noble ruler of our
Fatherland,* whom the world recognises and respects as prince of peace and as the representative
of a great and mighty nation that by its own power
has united its people and achieved its present prominent position among nations of the earth.

"May the Almighty grant that the visit of your
Royal Highness bear a rich fruit, that rulers and
their people may join together and thereby pro-
mote peace, harmony and good-will throughout the
world! May God grant this prayer!"

Everywhere the Prince went he was surrounded
by German-American and German influences. In
St. Louis, where the Prince spent about three and
a half hours, the German-Americans gave him a
great reception in the Grand Hall and lunch at the
St. Louis Club which was attended by many Germans. In Chicago, a reception was given after
the Mayor's banquet, in the First Regiment Armory, and attended by ten thousand Germans. The
following day in Chicago he went to a large luncheon at the Germania Club. In Milwaukee the officers of the Deutscher Kriegebund gave a reception
at the Exposition where ten thousand German-
Americans cheered the Prince, and also a luncheon
at the Hotel Pfister where many German-American officials were invited.

The speeches throughout had the same tone,
those of the German-Americans expressing their re-

spect for the Fatherland and those of the Prince
spurring on loyalty in the hearts of the German-
Americans. The Prince's speech in the Armory
in Chicago is quite typical. In reply to a speech
made by a German-American, the Prince said:

*"You have left your Fatherland, but if you still
have some love for the Fatherland then I ask you
to give three cheers for the one who has sent me
here as the representative of Prussia to bring this
greeting—the German Emperor and King of Prussia."*

In another speech which the Prince began with
"Mr. Chairman and Fellow-Germans," he said: "I
would like to say that the Germans in this country
have done a great deal for the literature and science
of this country and I hope they will continue in this
good work." The whole attitude of the Prince
seemed to be one of benevolence to his "Fellow-
Germans" and personal interest in them. Wher-
ever the Prince discovered a German wearing the
Iron Cross in the crowd, he would ask an aide to
bring the man up to him so that he could shake
hands and converse with him.

Talking with Prince Henry one day before the
war he told me he regretted that on his trip to
America he had seen so little of the Americans.
He said: "You know the Ambassador kept me always with the Germans and German Societies." I
suppose the poor Prince did not himself know what
was the real object of his visit. But undoubtedly
his shrewd trip manager and the clever propagandists who accompanied him knew only too well.

It is hard to understand why any German-Americans should take sides with German autocracy. There are many merchants of Frankfort and Hamburg and Bremen and the great industrial towns of Germany who do not approve of the cruelties practised in this war and many of these will leave Germany as soon as peace is concluded.

Any one had a right to sympathise, to side with Germany, before our entrance into the war. But now what the lawyers call "the time of repentance" has gone by, there is no middle course and every citizen must declare himself American or be thought a traitor.

It is hard to understand what the pro-Germans in our country want. They left Germany because of a lack of opportunity there, because of their dislike for military service under Prussian conditions, because of the caste system which kept them under the heel of autocracy and because here every avenue of business, and social and political advancement is thrown wide open for them and their children. And I am quite sure that if one of these prosperous Germans were deprived of the money that he has won here, given back the rags and wooden shoes in which he landed and told that he was on his way to Germany, no wild animal in all the mountains and swamps of the United States would scratch and bite and kick and squawk more vigorously than he would. These German-Americans do not want to be sent back to their Kaiser and their fatherland!

Certainly we Americans will not stop the war nor surrender our rights nor invite the invasion of our shores because of their stubborn devotion to a country which they were so glad to abandon. We must appeal to their sons and their daughters—to those who have become part and parcel of our nation, to see that these obstinate old codgers do not persist in an attitude which may end in creating a prejudice against those of German descent in America.

Those of us who are of Scotch or Irish or English descent can urge this with greater insistence because our ancestors were much nearer, in 1766, to the English fatherland, than German-Americans are to the German Empire and these ancestors did not hesitate in that year to turn against Great Britain on a mere question of commerce—did not hesitate again, in 1812, to face Great Britain in arms on a question of sea rights; and on account of this we expect all those of German-American descent to stand unreservedly by their adopted country,—forced into war by an autocracy that not only murdered our women and children in defiance of international law and common humanity but which threatens, if successful in this war, to invade our shores.

Do these stubborn German-Americans think that if a German force should occupy America their position would be any better than that of the other citizens of this country, that they would be put to rule over the rest of us and allowed to save their goods and houses from the indemnities that would be put upon this nation in case of our defeat?

Let me tell them one thing and that is, if by any

remote possibility the Germans did gain a foothold in this country through the aid of those of German descent here, before we, of other descent in this country submitted to German rule we would attend to every traitor!

We did not lure any citizens of foreign nations to our shores. They came here to escape serfdom and starvation and forced military service in an army where they could never be officers. We sent them no excursion tickets when they came here as half-starved peasants. We opened to them the doors of hospitality and of opportunity, and we do not propose that they shall pay us like the frozen snake in Æsop's fables.

Some of our finest citizens came from Germany in 1848 after the failure of the revolution against autocracy. Where do you think that General Siegel and Carl Schurz would stand if they were alive to-day?

The daughter of General Siegel has answered in giving her son, on whom she was dependent, to the army of the United States, saying, "His grandfather fought under Lincoln for liberty and he must take his place to-day in the great fight for freedom."

We are too good-natured, too soft, too easy in this country. Our great ex-President, that splendid American and patriot, Theodore Roosevelt, said not long ago of one of our United States Senators, if that Senator were a German and acted in Germany the way he acted in America as an American he would be put at digging a trench. I do not like

to differ with Theodore Roosevelt, but from my
knowledge of German conditions during this war,
I know that if this Senator acted as a German in
Germany as he has been acting as an American in
America, he would not be put by the Germans at
digging a trench but that with the ten bullets of a
firing squad in his chest he would be filling one!

Are these Germans in America imbued with the
belief that the German Kaiser has been sent by
heaven to rule the German Empire and bend the
world under German "Kultur"? President Wilson, in one of his notes in 1916, referred to the German government as "the mouthpiece of the people." A German conservative newspaper, I think
the *Tages Zeitung,* commenting upon this said that
"the German Emperor is not our 'mouthpiece' but
our truly beloved Emperor sent to us by God."

Does the German-American ever stop to consider
how the Hohenzollerns obtained possession of the
Mark of Brandenburg, the basis of modern Prussia? Five hundred years ago the Hohenzollerns
were Counts of Nuremberg, then as now a rich
trading city. Sigismund III wanted ready money
and this was advanced by the Hohenzollerns,
Counts of Nuremberg, on the security of the mark
of Brandenburg pledged as collateral to the loan
which totalled only $100,000. Later the Counts of
Neuremberg foreclosed their mortgage and took
possession of the Mark of Brandenburg and have
held it ever since.

Does a German-American in this country who
has placed a mortgage on his house think when he

fails to pay the interest or principal of the mortgage that the man who has sold him out was sent by God?

This calls to mind one of the great failures of the war—the failure of religion in the German Empire. I attended a great service, in the Protestant cathedral of Berlin, held to celebrate the five hundredth anniversary of the occasion when the first Hohenzollern, having foreclosed his mortgage, entered into possession of Brandenburg. The Emperor sat in an elevated gallery and across the great cathedral Dr. Dryander, the Court preacher, mounted the pulpit to deliver an eulogy on the Hohenzollern rule and the Hohenzollerns.

What an opportunity then if Dr. Dryander, lifting an accusing finger, had spoken of the rivers of innocent blood sacrificed to the Prussian Moloch of conquest, if he had demanded in the name of Christianity that the barbarities of Prussian rule should cease, that the Belgian workingmen, dragged from their homes to manufacture shells to be used against their own brothers, sons and fathers in Prussian factories, should be sent back; if he had demanded that the twenty thousand women and girls driven into worse than slavery from Lille and Tourcoing and Roubaix in the North of France should be given their freedom once more; if he had spoken of the whole nation of the Armenians, of the Syrians, of the Jews, massacred by the Turks while the German Generals in command of the Turkish armies stood by; if he had denounced the invasion of Belgium, the breaking of treaties, the starvation

298

of Poland, the horrors of poisoned gas and the cruelties exercised upon those of the opposing armies unfortunate enough to become prisoners of the Germans.

But no, Dr. Dryander droned on. No pastor in Germany has dared to risk his state-paid salary to stand up for Christianity and the right.

The Prussians cannot get away from the belief that they have a sort of personal God who takes a direct and kindly interest in their destinies, especially in the ordering of their bloody battles. Countless sermons were preached through Germany during the war, but the most ridiculous was that of a Protestant pastor in Berlin early in the war. He announced the title of his sermon as, "Is God neutral?", and in his fourteenthly proved to his own satisfaction, that the Deity, abandoning neutrality, had declared Himself unequivocally for the success of German arms!

CHAPTER XXII

THAT INTERVIEW WITH THE KAISER

AFTER the appearance, in August, 1917, in the *Philadelphia Public Ledger* and other newspapers in America and the *Telegraph* in England of the message of the Kaiser to President Wilson, the official *North German Gazette,* evidently unaware of the fact that the original message of the Kaiser in his own hand was in my possession, published the following:

"The *London Daily Telegraph* publishes from the memoirs of former Ambassador Gerard a telegram that His Majesty the Kaiser is alleged to have sent to President Wilson on August 10, 1914, and in which the events before the participation of England in the present war are set forth.

"We are, in these circumstances, in the position TO GIVE THE ASSURANCE THAT A TELEGRAM OF THE KAISER OF THIS NATURE DOES NOT EXIST.

"It is correct that an audience was granted to Ambassador Gerard on August 10, 1914, in order to give the opportunity to spread before His Majesty the peace mediation offer of President Wilson.

"The personal message of President Wilson to the Kaiser runs as follows: 'As official head of one of the Powers which signed the Hague Convention, I feel according to Article III of this Convention it is my right and my duty to declare to you in the spirit of the truest friendship that I would welcome every opportunity to act in the interest of the peace of Europe whether now or at another more fitting time.' . . .

"This proposition came at a time when the opposing armies had already crossed the frontiers and when it seemed out of the question to halt the march of events.

"His Majesty could, therefore, only transmit to the President his thanks for the mediation offered and to add thereto that it was too early for the mediation of a neutral Power, but that later the friendly proposition of President Wilson could be taken up again.

"His Majesty, the Emperor, then talked for some time with the American Ambassador and set forth to him separately the events which led to the outbreak of the war. Particularly did the Kaiser call attention to the equivocal and unloyal position of England which had destroyed the hope of a peaceful issue.

"The setting forth by Ambassador Gerard in his memoirs seems to be a contradiction of this conversation.

"If the press of enemy countries sees revelations in this that only shows that they are not acquainted with the German White Book which sets forth these events.

"Possibly, during the interviews, the Emperor wrote down notes for the Ambassador, in order that the latter should not send anything incorrect to Washington. In this case we have to do only with certain notes to aid the memory of the Ambassador, not with a communication of the Emperor to President Wilson."

The *Tageblatt* reprinted this lame and silly explanation in its issue of August 13, 1917, and complained that, although its correspondent at the Hague sent, on August 7, 1917, this part of my first book in a telegram, only on August 11, did the Government permit the delivery to the *Tageblatt* of this story from the correspondent. Then the newspaper despatch had to be submitted to the Censorship officials who only released it for publication at midnight. The *Tageblatt* says, "The form of the explanation which has now appeared in the *North German Gazette* can hardly be called very happy. What does this mean—'possibly during the interview the Kaiser wrote down notes for the Ambassador in order that the latter should not send anything incorrect to Washington'? Now, after a week the occurrence must have been fathomed and it was not necessary to make use of a 'possibly.' Could Mr. Gerard consider these 'notes' in the handwriting of the Emperor as a draft for a telegram? And do these notes read, as a telegram of the Emperor to Wilson—as Mr. Gerard repeats them?"

Does not the *Tageblatt* article give a glimpse not only of how the newspapers of Germany are hampered and censored, but of the positively glorious incompetency of the Government officials who denied the existence of an original document in the Kaiser's own hand which the most elementary inquiries in their own circle would have disclosed not only was in existence but in my possession?

The redoubtable Reventlow writing in the Conservative *Tages Zeitung* commented as follows:

"Kaiser William had possibly for his answer written down notes and given them to Gerard, but these were only helps for Gerard's memory and it was not a question of a direct communication of the German Kaiser to the President. In accordance with the Gerard reports it now seems that nevertheless the Ambassador telegraphed the Imperial notes immediately and literally to Washington. Mr. Gerard has, therefore, again in this respect lied, which is not surprising."

Reventlow, of course, had not then seen the facsimile of the Kaiser's telegram which is headed in his own hand "To the President, personally."

Later the other German newspapers took the Foreign Office to task for making such a weak denial of an incontrovertible fact. And note the charming parliamentary language of dear old Reventlow! The article, which appeared in the *Tages Zeitung* of August 14th last, is interesting because Reventlow is without doubt the oracle and mouthpiece of the Prussian Conservatives. He continues to attack me in this article but much of the attack is in reality praise, and, as we say in expressive slang, "every knock is a boost." The article continues:

"It is very desirable to know if the former Chancellor was present at the audience; it is regrettably not inconceivable, but is a new proof of the incompetence of the Chancellor, that he did not, according to his duty, inform his Imperial Lord of the political personality and character of a man like Gerard.

"In the U-boat crisis Mr. Gerard had been able to play a quite decisive part. He was like Mr. von Bethmann-Hollweg entirely of the view that the German Empire must give in to the demands of the United States and constantly showed himself wonderfully informed about what step each inner circle would for the moment take.

"The influence of Mr. Gerard is all the more a shameful and heavy reproach for the official leadership of Mr. von Bethmann-Hollweg, since this American Ambassador, while an intriguer, was not a personality.

"But when Gerard said anything, wished anything or threatened anything, that imported always a fear-exciting event, and he was finally sly enough to seize and use this halo to the limit. That a man like Gerard has been able through all these years to win and keep such a position and such an influence over German affairs is without example."

But I must really put aside the halo which Reventlow so graciously hands me. While I was informed of what was going on, I certainly did my best to persuade Bethmann-Hollweg and von Jagow and Zimmermann as well as the Emperor and numberless others from defying America. If von Bethmann-Hollweg and any of the others were against ruthless submarine war, seeing that to adopt any other policy would bring America into this war, then they took this position because it seemed to them best for their country and history will prove them right.

Reventlow says further:

"In the winter of 1916-17 one dreamed already of loans and imports from the United States during the peace negotiations. Mr. Gerard came back from America with alms for the wounded and the result of his sublime patience and of the sublime patience of Mr. von Beth-

PHOTOGRAPH TAKEN AFTER THE BANQUET GIVEN AMBASSADOR GERARD IN BERLIN ON JANUARY 6TH, 1917. PROBABLY THE ORDERS FOR THE RESUMPTION OF "RECKLESS" SUBMARINE WAR HAD BEEN GIVEN WHEN THIS LOVE-FEAST TOOK PLACE

Sitting, left to right—Von Wermuth, Mayor of Berlin; Ambassador Gerard; Zimmermann; Von Sydow, Minister of Commerce.
Standing, left to right—Unknown; Consul General Lay; Commander Gherardi, U. S. N.; First Secretary Grew; Unknown; Count Montgelas; Solf, Colonial Minister; General Friedrich, in charge of prisoners of war; Isaac Wolf, President of American Association of Commerce and Trade; John B. Jackson, former Minister to Cuba.

mann-Hollweg was pictured by the Gerard celebration in Berlin.

"Then came the decision for ruthless submarine war. The first time in his ambassadorial service was Mr. Gerard surprised and the men who entertained him were also surprised for they dreamed of and wished for quite other things. It is incorrect, if it has been stated, that at the time of the Gerard celebration ruthless submarine war had already been agreed on. That came later."

But I did know that ruthless submarine war was coming, knew of the orders given, and this is proved not only by my reports which are still secret, but by what I told not only many people in America but several editors who with my full approval published articles showing this belief.

I am obliged to Reventlow for what he says of me. I admire him as a powerful writer for whose ability I have a deep respect and perhaps if I were a Prussian Junker I would follow him as blindly and confidently as do the army and navy officers, the nobles, great and small, and the land-holding squires of Prussia, to whom his writings are as seductive as the pipings of the Pied Piper to the townsfolk of Hamlin.

Reventlow's charge of lying was made in the line of his duty as a Prussian Junker, according to the best traditions of Prussian government and diplomacy but it is so thoroughly disproved and the authenticity of the Kaiser's telegram so universally admitted in Germany, even in official circles there, that I feel only sorrow for a Prussian nobleman and Junker and editor compelled by the exigencies of his position to make so ridiculous a statement.

I think that the Germans just now are beginning to realise that I always told them the truth and treated them fairly, a procedure, I admit, far more disconcerting and disturbing to them than the most subtle wiles and moves of the old diplomacy.

Von Bethmann denied that the peace terms as set forth in my book were his (he did not deny that they are the terms of the Junkers) and criticised me for "unethically" publishing an account of my experiences in Germany. This is what he said:

"In his published report of this particular conversation Mr. Gerard attributed utterances to me which may have been made in other quarters in Germany and to which he frequently referred in the progress of our conversation but which were not my own. This applies especially to those references to Germany's alleged intentions to seize Liége and Namur, and of Germany's plans to take possession of the Belgian ports, the railways and to establish military and commercial dominion over that country.

"I never unfolded such German war aims to Mr. Gerard. In the course of my several conversations with him as also in our discussion last January I invariably referred to my Reichstag speeches in which I stated that Germany would exact positive guarantees that Belgian territory and politics would not in the future be exploited as a menacing factor against us. I did not make any statement as to the nature of these guarantees.

"In the progress of our conversation Mr. Gerard suggested that the realisation of far-reaching aspirations in Belgium would give King Albert merely a sham author-

ity and asked whether it would not be better for Germany
to forego such plans and instead of them endeavour to
acquire Liége which Mr. Gerard thought possible of
achievement.

"Perhaps this suggestion was a bait intended to pro-
voke a reply from me. If so, the attempt failed. In
all my discussions with the Ambassador on this subject
I referred to my public utterances in which I emphasised
that I was endeavouring to procure a peace that would
permit us to live in cordial and neighbourly relations with
Belgium.

"Mr. Gerard's memory would seem also to have served
him faultily when he wrote down what was said about
Russia. He dealt but superficially with Germany's eastern war aims, observing that the United States' interest
in this direction was very limited and that Germany undoubtedly would have a free hand there. For Roumania
and Serbia he also revealed very slender sympathy. Mr.
Gerard did not obtain out of my mouth any of the statements concerning these countries which he attributes to
me.

"When diplomats undertake to exploit their official
career for journalistic purposes they are very apt to be
misled into putting into mouths of foreign statesmen utterances which either are the creation of an ample imagination or are based on faulty memory. Discussion of
political opinions is bound to be transitory and fleeting.

"You Americans are impetuous people. You do not
seem to permit even your retiring diplomats to observe
the traditional silences nor have you the patience to abide
the post mortem publication of their memoirs. Sir Edward Goschen (former British Ambassador to Germany
and Austria) or Jules Cambon (former French Ambassador to Germany, the United States and Spain) probably could excel Mr. Gerard in revelations of entertain-

ing diplomatic history and gossip. Count von Bernstorff, former Ambassador to the United States, too, I imagine might startle us with a diary of his Washington experiences.

"In Europe, however, it was seen that publication of such matters was best postponed by common consent to a later period when judgments are both calm and more mature. Mr. Gerard, however, may hold the special license conferred by shirtsleeve diplomacy, as you call it, and I shall not dispute his prerogatives. But he must not give his imagination the free rein."

And this was my answer: published in the *New York Times* for September 2, 1917:

"Dr. Hollweg apparently did not have the exact copy of my articles for if he had read them he would have seen clearly that I said the peace terms described were the German peace terms and not the opinions of the Chancellor. Dr. Hollweg said he himself was subject to the rule of the military party of Germany and could not follow his own desires.

"In the second place, Dr. Hollweg admits that the German government intended to exact guarantees from Belgium and makes the admission himself after the interview in which he so sharply criticises me.

"Thirdly, I ask if those terms as cited are not the German peace terms, then what are the German peace terms?

"Dr. Hollweg gives nothing different from these and so it might be assumed they are the German terms after all. I consider it a matter of great regret that the German government put Dr. Hollweg out of office and I feel that personally he is bitterly opposed to the ruthless submarine warfare of the German government and that he only refrained from resigning his office out of deference to the wishes of Emperor Wilhelm.

"I presume he was put out because his ideals were too liberal for the German authorities to endure. This liberality is shown in the interview. I am sorry to take issue with Dr. Hollweg on this subject because I have a great admiration for him and I think he is a fine old fellow.

"The old-time diplomacy, which Dr. Hollweg advocated, has succeeded in plunging almost the whole world into the bloodiest war of history. When the people of a nation know what is going on in the seats of government such wars cannot happen.

"I do not believe in backstairs diplomacy any more than Dr. Hollweg. I believe the people of a nation are entitled to know what is going on. This German diplomacy may be all right in a monarchy of the most limited type but it will not go at all in a modern democracy.

"As to the ethics of publishing my memoirs now, I pass over the obvious repartee that to hear a German speak of ethics borders on the ludicrous and especially the man who openly in the Reichstag announced that necessity knows no law and that the German troops were at that moment deliberately violating the neutrality of Belgium.

"But I believe that the old style diplomacy in the dark caused this war. Of course, it is hard for a German ex-official to conceive that the people have a right to be enlightened about this awful calamity. But I hope one of the results of this war will be the end of backstairs diplomacy. When the Germans with the Chancellor's approval violated the usage of all nations and times and kept me as a hostage after I had demanded my passports, I think to talk of ethics comes with a bad grace from the German side."

Understand that Bethmann-Hollweg is not a bad man, but for one who openly announced that necessity knows no law and defended the invasion of Belgium, failed to stop the cruelties of the prison camps and gave official, if not private, consent to the murder of women and babies not only on the high seas but in undefended towns, to talk of ethics because I dared to tell the world what was happening in Germany is more than ridiculous. It verges on the ludicrous—but why attack poor Bethmann? Opportunity knocked at his door, but the want of a backbone prevented his becoming a great figure.

History will laud him for opposing ruthless submarine war so long, but will blame him for weakly yielding in the end. As for the "ethics," I have been careful to give only official conversations with the Emperor, interesting as the others are, and never shall disclose my private conversations with Bethmann, von Jagow, Zimmermann and others, including my talks with Bethmann and Zimmermann on the day I left Germany, because it was understood that these conversations should never be disclosed whatever happened.

And as time goes on more and more do I believe that history will vindicate von Jagow and teach the Emperor and the people of Germany that a faithful and skilful servant should never be sacrificed to the intrigues of a few gossiping politicians. It is part of the strength of President Wilson that he backs up his officials and refuses to listen even to widespread popular clamour for their heads. It was the business of von Jagow to conduct the Foreign policy of Germany, but the intriguers demanded his removal because he was too occupied to waste time talking to amateur politicians, and because his voice did not charm the Reichstag.

CHAPTER XXIII

THE FUTURE KAISER—THE CROWN PRINCE AND HIS BROTHERS

IN a country where the supreme power swings between the Emperor and the impersonal General Staff, all are interested, since even an Emperor is mortal, in learning something about the heir who succeeds in case of death. And we who face with the rest of the world the forces of Kaiserism desire to know about this heir.

The Crown Prince is about five feet nine, blond and slim. In fact, one of his weaknesses is his pride in an undeniably small waist which he pinches and his characteristic pose is with one foot thrown forward and one hand at the waist, elbow out and waist pressed in. He is well built, his face much better looking than his photographs show, nose rather long and eyes very keen and observing. Possessed of a great youthfulness of manner and a boyish liveliness and interest in life, his traits are somewhat American rather than German. He is a good sportsman and excels at many sports, is proud of his trophies but not afraid to meet other men in contest for them.

His manners are open and engaging and because of this he is very popular in Germany. Un-

312

like his father on whom a pretty woman makes no impression whatever, he is a great admirer of female beauty, so much so that when he is playing tennis, for example, if there is a good looking girl watching he can hardly keep his eye on the game. This weakness for the feminine has been the foundation for countless stories linking his name with that of various women, in all countries and of all classes of life, but personally, I think these rumours are untrue and that he is fond of his lovely wife, who is not in the least disturbed by his frank and open admiration of other members of the fair sex. A brood of strong, good-looking children have been born to the Crown Prince and Crown Princess.

A Prince so fond of a good time, one who loves dancing and racing, hunting and shooting, with a shrewd eye and cool head, might make an ideal king, but the one dark shadow in the background is the Crown Prince's real love for war. From his seat in the Royal Box in the Reichstag, he has applauded violently and ostentatiously utterances looking toward war: he had made himself the head of the war party, and the Militarists look to him as their chief. The great danger is that if this war ends in the defeat of Germany without the democratisation of Germany then the Crown Prince will lead the party of revenge, of preparation for war, and if the war ends in what the Germans can call a success or ends in a draw (which means German success) then the Crown Prince and the Militarists, crying that the military system has been justified, will seek new excuses to enter once more on a war of conquest. All paths or speculations turn to one gate; if the German people continue slavishly to leave the power to drive them into war in the hands of the Crown Prince, or the Emperor, or the General Staff, there will be no prospect of such a world peace as can justify a universal disarmament. Absolute monarchs and Emperors and Crown Princes and their attendant nobles, all spell war. They are the products of war and they can only continue to rule if the desire for war animates their people.

While the Crown Prince has not set himself in direct opposition to his father or at any rate taken a part in public affairs with the view either to force his father's hand or take a dominant political part, nevertheless he has allowed no occasion to pass when he could encourage the army and war party even if this brought him into conflict with the policy of the Emperor, and so there have been periods of coolness between the Emperor and the Crown Prince son.

Thus after one scene in the Reichstag when the Crown Prince applauded those in favour of aggression it was reported that he was banished to Dantzig. At any rate during the winter of 1913-14 the Crown Prince and his family were at Dantzig, the headquarters of the regiment he commands, the famous "Death's Head Hussars."

Some say that it is a tradition in the Hohenzollern family for the Crown Prince to appear to oppose the King. Then, when the King dies, the Crown Prince enjoys a certain popularity in the first years of his rule from those who have been

314

against the Government, and by the time this popularity has waned the new ruler is firmly seated on the throne

The Crown Prince, born in 1882, will be thirty-five in May next. His military education began long before he was ten years old. In accordance with Hohenzollern custom, on his tenth birthday, he became an officer of the 1st Regiment of Foot Guards and on this birthday was introduced to the other officers and took part in a regimental dinner. Before this great event he had learned enough of military drill and usages to carry himself as an officer.

In 1895, he and his brother Eitel entered as cadets at Ploen in Schwerin, where they were subjected to very strict discipline. After leaving Ploen the Crown Prince entered Bonn University, and there became a member of the "Borussia" student corps.

I never heard that he took part in the corps duels. His face is not scarred, so I imagine as heir to the throne he was excused from a custom in which other corps members are compelled by public sentiment to take part. From photographs I have seen and from what I have heard I believe that the Crown Prince entered cheerfully into the student life of the place and lived on terms of college equality with his brothers of the "Borussia" corps. These corps members, however, hold themselves aloof from other students.

The Crown Prince attended the Technical High School of Charlottenburg, that large building just across the canal which separates Berlin from Char-lottenburg. Here he gained some knowledge of machinery, chemistry, etc. In 1909, he went to work in the Ministry of the Interior, where he learned something of government administration, how to manage the constabulary and their activities,— something quite necessary for an absolute ruler in a country where every citizen's acts is noted in the copy books of the police.

Meantime, his military activities continued. He was gradually promoted and finally, in 1911, became Colonel in command of the Dantzig Black Hussars. This regiment owes its black uniform and white death's heads to the thrift of Friedrich II who utilised the black funeral hangings at the elaborate funeral of his father to make uniforms for this regiment. It has been in existence about 175 years. The white death's heads and bones which appeared in the funeral trappings were used to make ornaments for the front of the regimental headgear.

While stationed at Dantzig the Prince was taught agriculture so as to understand the needs of the Prussian Junkers. He even studied the methods of brewing beer in the Dantzig brewery. His education has been strenuous. He has not been coddled or spoiled and is far better fitted for the battle of life than most graduates of our colleges.

The father of the Crown Princess was a Grand Duke of Mecklenburg-Schwerin and her mother a Russian Grand Duchess. In appearance the Crown Princess is very attractive, her face rather Russian,

THE CROWN PRINCE AND CROWN PRINCESS. FROM A
PHOTOGRAPH TAKEN IN THEIR PALACE ON THE
NIGHT OF A FANCY DRESS BALL. THE CROWN
PRINCESS IS IN RUSSIAN COSTUME, AND THE
CROWN PRINCE WEARS THE UNIFORM OF ONE
HUNDRED YEARS AGO OF HIS REGIMENT, THE
DEATH'S HEAD HUSSARS

with an expression of good nature and cleverness. Although the Crown Prince is tall (about five feet ten), the Crown Princess overtops him, and on occasions when they appear together she wears shoes with very low heels and keeps her head bowed.

The marriage took place in 1905 and was undoubtedly a love match, the young couple having met in 1904 and become devotedly attached to each other.

There is only one defect in the character of the Crown Prince and that is his fondness for war, his regard for war not as a horror, but as a necessity, an honourable and desirable state.

I have long been apprehensive that when he came to the throne the world might again be hurried into a universal conflict and that vast military preparations would burden every State.

The Crown Prince and I often talked over shooting in various parts of the world. He wishes to see America and especially to kill game in Alaska where the heavily horned heads and enormous bears make such magnificent trophies. When I told him once how my friend, Paul Rainey, had killed seventy-four lions in Africa he could talk of nothing else at that interview.

The Crown Prince has been pictured as a libertine and a pillager. His face has been caricatured so often that people have the cartooned impression of him and believe him to be a sort of monstrous idiot.

On the contrary, he is a good sport, a clever man, a charming companion, but the shadow of military ambition hangs over all and I doubt if the effect of his infernal military education, commencing when he was a child, can be entirely removed.

If some day he learns the idiocy of war, if he recognises that the world has progressed, and allows the people some share in their own government, he will make a splendid constitutional ruler of Prussia and the German Empire.

Should the German people fail to take unto themselves the war-making power, they will, before long, be decimated again for the amusement of the Crown Prince, or as he once put it, "for his fun."

The favourite son of the Kaiser is presumed to be Prince Eitel Friedrich. A large, fat, healthy, good natured young man, married to the daughter of the Grand Duke of Oldenburg, a rather pretty but discontented looking Princess. It is said of him that he has shown not only great bravery in this war but real military capacity. Ridiculous scandals have been circulated about him in Berlin, but this is only the usual gossip circulated about persons in prominent positions.

Adalbert, the sailor Prince, is now married to a German Princess. He is the best looking of the Kaiser's sons, possessing all the charm, and vivacity of manners of the Crown Prince, but is without that Prince's absurd ideas about the necessity of war. Any one of those three sons of the Kaiser can give yards to any other young Royalty in Germany and win easily in capacity for administration and the King business.

Certainly if the German people insist on being

ruled by some one and on being occasionally dragged out to be shot or maimed in an unnecessary war, they could not find more capable rulers than the Hohenzollerns.

Prince August Wilhelm is of a milder character. He, of course, wears the uniform of an officer, but has entered the civil service of the government. He is now a landrat or government official, and some day will be given charge of one of the provinces of Prussia such as Silesia or Posen. He is married to his first cousin, a niece of the Empress, the Princess Alexandria Victoria, daughter of H. H. Frederick Ferdinand, Duke of Schleswig-Holstein-Sonderburg-Glücksburg. They have one son, a fine healthy specimen. The August Wilhelms live very simply in a palace in the Wilhelmstrasse, very plainly furnished. They are fond of amusements, riding, theatres and dancing. August Wilhelm has none of that desire of war so characteristic of the Crown Prince.

Of Princes Oscar and Joachim, little is known. Oscar, during the war, married Countess Bassewitz, who has been a Maid of Honour in the Palace. The marriage was of course morganatic, and on marrying the young Countess was given the title of Countess Ruppin. Her children will be Count and Countess Ruppin and cannot inherit in any contingency, the Kingdom of Prussia.

Adalbert had no resting place in Berlin, but perhaps now that he is married a palace may be assigned to him. Eitel Fritz and his wife occupy the Bellevue Château between the Tiergarten and the River Spree. His wife is childless.

The Kaiser, the Crown Prince or some of the numerous Princes of Prussia are always rushing about the streets in motors, each one heralded by a blast on the cornet. Beside the chauffeur on each royal motor sits a horn player who plays the particular few notes of music assigned to that Prince. The Kaiser's call goes well to the words fitted to it by the Berliners, "celeri salade" (celery salad) and has quite a cheerful sound.

On days of an outdoor function the streets ring with these calls as the royal automobiles whizz back and forth. It is forbidden by law for any one other than royalty to announce his coming by more than one note on a Gabriel horn, or other device. I do not know whether out of town or suburban royalties from Mecklenburg-Schwerin, Strelitz, Lippe, etc., are allowed this privilege when in Berlin; I think not, and that is perhaps one reason why they so consistently shun the capital of Prussia.

When the Kaiser motors to Potsdam he usually sits in one of three motors which travel very fast, one behind the other. I do not know whether this is by design or not, but of course, it makes an attempt on his life more difficult.

I used one of the Kaiser's motors in occupied France—a large Mercedes, run by a skilful driver at a great rate of speed.

The Crown Prince is especially fond of horses and if he succeeds to the throne will undoubtedly keep up the Royal stable or Marstall. This is situated on the bank of the Spree across the square from the Royal Schloss in Berlin. There are kept the carriages of state, those sent to bring Ambassadors to the Palace when they first present their letters, two hundred splendid saddle and driving horses, with modern carriages, four-in-hand coaches, dog carts, etc. Most of the Foreign Ambassadors use state carriages for great occasions, with bewigged coachmen and standing footmen. I think Ambassador White was the last American who indulged in the luxury of a state carriage. As a plain dress suit did not exactly fit with a Cinderella coach, I went to functions, such as the Emperor's birthday reception, in a large automobile, retaining only of the former state the necessary body huntsman who acted as footman on these occasions and who wore a livery of hunting green, a cocked hat, with red, white and blue plumes and a long hunting dagger in his belt.

Out of consideration for the feelings of others I retained the porter in his old finery, a Berlin institution. At state dinners the porter of a Royalty or Ambassador stands at the house entrance, clad in a long coat, wearing a silver belt diagonally across his chest, and crowned by an enormous cocked hat worn sideways. The porter carries also a great silver headed staff, like a drum major's baton, and when guests of particular importance arrive he pounds this stick three times on the pavement.

It used to amuse the Berlin crowd lining Unter

den Linden to see the Ambassadors and Ministers leave the Palace or Cathedral on the Kaiser's birthday, New Year's day, etc., to see the state carriages of the other Ambassadors overtaken by the modern automobile from America.

The Berlin lower classes are renowned for their dry wit and they find much to amuse them in the tasteless statues and monuments of Berlin.

In the square outside our house was a statue of one of Friedrich the Great's generals which seemed to afford the boys great fun. The General is shown in the act of reflectively feeling his chin and by chance is gazing uncertainly at the barber shop of the neighbouring hotel Kaiserhof.

Nobody knows, of course, whether the present Crown Prince will succeed Emperor William—nobody knows the fortunes of war or the fate that this war has in store for the Hohenzollerns but while I personally like the Crown Prince, admire his skill in sports, his amiable ways, his smiles to the crowd, I know also of his crazy belief in war. And so long as a ruler persists in this, he is as dangerous to the peace of the world as a man with a plague to the health of a small community.

CHAPTER XXIV

WHEN GERMANY WILL BREAK DOWN

I REMEMBER a picture exhibited in the Academy at London, some years ago, representing a custom of the wars of the Middle Ages.

A great fortress besieged, frowns down on the plain under the cold moonlight. From its towering walls the useless mouths are thrust forth—if refused food by the enemy, to die—the children, the maimed, the old, the halt, the blind, all those who cannot help in the defence, who consume food needed to strengthen the weakened garrison.

Every country of the world to-day is in a state of siege, is conserving food and materials, but not yet has Germany sent forth her useless mouths, to Holland, to Scandinavia and to Switzerland, a sign that not yet is the pinch of hunger in the Empire imperative.

Since I arrived in America in March, 1917, I have been like Cassandra, the prophetess fated to be right, but never believed. I said then Germany would never break because of starvation, or fail because of revolution, and that her man-power was great.

We have not made sacrifices enough in this war, there are too many useless mouths. I believe that there are in the States of New York and Pennsylvania alone 175,000 professional chauffeurs, a great number of them employed on automobiles not used for business or trucking. And then think of the thousands of skilled mechanics employed in garages and factories repairing and making mere pleasure vehicles. If all these chauffeurs (nearly all with some knowledge of machinery) and mechanics were put at work building ships or making rifles there would be no loss to the country, but certain overfed women and their poodles would have to walk, greatly to the advantage of their health and figures.

Private automobiles disappeared very quickly in Germany. At first a man who could not reach his business in any other way was allowed to use his own automobile but even these soon went out of commission and then bicycles were forbidden except for rides to and from business, work or school. A few ramshackle taxicabs still survive in Berlin at the railway stations, driven by benzol instead of gasoline and shod with spring tires. No one can keep a taxi waiting, it is subject when waiting to be commandeered by the first comer.

Gradually as we realise the gravity of the conflict our lives will become more earnest and luxuries will be given up to meet the changed condition. There must be a committee who will tide over the workers in luxury industries and help them to learn new war trades. This was done in Germany by the great organisation of the Woman's Service. Already Fifth Avenue dressmakers have dismissed many of their workers, who, being without resources, should receive assistance and advice until they have learned other trades.

Our farmers are entitled to cheaper labour. Why should not enemy aliens work our farms? We do not propose to make the Austrian and German and Hungarian women agricultural slaves as the Germans made the Russian women caught by the war within the borders of Germany, nor have we the right, I believe, to force civilian prisoners to work. But we can give these civilian men instead of meat twice a day, now given them, the same food which the Germans give their prisoners, until the enemy aliens volunteer to work in our fields. They should, of course, work as in Germany under guard. They should be used also in mines, factories, etc. The sooner we use every ounce of war energy, the sooner we shall beat Germany and obtain a lasting peace.

Eventually forced by the hopelessness of the economic situation, the nerve of Germany will break. There is a suicide point in the German character. The German has been sustained since the war by victories somewhere. No defeats were brought home to the German people. Viewed from inside the German Empire what are the loss of a few villages on the West front or even of distant colonies compared to the conquest of Belgium, of the richest part of France, of thousands of square miles of Russia, of Roumania, Montenegro and Serbia? With the exception of a very small bit of Alsace the war is being fought far from German territory. The German can swagger down the streets of the capitals of his enemies, in Brussels, Belgrade, Bucharest, Warsaw and Cettinje and Prussian greed exacts tribute from rich cities from Lille on the West to Wilna far within the frontiers of Russia.

Our President has never faltered. He will convince the Germans at last that we are unfaltering, in the war, that nothing can swerve us from our goal,—the destruction of the autocracy which looks on war as good and seeks the dominion of the earth. When the Germans grasp that, then will come the suicide point.

There is nothing in the war for the German who is not a noble or a junker, an officer or an official. German victory will only bend the collar of caste and servitude, low wages and militarism tighter on the German neck. Sooner or later the deceived German will discover this; revolution will not come during the war, but after it, unless it closes with a German peace, or unless in anticipation of revolt, rights are granted to the people.

We cannot stop, we cannot bear the burden of the debts of this war and at the same time burden ourselves with future military preparation to meet a confident conquering Germany ready to carry the sword into South America. Whatever the sacrifice, we must go on.

And for each country and for the Allies as a whole there is one word, Unity.

When all had signed our Declaration of Independence, Benjamin Franklin said, "And now we must all hang together or we all shall hang separately."

Russia has, for the moment, failed and unless she recovers herself she will pay the penalty by submission to German rule.

Is there a defect in the Russian character? Is persistency lacking? In 1760, the Russian troops had taken Berlin. If Russia had gone on strongly with the war, the power of Frederick the Great might have been broken. But apparently the Russian troops simply turned around and went back to Russia. In 1854, in the Crimean War, after a long siege and bitter losses, the French, Turks, English and Sardinians succeeded in taking one Russian city, Sebastopol, in the extreme southern part of Russia. With this exception, Russian territory was intact and yet the Czar Alexander II, shortly after the death of Nicholas, begged for peace. As a result the Black Sea was made for a time neutral and no state could have warships or arsenals on it with the exception of small gunboats for police purposes.

In 1878, after the Russo-Turkish war, when the Russian troops were in sight of the minarets of Constantinople, the Russians allowed themselves to be bluffed by the diplomats of Europe from obtaining the fruits of victory.

Secretly or openly, Germany will propose to the world to take her pay from the skin of the Bear, from the conquered territories of Russia which remain in her possession. The inhabitants of those territories would have to become the slaves of

Prussia as did the inhabitants of Belgium and
Northern France. Prussians of Russia paid the
agitators to talk about peace without indemnities.
Germany, since the first days of the war, has been
taking indemnities not only in money, but in property and in labour from the conquered countries.
Belgium alone has been compelled to pay a tribute
of forty-million francs a month (lately sixty million) to her conquerors and vast sums have been exacted from Lille and other conquered cities. Property, including machinery, has been seized and
transported to Germany in the effort, not only to
obtain a temporary advantage, but to destroy forever factories that compete with German manufacturers.

Especially do the German autocrats hope to obtain the so-called Baltic provinces as a spoil of war.
Of Courland, Livonia and Esthonia now largely occupied by the German invaders, Courland and Livonia were originally possessions of the Teutonic
Knights, then became a part of Poland and finally
passed to Russia. The three provinces were governed semi-independently, until 1876, when they
became in all respects an integral part of the Russian Empire. The land in the provinces is held by
great landowners, mostly of German blood—and
the mass of the population belongs to the Lutheran
Church. The peasants have been kept down by the
lords of the soil, whose sympathies turn to Germany.

In 1913-1914 I met in Berlin several landlords
from these provinces who acted in Berlin and were

treated in Berlin like Germans, although subjects of the Russian Czar. So backward were these provinces in liberty under their German landlords that it was not until 1848 that the infamous "right of the lord" (*droit du Seigneur* or *Jus primæ noctae*) was abolished.

What Tannenberg has to say about Courland, Livonia and Esthonia is well worth studying. He writes:

"The most precious portions for us of the Russian heritage are the German Baltic provinces, Courland, Livonia, Esthonia.

"To the north in Esthonia and in the northern part of Livonia live the Esthonians. In the South, the Livonians of the Lithuanian branch. Esthonians and Livonians are Lutherans and form the principal part of the population. There are 250,000 Germans. But the civilisation is German and gives to the whole country a German stamp. In the rural districts, the great landlords, the ministers of the Gospel and the school masters are German. In the cities the middle classes are Germans. But the workingmen are Esthonians or Livonians. The Russians are only represented in the large cities by officials.

"It was in the middle of the twelfth century that the first German settlements were made at the mouth of the Dina. In 1201, Riga was founded, and, in 1202, the Order of the Knights of the Sword. In 1237 this Order was united with the powerful Order of the Teutonic Knights. There was no thought then of the Muscovites. From Marienburg to Riga it is five hundred kilometres, from Koenigsburg to Riga, three hundred and fifty, to Moscow eight hundred and fifty. Moscow was then going through a very difficult period. In 1225, the battle of the Kalka took place which put an end to the power of the great Russian Princes.

"From Riga to Kalka, Dantzig, Stettin and Lubeck, there was sea communication. The all powerful merchant marine of the Hanseatic League was at its height." . . .

Tannenberg describes how these provinces finally became part of Russia and adds:

"Courland, Livonia and Esthonia became the model provinces of the whole Empire. The German nobility furnished Russia with its generals and its high officials: the University of Dorpat was founded and was the model of the high schools created later in Russia. . . . The University of Dorpat exchanged its professors with the other German high schools of the Russian Empire. The students of the Baltic provinces passed several terms in the German Universities of the South and East of Germany and then returned to Dorpat to undergo their examinations to enter in the service of the Baltic or Russian State.

"One encounters constantly in our literature allusions to the Baltic provinces. Kant, the philosopher of pure reason, published his work at Riga. . . . In the time of Goethe students from Courland and Livonia visited the great of Weimar. Richard Wagner commenced at Riga his theatrical and musical career."

Tannenberg speaks of the revolution after the defeat by the Japanese of the Russian troops in these provinces when the castles of the German Barons were besieged by the people and says, "The cry of indignation resounded through all Germany. A military German intervention was generally expected. Against all expectation nothing of the kind happened." . . . "When the Russian Government finally got control the Russian troops treated the rebels mildly and it was finally the sparkling on the horizon of five million German bayonets that hastened matters so well that superficially, at least, order was re-established."

Speaking on the annexation of those provinces to Germany he says:

"There is no money to be seized in the East but there is something which is of more value than cash and that is lands, lands of colonisation for new German peasants." And he points out that the Baltic provinces are about the same size as Bavaria and Württemberg, but in Bavaria and Würrtemberg there are eight and a half millions of inhabitants while the Baltic provinces support a little over two millions.

"The Baltic provinces have always occupied an important place in the thought and sentiments of the German people. The public as a whole does not inquire if it's true that only fifteen per cent of the population is German. For the public they are simply the German provinces of the Baltic and the German people are right, because since seven hundred years the proprietors of the land there are Germans and the civilisation has always been German."

Should Germany be allowed to seize these provinces, to increase her population and man power enormously, a second great war like this one will not be far off and Russia, deprived of what Peter the Great called "His window on the Baltic," will lose her place as an European Power.

The Germans will endeavour, during any peace negotiations, to keep their troops there in the hope that they will be permitted to occupy these provinces or that, if a vote should be taken to determine to which country the inhabitants wish to be annexed, the latter would be coerced through the German landlords, and by the use of money and terror made to appear as desirous of annexation to Germany.

Prince Münster, who had been in this section during the war, told me once how easy it was to observe that the more prosperous sections of the population were German and how anxious these people were to become Germans. In this case I think he was right to the extent that the feudal landlords of the Baltic provinces believe that as Prussian Junkers they would have a greater chance to continue to oppress the people than as Russian citizens, especially citizens of a new Russian republic.

The Allies must guard against any move which can add to the man power of the Central Powers, and this reason alone is sufficient reason never to permit the Arabs and Syrians, who have been so oppressed by the Turks, to suffer again under the rule of the Young Turks.

The world must not be disturbed again by Prussian dreams of world conquest, nor must Jerusalem and the Holy Land, towards which the eyes of all Christians have turned for twenty centuries, be voluntarily given back to the Turks.

To allow the Germans access to Bagdad is to

invite trouble—a second attempt of the Kaiser to don the turban and proclaim a Holy War in the interest of the fat merchants of Hamburg and Frankfort.

If this were an old time war, when sly diplomats sat at a green table, exchanging territories and peoples like poker chips, we might consent to the partition and destruction of Russia as most natural. But this war is between two systems, and wars either will be continued or cease hereafter. We who hope for the end of war cannot permit Germany to add to her man power any part of the rapidly multiplying population of that great territory which we now call Russia.

It is probable that Russia will go through the stages of the great French Revolution. We have had already the revolution made by the whole nation, Duma, army, and the control of the respectable moderate Republicans. The period of the Jacobins, the extremists, has come, too, and we must in the end expect the appearance of the military leader, a strong man who will bring order. That is what will happen, for Russia cannot remain a nation under the control of any government which cheerfully consents to dismemberment of her territory. Perhaps Trotzky will be clever enough to transform himself into a patriotic militant leader, if not, then he will not long remain at the head.

All these movements of lesser so-called nationalities are fostered by Prussian propagandists.

The region of the Ukraine, in Southern Russia, is supposed to be clamouring for freedom and independent existence. Long before the Russian revolution, I and all the diplomats of Germany were flooded with newspapers, pamphlets and literature about the longing of the Ukraine—all as plainly issued by the Germans as if they had been stamped with the Royal arms of Prussia and the seal of the General Staff.

The Lithuanians, too, stir uneasily. There is, perhaps, more in their claim; they request the world not to confuse them with the Poles and they protest against incorporation with Poland. But should a number of little states be created, sliced from the map of Russia, they would enjoy but a short independence before falling, one by one, into the maw of Prussia.

Every one sympathises with the Poles and hopes for the establishment of a really free and independent Poland, and not a Poland under the rule or protection of either Austria or Germany. It will be a great experiment, because in the past the great state of Poland, one of the greatest in Europe, was broken because of the incapacity of the Poles to rule themselves. Their armies showed great bravery, the Polish cavalry, winged like angels, terrified enemy cavalry horses and charged often to victory; but the Polish aristocrats, camped with thousands of retainers at the place where the King was elected, sat patiently waiting for the highest bidder before giving their votes.

And the King once elected, the Polish diet accomplished nothing, because any noble who voted against a proposition could defeat it. This was the so-called "liberum veto" so fatal to Poland. Katharine of Russia, that clever, wise, dissolute but great German Princess, placing a puppet favourite on the Polish throne, insisted on the retention of the "liberum veto" in the Polish Constitution, because she knew that by the mere existence of this asinine institution Poland could be counted on to commit suicide for the benefit of the watching spoilers, Russia, Prussia and Austria.

But a new, real Poland would not be governed by its aristocracy, and under a democratic government the splendid Polish race could be trusted to work out successfully their political salvation.

Should the strong man fail to appear in Russia and the Bolsheviki continue to rule, then the confusion of Russia may not prove an immediate help to Germany.

In the first place, no one now works in Russia; the population will be in want of food and will not have any great surplus to export; and it will be a long time before Germany can draw any material help from the Steppes of incompetency. Had Russia immediately settled down to a new form of government, the case might have been different, but now Germany or some power in Russia must first organise that vast country for production under new conditions before Germany can begin to profit from the withdrawal of Russia from the war except, perhaps, in that important factor—the release of German troops from the Eastern frontier. But as time passes the Germans may use food from

335

Russia to bribe northern neutral nations into an alliance with the Central Empires.

Revolutions are contagious. In 1848, the movement started in France spread all over Europe. The burdened horse on the road evinces a tendency to get out of hand at the mere sight of another horse cavorting about a pasture. The Germans are in blinders and driven by heavy hand, but forgotten as liberty is in Germany, the German Michael, the peasant chained to the soil, the hard-driven, poorly paid worker of the cities, at least, will exhibit a spirit of uneasiness, when across the line he sees Ivan, the Russian moujik, capering about, free from restraint and running things at his own sweet will. The yoke fits tight to Michael's neck, the German Kaiser drives hard from his All Highest Place; but no Emperor seemed more secure than the head of the Romanoffs, and the very fact that the chains of the yoke seem so strong may make the driven cattle all the more ready to toss the yoke aside when knowledge of power comes to the lower castes of Germany and Austria.

On the question of war Prussia is a civilisation as different from that of France, Great Britain and America as is China.

Ministers of the Gospel, professors, poets, writers, teach war; the necessity, the glory, the nobility of war. Long before Nietzsche wrote and Treitschke taught war as a part of the Prussian creed the teachings of these mad philosophers expressed an indigenous feeling in Germany. It is

REPRODUCTION OF A POST CARD CELEBRATING THE PROWESS
OF THE ZEPPELIN, SOLD IN GERMANY

ZEPPELIN POST CARD OF PATRIOTIC SENTIMENT SOLD IN GERMANY
POPULARIZING THE AIR RAID ON DEFENSELESS CITIES

not some abstract belief to be studied. It is a vital, burning, ever-present question which affects deeply, intimately, every man in this world. For until the Prussians are made weary of this belief and converted to a milder life, there is no woman in any corner of the earth, however remote, who may not have to see her son or husband go out to die in the fight against Prussian aggression, who may not, if this fight fails, be dragged away with her daughters to become slaves or endure that which is far worse than slavery.

If the Prussian people themselves cling to their Gods of War, if Kaiser and Crown Prince fulfil their ideals, if the Prussian leave the reins in the hands of these warlike task masters and refuse to join the other peoples in stamping out the devil of war, then the conflict must go on, go on until the Germans get their stomachs full of war, until they forget their easy victories of the last century, until their leaders learn that war as a national industry does not pay, until their wealth and their trade has disappeared, until their sons are maimed and killed and their land laid waste, until the blinders fall from their eyes and they sicken of Emperor and Crown Prince, of the almost countless Kings and Grand Dukes and Princes, Generals and Admirals, Court Marshals and Chamberlains and Majors and Adjutants, Captains and Lieutenants, who now, like fat, green, distended flies, feed on the blood of Germany. What is there in war for any one but those men of froth at the top? It is this infernal king business that is responsible; so much of the king tradition is bound up with war that a king with power feels that he is untrue to the traditions of his ancestors if he fails at some period of his career to give the court painters and the court poets and the court historians a chance to portray him as a successful warrior.

The British air minister recently announced that reprisal raids were to be made on German towns. Who is not sorry for the poor people who may suffer, but the war must be brought home to them. They have made no protest while Zeppelins killed babies and women and children in the "fortress" of London. The "fortress" of London, indeed! First the Germans attack an open town, contrary to every rule, and then, when guns are mounted to ward off future attacks, the Germans christen the town a "fortress" and claim the right to continue this slaughter of non-combatants.

Postcards were sold and eagerly bought all over Germany showing the Zeppelins bombing towns. When some German father sits by the hospital bed of his dying daughter, who sobs out her life torn with a fatal wound, let him tack one of these postcards over the bed and in looking on it remember that "he who lives by the sword shall perish by the sword," that it was at the command of the Kaiser and the Crown Prince when they thought only the German Zeppelins could make a successful air raid that these massacres were ordered and that the German people at the time yelled their approval of deliberate dastardly murder.

"Te Deum" has been always the favourite psalm

338

sung in cathedrals for all Christian conquerors, but neither psalms nor the paid pastor's praises of the Emperor will satisfy the German people, who have made awful sacrifices for intangible victories.

CHAPTER XXV

THE ERRORS OF EFFICIENT GERMANY

THE Yankee finding himself, like Mark Twain's hero, suddenly transported back to King Arthur's Court is landed in a surprising and unknown world. But one of King Arthur's knights brought to life at the court of the present German Emperor aside from steam, electricity, gun powder, telegraph and telephones would find the system as despotic as in the days when the enchanter, Merlin, wove his spells and the sword Excalibur appeared from the depths of the magic lake. But while the system is as royal and as despotic as in King Arthur's day, while the king and his military nobles look down on the merchants and the toilers and the plain people, no knights ride forth intent upon good deeds, to protect the poor or avenge the wrongs of the innocent.

It was the cold realists of the General Staff who battered down the defences of Belgium and the forts of France, destroyed the monuments of art and levied a tax of sixty million francs a month upon a little country deprived of its means to produce wealth, took the food from the inhabitants, shipped the machinery and raw material into Germany, deported the men and insulted the women and drove whole populations from their homes to work as slaves for the conquerors.

But while they can plan military successes in the first rush of assault on the chessboard of Europe they have failed to understand other nations—failed even to learn the lessons of history. They did not know that in every land, in every walk of life, there are men who will "reject a bribe and who will die for an idea."

Imagine a German Staff officer reporting in Berlin that over a hundred thousand Alsatians were armed and organised and that they threatened, unless certain proposed legislation uniting them, for example, with Baden, was withdrawn, to resist forcibly any attempt to incorporate them in that Grand Duchy. Would not this look to a German officer like real revolution and nothing else? And when, in addition, there came news of the landing of arms for the Nationalists in Ireland and of the organisation of the Nationalist army, the Germans, without knowledge of the psychology of other peoples, believed that Great Britain had her hands full and that the moment had come when they could go to war and leave Great Britain out of all calculations. So studying only the German mind, believing that all peoples in national character are like the Germans, the Great General Staff, the greatest military aggregation the world has ever seen, failed lamentably, whenever the human element became the factor in the situation. Its military successes have been marvellous; its judgments of mankind ridiculous. Its errors of judgment may be arranged as follows:

Error Number One.

Italy was in alliance with Germany and Austria, although there was no greater hate before the war than that between Italians and Austrians; and the Great General Staff believed that Italy would remain in this unnatural alliance, would fight in order to give the Germans and the German-Austrians the domination of Europe. The victory of the Central Empires would have placed Italy under that Austrian influence from which in her struggle for freedom under the leadership of Cavour, Garibaldi and Victor Emanuel she had liberated herself.

Prince Buelow, who early in his career romantically married a charming Italian of good family, was sent to Rome to keep Italy neutral. But he failed.

Error Number Two.

Germany's belief that because of the Carson movement Great Britain was immobilised and could take no part in the war.

Error Number Three.

The theory cherished especially in military circles that because the Japanese army had been trained by Prussians Japan would join Germany. Indeed, at the moment when the Japanese were packing their trunks and preparing to leave their Embassy, a German crowd with flags and torches was assembled in front cheering Japan, the latest ally of the Entente.

Error Number Four.

The belief by the General Staff that the British Colonies would render no assistance to the mother country.

In the first days after England entered the war many German statesmen said to me, "Of course, now Canada will be incorporated in the United States." The Germans believed that the practical thing, for the moment, for the Canadians was to avoid war, to disavow all their obligations and ties of blood and permit Britain to be destroyed. The General Staff thought that because the world did not have actual proof of the German designs of world conquest, because that design had not been publicly proclaimed, that no people or nation would either know or understand the vast enterprise of conquest on which Prussian autocracy had embarked.

Error Number Five.

The unexpected resistance of the Belgians.

The German armies were held only a few days, yet the delay of those few days changed the fortunes of the world.

Error Number Six.

The splendid stand of France which was a complete surprise to the Great General Staff. They believed that France was degenerate, torn by scandals, and that a sudden assault would land the German army in Paris. In this connection it was another great error for the Germans to have sought Paris, important from a sentimental but not a military point of view. They might better have occupied first the north coast of France, and from there could have conducted the German submarine campaign with deadly effect.

Error Number Seven.

We have seen what a shell the Russian Empire was, but in July, 1914, the Great General Staff believed that Russia was on the edge of a revolution. Barricades had been erected in the streets of Petrograd and the Staff believed that the revolution, which has since divided Russia, was in the making. Instead of this the Russian Empire lasted for nearly three years and the Russian troops and generals inflicted many a hard blow not only on the Austrians but on the German forces.

Error Number Eight.

Germany was confident that the United States had been so propagandised, so covered by bribes, by paid newspapers, that the export of supplies to the Allies could be prevented. Another error was the barbarity shown in the sinking of the *Lusitania* by which it was sought to terrorise Americans into withholding from England and France the privileges of international law, and of the definite treaty of The Hague in 1907, in which Germany had joined

344

and which gave to private individuals the right to supply munitions of war to any belligerent.

Error Number Nine.

Thinking that the Emperor, by posing as a Mohammedan in the East, could with the aid of the Turks stir all Mohammedans to a Holy War.

The Germans laboured with the Mohammedan soldiers captured by them. I saw many fine looking old Sheiks from the desert entering the Foreign Office in Berlin. The Eastern world was filled with German spies. But the Holy War was a failure, and the hope that the races of Asia and Africa would rise in favour of Germany was not borne out by events. The men of the East are wise, the rulers of India are enlightened and were not silly enough to place themselves voluntarily under the harsh rule of Prussia.

Error Number Ten.

The belief that President Wilson had been elected with an absolute mandate to keep the peace at all costs, the Germans declared for unrestricted submarine warfare, expecting a craven neutrality from the United States.

CHAPTER XXVI

ONCE the Kaiser said to me, "I wish I had as much power as your President. He has far more power than I have."

What would the Kaiser say of the power and prestige now enjoyed by the President of the United States?

At first blush it seems almost ridiculous for us to rush to war shouting against autocracy while the man with the greatest power the world has ever seen announces to the world that we fight "to make the world safe for Democracy."

Charles I must turn enviously in his grave when his spirit sees the obedient Parliament of Washington; and a line of fallen Kings, from Charles to Nicky Romanoff, must wish that they had had the opportunity to attend lectures at Princeton University where our President, Woodrow Wilson, once held forth on the science of government.

But it is characteristic of the high intelligence of our people that we have recognised that war to be waged effectively must be directed by one head. We know that after the war we shall be able to recover all the powers delegated to the President. We have gained by our temporary surrender all the efficiency of autocracy and risked none of its dangers, and have simply followed the custom of the free German tribes which elected a leader for war and gave him a power never given the chiefs in time of peace.

How much more enduring is our Government! Since the war the government cabinets of England have twice changed radically, that of France five times, and Italy very frequently indeed. Few realise that our Constitution is the oldest in the world to-day. Since its adoption the government of every land in some material particular has changed many times, France, for instance, from King and Republic, then to citizen kingship, then to Republic, then to Empire, and finally to Republic. In England the form has remained the same, but the power passed, in 1830, with the passage of the Reform Bill, from nobles to commoners, as great a revolution as any in France.

And I admire the very inaccessibility of President Wilson. He does not waste time on non-essentials, on useless, polite conversation or pointless discussion. This may add to his enemies but makes for efficiency.

When I saw the President on one occasion about German affairs we talked for four and a quarter hours without intermission. In that period he extracted from me all the information he required at the time. He is a wonderful man to have at the head of our nation in war or peace.

Gradually the splendid peace message of our

347

President (Jan. 8, 1918) will sink into the consciousness of the German people.

There are liberal and reasonable men among them striving for peace and for disarmament.

In January of 1917, just at the moment when the military autocracy brought on war with America by their sudden announcement of ruthless submarine warfare, the liberals of Germany were preparing to co-operate with our President in the efforts that he was then making for peace.

A Socialist member of the Reichstag, a man whose name is known throughout the world, wrote at that time two articles to be used in the effort for peace, and I print them in order that those outside of Germany may obtain a glimpse of the mind of one of the leading Socialists of that country. These articles have never before been published.

I feel that now when we are at war with Germany perhaps it would cause embarrassment to this man should I publish his name. In a country where a man may be sent to jail for speaking without respect of some act of the Kaiser's ancestors, committed more than four hundred years ago, it is dangerous for any German to put his name to utterances which might not march with the wishes of despotic Germany.

It has always been the desire of the Kaiser's government to draw the Allies into a peace conference with the hope of detaching some of the Allies from their combination. Perhaps these articles, although written by a Socialist, were part of a clever governmental peace propaganda to which

348

the majority Socialists so readily lent themselves during the year 1917. But on the other hand I think these articles represent the sincere real expression of the writer who is still a member of the Minority or Haase faction of the German Socialist Party. Though written a year ago they discuss points still unsolved and which must come before the peace conference that settles the war:

HOW AMERICA CAN HELP EUROPE

BY ——— ———, MEMBER OF THE REICHSTAG

The immediate reply of the Central Powers to President Wilson's note (Dec., 1916) has been a polite refusal to indicate, beyond some generalities open to the blame of ambiguity, in a clear way what their demands of peace would be. It has been followed by their note to the neutrals of the 11th of January, which also avoids giving a distinct delineation of their demands. The Central Powers maintain that only a peace conference of the belligerents themselves would be the proper place to bring forth the respective peace conditions, and they state they would produce theirs when once the conference has met. Putting aside every insinuation of motives one cannot help being reminded by this of the attitude of the Central Powers during the fateful twelve days of July-August, 1914, when they refused any outside mediation and insisted on direct conversations between Russia and Austria, whilst the punitive military expedition of the latter against Servia had to take its course. In so far their suggestion would not augur well for the execution.

The Entente Allies, on their side, have been somewhat more explicit. Their answer to President Wilson in-

349

cludes the delineation of demands that certainly are open to criticism, but just for this call for a reply or even compel it. At the time these lines are written only newspaper comments have so far come forward, and it is not necessary to dwell upon these. Nor does it seem appropriate to anticipate the reply of the Chancellor, which in some form or other will surely be given in the course of the next weeks. What matters is that there is a programme given for discussion and we are able to scrutinise its nature and bearing.

The demands explicitly or implicitly contained in the note of the Allies can be summarised under five heads, viz.:

1. Restitution of occupied territory to its former political community,
2. Reparation for inflicted material and moral wrongs,
3. Territorial changes motivated by alleged
    a. rights of nationality,
    b. need for freeing suppressed or protecting consistently maltreated nationalities,
4. Reform of International Law,
5. National and international treaties for the protection of inland and maritime boundaries.

Of these the demands under 1 and 2 are certainly in their principle quite reasonable, and if it comes to actual and exact formulation are apt to lead to a fair agreement.

The demands under 3 are partly on principle also unobjectionable, whilst some, as e. g., the cession of the Polish provinces of Prussia to a Polish state under Russian tutelage or the cession of the European vilayets of Turkey to Russia or some newly created community under Russian tutelage, can hardly be supported by reasonable argument in the face of the fact that they could only be carried out by dictation after a complete and crushing victory of the Allies over the Central Powers. That is to say, after a prolonged war more murderous and more embittered than that behind us. It is to be expected that public discussion will in regard to demands of this nature create an opinion resulting in their reduction if not disappearance. What is reasonable in them falls either under number 3, letter "a," or under numbers 4 and 5.

Now as regards the demands under 4 and 5, the settlement of most of them belongs rightly to an International Conference of all the nations. In their good and efficient regulation all are interested. They are also of the greatest concern to the future of mankind as a whole. The demands or questions can as regards their general character also be divided under three other heads, viz.:

Firstly, questions of justice to nations or nationalities as political or sociological entities,

Secondly, questions of the most expedient settlement of disputes between individual Powers or groups of such where no fundamental principles of nationality or similar rights are concerned, and

Thirdly, questions which concern all the nations through their common interest in general security and protection against the disturbance of international peace and traffic.

Both the Allies and the Central Powers agree to the idea of settling these latter questions in a better way than before; i. e., by an International League of the Nations to enforce peace. But both want the creation of this League to be settled after the war. It can, however, with good reason be upheld that there is in this a fault against logic which would have to be paid dearly by them

as well as by the neutral world. Both base a number of
their demands on the necessity of protecting themselves
against renewed onslaughts by their opponents. Now
such protection might be a necessary thing under the
present state of an International Law which has been
outraged and partly been made inane by themselves and
has partly turned out not to meet the conditions of modern warfare as they result from the modern weapons of
destruction. But it would be made unnecessary or its
requirements be greatly reduced if the League of the
Nations, such as is in principle accepted by them, did already exist or had its rules and regulations already laid
down in detail. Is it reasonable to allow this contradiction to cause now innumerable deaths and mutilations
of human beings and unbounded destruction of material
wealth instead of seeking means to dissolve it as early
as possible? Ought not all our wits be exerted to find
this earlier solution?

There are within the means of the neutrals, if acting
together, two ways to bring the war to an earlier end
than that to be expected from the free decision of the
belligerents. The one is to drop all considerations of
neutrality such as at present regarded and, without directly supporting the one section to the detriment of
the other, withdraw from both of them all supplies in
food, raw material, half and wholly manufactured goods,
not minding which section would by this be more dam-
aged than its opponents. In fact, it would most likely
be a decidedly unneutral measure against the one section
which now benefits more than the other by these supplies,
and because of this and from other reasons there is
little probability that it would find general acceptance.
The other way is to reduce the justification of the continuation of the war by minimising the objects for which

352

it is led in the belief of the great masses of the people engaged as much as in the eyes of the outside world.

Both belligerents, to say it again, put in the first line of their requirements security against renewed attacks, protection against the continuation of the insecurity of peace. Both admit that the proposed League of the Nations has become a necessity; both admit that it might indeed protect mankind against new wars and a state of incessantly endangered peace. Why then wait and let the disaster go on instead of proceeding at once to lay the foundation of this League?

The step is not so impossible as it might appear. Supposing one neutral state took the matter in hand and, after having ascertained the consent of the other neutrals or at least a majority of them—which it is almost sure to obtain—would invite all the nations, the belligerents included, to a conference or a congress at a neutral place for the discussion and the arrangement of the principles and rules of the proposed League of the Nations. Would the belligerent nations refuse to send their delegates to such a conference? Could they do it without damaging their case before the world of the neutrals and the masses of their own people? It is most improbable that they would do such a thing. And even if they did they would not by this put the conference to naught. It would be there and would give palpable substance to an idea which until now lived, in spite of great and most ingenuous work spent on it, politically only in the sphere of lofty speculation or projects.

And the conference could do more. Starting from the maxim which finds such impressive accentuation in President Wilson's note that war in general must not, and the present war in particular can not, be regarded as the private affair of the individual states that engage in it, the conference could also take into consideration some questions of consequence connected with the present war. It could, e. g., whilst laying the foundations for the security of countries against wilful attacks lay down opinions about the just settlement of disputed questions of nationality and the liberation of nations or part of such from allegiance to a state or empire of different or mixed nationalities. It seems to become a necessity to make clear whether a Power or coalition of such can be justified to put in the list of their war aims the liberation of nationalities without sufficient proof that the latter all want to sever their connection with the state or empire to which they just belong.

The Tcheques in Austria and the Finns in Russia strive for their full autonomy within these empires, but they have very little shown of a desire to become a separate state. An opinion that wars for abstruse benefits never asked for can under no circumstances be regarded as liberation wars would wrong nobody because it would apply to all, but it may contribute much to have designs given up which otherwise would uselessly cause bloodshed and prolonged enmities.

The conference would also be justified in taking measures to procure an impartial expert opinion on the origin and the legal conduct of the war and the general principles of national and international right involved.

If the conference would invite neutral experts in international law of general renown to investigate the questions indicated above and draw up reports it would not by this offend in the smallest degree against the requirements of impartiality. But the reports could, if based on careful examination and considerately worded, contribute very much to soften the excited minds in the countries engaged and facilitate the preliminaries of a genuine peace.

There are, no doubt, all sorts of objections that could

be raised against this suggestion. But they can be met satisfactorily if the matter is taken up in earnest and with practical mind. The principal difficulty to overcome is *time;* no time must be wasted by research in far-fetched details. It is a comparatively short list of pertinent questions which would have to be answered, and the materials of their examination are already at hand in the declarations and documentary publications of the different governments themselves which want to be verified by juxtaposition with the corresponding publications of the other side and to be scrutinised upon their intrinsic significance. Works of conscientious legists and historians that could serve as specimens are not missing. But they are occasioned by private enterprise and express opinions not always in the measured language that would alone fit the purpose here in view.

This purpose is to direct the minds of the greatest possible number of people in the affected countries to such way of regarding the questions of the war and to such comprehension of the feeling of the other side as are the necessary conditions of a sane and sober appreciation of the nature and the possibilities of a reasonable peace. The present feeling in these sections of the public which form public opinion in this country as in England and in France, is as full of bitterness as can be. A cure is badly wanted, but it does not proceed automatically. Weariness of the war is there, but it is counteracted partly by the manifold incidents of the war itself, by the appetites it has awakened, by the mutual distrust it has created.

It might be objected that one can hardly expect a number of even neutral experts to come to a concerted opinion on these points. But it would be of little consequence if the experts, instead of agreeing on a common report, would publish majority and minority reports.

What matters is that opinions of qualified experts are at all drawn up and published, so that discussion is as much as possible free from the effects of the biased speeches of interested statesmen and other politicians and their press. The report or reports would also be of use when an armistice at least had been agreed upon and a conference for the conclusion of a peace is sitting. And even if the work of the invited experts should take more time than the conclusion of the peace itself, the reports might still be of considerable value. For what matters is not only that a peace is come to but also that the nations should afterward possess authoritative impartial opinions on the main questions of consequence connected with the origin and the conduct of the war. For such opinions would educate the poisoned minds to an objective and argumentative discussion of the means to prevent a repetition of the present disaster.

Only those who live in the affected countries can be aware how great the need is for providing the general public with unbiased authoritative expositions of these questions.

Finally the conference could and should also discuss in a pertinent way the question of *disarmament*. This question has to-day reached a stage much beyond that of mere desirability. It is now a question of commanding necessity, one can justly say of life and death of the reached stage of civilisation. Not pious wishes or theoretical expositions will in regard to it now suffice. We must have practical proposals, proposals of a scheme to put disarmament into practice and proposals of the means to induce the different states to accept the scheme and to carry it out.

It is a big and pretentious programme here suggested, the first to be decided by breaks with the old principle of non-interference in state affairs. But the times are so exceptional that extraordinary measures cannot be shunned. If one sees two lads fight each other with their fists or even sticks one may well say, "Let them first fight it out and then we shall see to bring them to reason." But if they stand on board a ship and, mad with rage, and, without interruption and unremittingly, throw incendiary matter at each other you would rather stop them before the ship is in flames. Under other conditions it might be the right thing to convoke a conference to be held after the war is over. As it is now, reason would demand not to adjourn the term to that juncture. This is not the place to adjudicate responsibilities. Suffice it to say that the present aspect of the conflict is the worst since its beginnings and threatens aggravations of its horrors.

Of all the neutrals none is more predestined to take the initiative in this grave matter than the United States of America, by their great power, by their geographical position, by the ethnological composition of their citizens and last, but not least, by their historical traditions they before all are called to act. The small European nations are already, as it were, too much under the fire around them to be so free in their action as is the government of the giant republic on the western hemisphere. But that they would with the greatest readiness join in the convocation of a conference for the settlement of at least the two first of the described subjects is sure beyond any doubt.

The leader in the arrangement of this conference is, in my opinion, the least objectionable, and at the same time it is the most promising help that in the present appallingly entangled situation America can give Europe. The Old World is poisoned. The virus of the most irrational hatred of its component sections against each other, inoculated into them by all sorts of false leaders

357

of opinion, eats deeper and deeper and threatens to mortify all the roots of a wholesome life. May the United States of America help a disunited Europe to find the way out of the deadly miasmatic jungle into which it has lost itself.

THE HELPLESSNESS OF EUROPE

BY —— ——, MEMBER OF THE REICHSTAG

Europe is in the position of a wanderer who has gone astray into a swamp. In vain he labours to regain firm ground. The more frantically he struggles the surer he is to become submerged. Like an infant child he is unable to help himself. Help must come from people outside the swamp.

We are now in the third year of the biggest, the most fratricidal and the most hopeless war the world has ever seen. It is hopeless in so far as on the one side none of the two coalitions is likely to be in a visible time as much the victor over the other that it can dictate it its own terms, and as on the other side there is no common basis to be seen for a sensible compromise. It is not the extravagance of demands that forms an insuperable barrier for peace. Extravagant terms of peace have indeed been formulated by unauthorised persons or groups but they have nowhere received the sanctioning stamp of the responsible governments. The latter prefer rather to shine by the moderation of their demands, at least as far as territory is concerned. But it is just this apparent moderation that makes peace such an almost insoluble problem.

Far behind this moderation in regard to territorial demands looms the desire to destroy the opponents' chances of political predominance. The war is, for the present at least, in the first instance a struggle about the supremacy in Europe. And this perhaps more in a negative sense than otherwise. Jingoes are, of course, everywhere in high and low quarters, but it is very doubtful whether one of the responsible heads of the belligerent nations pursues for himself or his nation seriously and consistently what might be called the mastery of Europe. All are, however, dead against the idea that this mastery might pass into the other camp. Comparatively easy as it is to settle a dispute on questions of territory by arbitration or to work out schemes for compromise in regard to such, so difficult or almost impossible it would be to arbitrate on a question of actual supremacy or to settle it by compromise.

Particularly in the camp of the Allies is the possibility lest Germany might emerge out of the war the actual arbiter of Europe conceived as an unbearable thought. None of the allied Powers, neither England nor France and not even Russia, Italy being in this respect quite out of question, has during the last decades shown a disposition or a pretence to play up to such a part.

But Germany is suspected of nourishing ideas of this kind, and utterances of some of their prominent men, *occasional sayings of the Kaiser included,* tend to give substance to this suspicion. In vain Germans object that their country has all the 44 years since 1870 kept the peace in Europe. We have done the same, would the others reply, and we have not, as Germany has done, again and again threatened war when things did not run according to her wishes or humours. *Germany has in fact abstained from actual peace breaking. But she was regarded and has not a little done to acquire the fame, as the latent or virtual disturbing element in European politics.*

359

This view in regard to political Germany has greatly been enhanced through many of her actions during the present war. It is natural enough, though not particularly edifying, that in a war each party ascribes all the guilt thereof to the opponents and poses as the innocent who maliciously was surprised when not dreaming of any harm. But the cantankerous way in which almost the whole political and intellectual Germany has handled this question and has treated it as a crime not to take in every respect the German view of the case and of all the details of warfare has strengthened the feeling that this nation has come to regard itself as a sort of high judge of Europe. People were reminded of that ill-considered harangue to German soldiers at the time of the China expedition when they were entreated to act towards the Chinese like the Huns under Attila. *This and the eagerness to crush by overwhelming power every small nation that ventures to take sides with the Allies as well as the proclaiming of rights for submarines and Zeppelins upon her own authority—these and similar measures have only been too suited to nourish the conception that Germany places herself in the rôle of the scourge of God.*

How this feeling reacts upon political thought is illustrated by a conversation a German socialist has had in the summer of 1915 on neutral ground with a French socialist politician of no jingoish leanings at all on the possibilities of peace. Even if Germany declared herself ready to relinquish Belgium and to return to France every inch of ground occupied, his countrymen would not accept peace from her, explained the Frenchman. And on the question, "Why not?" he replied passionately: "Because it would be the German peace; because it would yet leave Germany the all powerful of Europe; because it would make us depend upon the whims and tempers of that conceited military nation."

"But are you going to bleed yourself to death?" was the next question, and the reply, uttered in a voice where sadness mingled with determination, was:

"Yes, rather be ruined!"

This is a specimen of the feeling created by the present war, and I am afraid the sentiment has not abated a whit yet. Germans have done a good deal in attempts to detach the French from the English. They have told them that they are only the poor seduced tools of the base and egotistic Britishers, that Germans did not bear them any malice, that they rather pitied them and would fain be ready to come to terms with them. But declarations of this sort proved only how little the French mentality was understood this side of the Vosges. The French nation is too much impressed by the memory of her great past and the part played by her in European politics to stand being pitied and patted like children of tender age. It will be respected as an equal who acts with the full knowledge of the state of things and is too much given to political reflection to accept willingly any view of the war that visibly is coloured by the interest of Germany in the dissension between the two great Powers of Western Europe. The anti-German feeling runs still very high in France; her leading papers excel without any exception in extremely harsh language against everything German, and the great mass of those who in former years had propagated the idea of a Franco-German understanding are now dead against it.

A similar feeling has step by step got hold of the British nation. From not being very popular at its beginning in England, the war has come to be regarded as a greater national concern than any of its predecessors. The frantic if not hysterical outbursts of hatred against England in Germany when the former decided to stand by France in the war were at first not taken too seriously. But by and by the unceasing utterances of spite have, together with the known acts of German aerial and submarine warfare, deeply reacted on the British mind. The feeling is now general that England has never before had an enemy so full of hatred against her, so ardently desirous of causing her irreparable harm as she now has in present day Germany.

Even such socialist papers as the *New Statesman,* which before the war had no anti-German bias at all, have arrived at the same conclusion concerning what may be called a German peace as the French socialist politician whose opinions were given above characterised it. In an article called "The Case for the Allies," and especially addressed to Americans, the *New Statesman* explains in its number of December 30th that peace with an unbeaten Germany would mean "Mittel Europa from the Baltic to the Black Sea," that nothing would prevent its expansion through the Balkans to El Arish and Bagdad, that throughout this vast area the authority, if not the suzerainty, of Berlin would be acknowledged and that the small European States north and northwest of Germany would without any resistance—by the mere force of things—come to be subjected to the dictate of Germany. In the words of the *New Statesman,* as the result of an inconclusive peace, "militarism would be more firmly established than ever by the record of its marvellous success and by the manifest need for a military organisation proportionate to so vast an expansion."

Is this feeling justified? Does it appreciate facts at their exact value? *There is undoubtedly an influential section in Germany which entertains feelings of this kind.* It has its adherents particularly in naval circles and amongst the intellectuals of the nation and in a con-

362

siderable degree also in the financial world. These sections hate in England partly the happy possessor of what in their opinion ought by right to belong to the German race and partly the power without which German expansion would meet with no resistance worth speaking of by European nations. *This section of anti-English on principle or by deeply rooted hatred, influential as it is, is, however, not the whole nation.* It has only now the hold of her mind because it has succeeded in instilling into her the belief that England is the secret manufacturer of the present war, that she is the selfish fermenter of hatred in Europe, the scheming brewer of strife on the Continent. England has become to the average German mind a real nightmare, a sort of a Frankenstein or any such spookish monster, and as she now, by the vicissitudes of the war, has indeed become the most dangerous of Germany's opponents it is not possible to educate people from the inside to a more rational view of her part in this war and in European politics altogether.

There you have the greatest hindrances to peace in Europe. I did not mention Russia. But the war between Germany, inclusive of Austria-Hungary, and Russia is of quite a different nature. It is more of a war of the older order. It has, of course, also evoked a good deal of hatred. But on the whole it is as wars go, more of an objective nature. There are material differences on which it would not be impossible to compromise. But there is no such deeply-seated irrational opposition, which now sets Germans and English and French and Germans against each other. The war between the Central Powers and Russia is, comparatively speaking, an accident in the political history of Europe. *The war between England, France and Germany is a catastrophe in European civilisation. As a war it is most irrational, and just because of its absurdity it is so utterly difficult to find*

*a solution for it, and there is little hope that unless some
outside force intervenes, it may end otherwise than by
absolute general exhaustion.*

Things would be otherwise if there were reasonable
hopes of a concerted action on the part of the international union of the socialist parties. But such hopes, if
they ever could be entertained, have by now become a
thing of the past. In the three countries named the majority of the leaders of organised labour have taken
sides in the war alongside of their governments and
have by this more or less given up independency and
lost the confidence of their former comrades in the opposite camp. Distrust, which in general has so much contributed to bring about this war, prevails also in the
ranks of the socialists in regard to the leaders of the
movement on the other side of the frontier. Minorities
everywhere work for a greater independency as a step
to a better international understanding. But they have
as yet nowhere succeeded in winning the majority of
the movement over to their views and policy, and even
if they did, all sorts of hindrances would by the governments be put in the way of these Socialists to assem-
ble internationally in sufficient number for work of this
nature.

Nor is it to be expected that revolts of the discontented
masses will be vast enough to force the governments
into peace negotiations against their will. The possibilities of centralised governments against revolutionary up-
heavals as long as these remain locally isolated, which
in the face of the enormous extent of the section of the
globe directly drawn into the war is most probable, are
too great to let these movements have a great chance of
changing the policy of the rulers. This would only happen when at least some of these classes or parties which
at present support the war come round to their opinion,

of which very few signs are at present to be seen. The work of small minorities everywhere, the war has got hold of the minds of the millions in all countries and has filled nations against nations with such distrust and spite as in the history of civilised mankind never before have been witnessed.

How little we are justified to expect peace from the action of these socialists who stand by governments in the war is, as far as my own country is concerned, shown by the fact that the big meetings now (and, I am willing to admit, it is the intention of the initiators to hold them in favour of peace) led by the leaders of the majority of the social-democratic party, such as Messrs. Scheidemann, David, Ebert and others, turn out in practice as meetings in support of the policy of the government in regard to the question of war and peace. In order to defend their own political attitude the speakers are compelled to shift the responsibility for the war and its continuation wholly on the shoulders of the governments of the opposite countries and their supporters, and by this they increase in the mind of their hearers the conviction that nothing short of a defeat of these countries will bring the war to a desirable end. In England the majority of the Labour Party and a considerable number of the best known socialist leaders and in France the most influential leaders of socialist party support also the war policy of their respective governments in all principal issues. The well meant and praiseworthy attempts to convene a full International Socialist Congress for the purpose of settling these differences by finding a common line of action are, I am sorry to say, under the circumstances most likely to prove abortive. *They will founder on the self-contradiction that the Socialists of the Entente countries argue that their governments hate the idea of German militarism coming out unbeaten and unreduced out of this war which in their opinion was provoked by it, whilst the leaders of the German Socialists in power would rather see this same militarism which they in former years have so violently attacked and denounced, come out victorious than have it interfered with by outside influence.*

In short, sections of the socialist movement will assist other forces in the action for peace, but the movement as a whole is incapable to act in the matter as a force of compelling strength.

Help must in the main come from outside. Consequently President Wilson's action in his note to the belligerents of December 20th would have been the right thing, even if it had offended in some way against the rules of diplomatic procedure. Under so exceptional circumstances as these occasioned by the present war extraordinary steps are certainly justified and breaches of etiquette of little significance. But the note was faultless in this respect, and it can morever be said that in no way did it endanger legitimate interests of the one or the other section of the belligerents. It offends only in spirit against Cain's word, "Am I my brother's keeper?" and in distinct words against the conception that war is a private affair of states may it ever so much interfere with the material and moral welfare of other nations.

The step has not at once succeeded. But it has opened the way; nay, it has forced the door open for discussion in a fashion that nobody will be strong enough to shut it again. True, the Central Powers have by their offer of peace negotiations forestalled the note by a week. But this offer would have come to naught without Mr. Wilson's action. Harsh as the reply of the Allies is to the offer, it would most likely have been put in much more negating terms had not the American note caused the Entente Allies to avoid a blunt "No" and content themselves with raising objections and interjecting accusations. By this they have willy-nilly provoked a debate and instead of shutting the door kept it well open.

People may call this a small success. In fact it is a beginning, and for the first as such sufficient. The question is now what shall the next step be and how can the debate be directed to positive proposals?

Of course, as these articles were given by this Socialist-Author for publication any one is at liberty to reproduce them.

In conducting the peace negotiations, President Wilson will have the benefit of the services of Colonel House, the one man who, I believe, is best fitted to protect the interests of America and of humanity at such a conference. I, of course, saw Colonel House during the war in Berlin and in America and I consider that no man alive is his superior in either knowledge of the whole situation or in ability to cope with the trained diplomats of Europe. Human nature is much the same and the gentle mannered Texan who has been so successful in American politics will not fail when representing us at the table of Peace.

CHAPTER XXVII

AFTER THE WAR, WHAT?

NO one but a fortune teller or professional seer dares to predict the condition of the world after this war. Only mere suggestions can be thrown out, shadows of prophecy as to what may come.

Will the tide of emigration turn from Europe and the United States to other countries or will people of German birth and descent leave America to return to the Fatherland after the war?

I made it my business after I had learned German to talk to many of the plain people in Berlin and elsewhere, to get their views. I found that the common soldiers, especially those representing the class of skilled workingmen in the industrial centres were almost unanimous in saying that after the war and at the first opportunity they intended to leave Germany, to turn from a country capable of perpetrating this calamity on the world, a country where they have been subject not alone to military service but to a cruel and oppressive caste system of discipline. I believe that Germany will enact laws against emigration and that there will be zones of espionage on all German frontiers de-

368

signed to watch and keep back such Germans as may seek to escape to other countries.

In Austria even more stringent laws will be necessary to keep the unmarried males from leaving.

I know that experts of the United States Government believe at least three millions of Slovaks, Greeks, etc., will leave America after the war, taking with them the money they have earned, for investment in new opportunities in the Old Country.

With this view I cannot agree. The soil of the European continent is too poor, wages too small, hours too long, and distaste for the military and caste systems too great, to tempt those who have tasted the equality and the freedom of America. Why to-day an ordinary coal miner in Pennsylvania can earn $5,000 a year—a sum greater than the pay of a Prussian or Austrian general! Why should this miner go back to insult and slavery?

The greatest problem of Germany comes after the war—when these millions of men, trained for four years or more to murder, shall return. It will be hard for them to settle down to regular work, impossible for them to submit again to the iron discipline of German civil life. Will they not, as Bloch predicts, possibly, re-enact the horrors of the French Commune, or even those of the French Revolution?

It is hard to understand why Prussian autocracy does not freely offer what it will be compelled to give after the war—equal suffrage in Prussia, fair

369

representation in the Reichstag—a government responsible to the Reichstag. Is it not better for the Emperor to offer this—following Bismarck's saying that "in Prussia the revolutions are made by the rulers."

And who of all rulers in history seemed to sit more securely on his throne than Nicholas who is now learning from his keepers what a Czar really is?

The Emperor said to me once, "Is it not wonderful how the German people bear their sufferings in this war?" I said I thought it was wonderful. It is that and more,—it is almost a miracle—that a whole nation can so nearly approach this delirium.

The autocratic idea survives in Germany—on November 22, 1917, the Conservative Union of the Province of Brandenburg unanimously adopted the following resolution.

"The Prussian State, fundamentally a people of its Princes, is the foundation on which the German Empire rests.

"Not sovereignty of the people but Kingship by Divine Right is its corner stone.

"We implore our deputies to do their best to prevent the Kingship being debased into a sham Kingship and being replaced by that sovereignty of the people by means of the alteration of the Prussian franchise."

After reading this can any one wonder that the Kaiser believes he is called by God to rule the Germans?

"Kingship by Divine Right"—is quite a development of a Kingship that originated in foreclosure proceedings, when Prussia was taken for a debt by the crafty, rich Hohenzollern Burgraf of Nuremberg.

Is it any wonder that the Kaiser once said to me during the war, "Everything seems to be going my way—don't you think God is helping me?"

The efforts of those in charge of the German propaganda to sow dissensions among the Allies are more than awkward.

For some time after the landing in force of the British troops in France, the newspapers of Germany were filled with cartoons representing the British refusing to leave Calais; and now that America has entered the war even so intelligent a philosopher as Chancellor Hertling speaks as follows:

"If those who hold power in France forcibly repress every suggestion of peace, and try to rouse fresh will for war by a show of assurance of victory, in spite of the frightful sacrifices the war has cost the country, and must cost still further, it is because they are sustained by the hope of help from America. In this hope they patiently tolerate the Americans also making themselves at home in France, turning Bordeaux into a great American harbour with immense loading and unloading wharves, and cutting down the forests of the Gironde in order to build a camp in the neighbourhood of Bordeaux for the expected army. French workmen tolerate in their factories the competition of American workmen, with whom they are not in sympathy, and the owners allow them to look into the secrets of their business, all so that the new Ally may help to take the revenge on the hated Germans."

Misguided old Philosopher!

The most stupid peasant of the Bordeaux country does not believe that the Americans have come to France in order to occupy permanently a section of that sandy, barren scrub pine desert which stretches to the south of Bordeaux.

And President Wilson and his cabinet, Lloyd George and the statesmen of France and Italy, Portugal and Russia must be on their guard—Wolff's agency is at work, spreading poisonous propaganda. Here is an excerpt that speaks for itself:

"The Imperial and Royal Propaganda Department, Section of Foreign Affairs, calls the editor's attention to the practice of the enemy press in caricaturing the Kaiser, the Crown Prince, Hindenburg and alleged German militarism, with the evident intention of an odius anti-German propaganda. It would, therefore, be important from the patriotic point of view for the daily newspapers also to occupy themselves by means of caricatures with the principal events of the day.

"The idea of such propaganda has been conceived by the supreme military command. And it is therefore desirable that all should conform to it. The official cinema has been ordered by the supreme command to enter into direct communication with the daily press, and many leading newspapers have hastened to express their readiness to insert these patriotic caricatures, for the drawing of which the service of the best artists in Munich and Berlin have been secured. These caricatures will regard chiefly the heads of state of the Entente powers, their political leaders and those who make no mystery of their hatred for Germany. The blocks will be supplied free of expense."

German employers will never be able to grind down their workmen as before the war. The men who have fought in the trenches will return with a new feeling of independence, a new spirit of revolt against the caste prejudices, a disinclination to do the same work in the same hours and for the same wages.

My tailor in Berlin told me that several of his men who had returned after being discharged from the army because of some physical disability or wounds took an entirely different attitude and that one of them, for example, had said to him: "Do not think that I have come back to work as before. I have the Iron Cross, I have helped to save Germany. I am a hero and I do not propose again to be your industrial slave."

That is the new spirit which after the war will animate the deceived, hitherto down-trodden lower classes of Germany.

In our own country, the balance of political power may be held by the soldiers who are enlisted in the war and who, like the G. A. R.'s after our Civil War, may doubtless organise not only for protec-

tion but for political purposes. And this great restless body of returned troops, veterans of wars beyond the seas, may change our whole foreign policy in ways of which we do not dream. We shall
be a more warlike nation, less patient to bear insult,
more ready for war, unless this war ends all wars.

The war after the war, in trade and commerce,
may be long and bitter. The rivers of Germany
are lined with ships of seven or eight thousand tons,
many of them built or completed since the war,
and Germany designs as her first play in this commercial war to seize the carrying trade of the world.
The German exporter has lost his trade for years.
Alliances have already been made in great industries, such as the dyestuff industry, in preparation
for a sudden and sustained attack upon that new
industry in America. Prices will be cut to far below the cost of production in order that the new industry of America fighting single handed against
the single head German trust may be driven from
the field. The German Government will take a
practical hand in this contest and only the combination of American manufacturers and the erec-
tion of a tariff wall of defence can prevent the
Americans, if each fights single handed and for his
own end, from falling before the united, efficient
and bitter assault of German trade rivals.

The war has brought new power and new responsibility to women. Armed with the franchise they
will demand not only equal rights but equal pay.
In Great Britain alone, before the war, there were

less than five hundred thousand women workers where now over five million carry the burden even of the war industries of the country.

Unless the war ends with a victory so decisive for the Allies that an era of universal peace shall dawn for the world, each nation will constitute itself an armed camp fearing always that the German, with his lust for war and conquest, will again terrorise the world by a sudden assault.

And a necessary sequence of this preparation for war will be the desire of each nation to be self-sufficient—to produce within itself those materials indispensable for the waging of war. Capital will be wasted because each nation will store up quantities of these materials necessary to war which it is compelled to import from other countries.

For instance, Germany will always carry great stocks of grain and of fats, of copper and cotton and wool, all of the materials for the lack of which she suffered during the present war.

In my first book, I touched on the change in the industrial system that will be brought about by the socialised buying and selling introduced first by Germany and which must be copied by the other nations if they desire to compete on equal terms with that country. In Germany for several years after the war at least, and perhaps as a permanent regulation, the purchase of all luxuries outside of Germany will be forbidden because of the desire to keep German gold and credits at home.

Germans have even stated to me that they do not fear in a trade way any prejudice created against them in other countries by their actions during this war. They say that a man always will buy where he can buy the cheapest, and that however much a merchant may hate the Germans after the war, if he can buy the goods he wants for his use from Germany at a cheaper rate than anywhere else, he will forget his prejudices in the interest of his pocketbook.

This is a question which each reader will have to solve for himself. Personally, I believe that in England, in France, and in America, too, if the war should last a long time, the prejudice against German trickery and brutality in war will become so great that many a merchant will prefer to lose a little money than deal with German sellers. However, the appeal of the pocketbook is always so earnest and so insistent that the Germans may be right in the view that financial considerations will weigh down the balance as against the prejudice engendered in this struggle. And if there comes a change of government in Germany, if the Hohenzollerns no longer control, or if in a liberalised Germany the ministers are responsible to a popular parliament, while kings sink to the political position of the kings of Great Britain or of Spain, then the commercial prejudice certainly will not last long. The boycott of Germany for fifty years suggested by the American Chamber of Commerce is a most powerful weapon.

And why, if wars are to continue after this one, should we contribute to German trade profits and consequently to German preparations for another war? The nations of the Allies must reckon, too, with the bitter, bitter hate felt for them by the whole German people—and only one who has been in Germany since the war can realise its intensity.

One great factor in forcing a change of government will be the desire of the individual German after the war to say that the government of his country existing then is not the government that ordered the shooting of Edith Cavell, the enslavement of the women and girls of northern France, the deportation of the Belgian workingmen, the horrors of the prison camps, the burning of Louvain and all the other countless barbarities and cruelties ordered by the German military commanders.

Imagine after this war in some distant island, perhaps, a Frenchman, an Englishman, an American, a Portuguese, an Italian all seated at the dining table of a little hotel. A German comes in and seeks to join them. Will he be treated on an equality? Will he be taken into their society? Or will he be treated as a leper and a pariah?

The Germans will wish to be in a position to say: "Why, gentlemen, I was against all these cruelties. I was against the sinking of the *Lusitania,* and the murder of its women and children. I was against the starving of Poland and the slaughter of the Armenians and the crucifixion of prisoners, and we Germans have thrown out the government that was responsible for these horrors."

Stronger than any other consideration will be the desire of the German to repudiate these acts which have made the Germany of to-day a Cain among the nations,—an outcast branded with the mark of shame.

The Russian author Bloch whom I have quoted, says, referring to the future war:

"Behind all conflicts of interest between nations statesmen must balance the chances of success of their nation, promised by the recourse to arms, against the terrible miseries of the victims caused by war as well as the social peril which can be the consequence of war.

"They who ask themselves when it will be possible to propose to the people of any nation after the war a compensation for its enormous sacrifices, forget that the conquered will be so exhausted that there will be no question of being able to draw from a conquered nation the least pecuniary indemnity. All that can be imposed on the conquered will be the abandonment of some rags of frontier territory.

"In these conditions, up to what point can calm be counted on to reign among the millions of men called to the colours, when in their ranks there is not more than a handful of old officers and when the command will be in the hands of those newly promoted from among the non-commissioned officers? That is to say, men belonging to the working classes. Will these workingmen surrender their arms in the states of Central Europe where the propaganda has spread already among the masses?

"Will they allow themselves to be disarmed after the war and could there not come events more horrible than those which signalised the rapid triumph of the Commune of Paris?"

Just as to-day it is not isolated armies but whole peoples in arms that are opposed, so in the war of commerce after the war not single producers and exporters, corporations or individuals, but whole nations will meet in the markets of the world.

Germany has favoured trusts—controlling prices and unfair competition—and we shall encounter in buying and in selling the whole German nation ranked behind their Central Buying Company in buying and their Kartels in selling.

Isolated firms and individuals cannot on our side cope with such an offensive—but we are hampered in effectiveness by the so-called Sherman law—a law from which England is free.

The war will produce great and sudden alterations and President Wilson in meeting new problems has pursued a progressive course; witness his support of the Webb law, which enables our manufacturers to combine in export trade.

Every sign points to a new era in business—an era in which the Government will permit—even encourage—enlightened business combinations.

The railroads of the country in the efficient hands of McAdoo have already bettered service, and the rights of the Savings Banks and of other holders of the securities of each road have been secured.

We must, on the one hand, permit the abolition of ruinous competition and on the other safeguard the public from high prices, and the smaller firms and corporations from the unfair competition of a powerful rival.

Great changes are coming in the social structure of the world. We are on the threshold of a great readjustment. Whatever else our entrance into the war may accomplish, let us hope that it will have made of us a nation with the throb of a single patriotism and the steady pulse of an energetic efficiency that shall not merely seek in honest rivalry to compete with other nations but in an enlightened and helpful way shall strive truly to heal a wounded civilisation in the God-given days of peace.

THE END